FEDERALISM

DAVID L. SHAPIRO

FEDERALISM

A DIALOGUE

Northwestern University Press
Evanston, Illinois

Northwestern University Press
Evanston, Illinois 60208-4210

Library of Congress Cataloging-in-Publication Data

Shapiro, David L., 1932–
Federalism : a dialogue / David L. Shapiro.
p.   cm.
Includes bibliographical references.
ISBN 0-8101-1262-0 (alk. paper). — ISBN 0-8101-1280-9 (pbk. :
alk. paper)
1. Federal government—United States.   2. United States—
Constitutional history.   I. Title.
KF4600.S53   1995
342.73'042—dc20
[347.30242]   95-8595
                                                                                CIP

The paper used in this publication meets the minimum
requirements of the American National Standard for Information
Sciences—Permanence of Paper for Printed Library
Materials, ANSI Z39.48-1984.

To Jane

Contents

Acknowledgments

This book grew out of the Julius Rosenthal Lectures, delivered at Northwestern University School of Law on April 4–6, 1994. I am indebted to the Dean and Faculty of that school for inviting me to join such a distinguished list of earlier lecturers in this series, for their hospitality and helpfulness, and for their valuable comments and suggestions. I am also grateful to my colleagues at Harvard, Charles Fried, Bruce Hay, and Daniel Meltzer, for their rigorous review of earlier drafts, and to Ted Cruz, Gail Levine, and Howard Slavitt for their research and editorial assistance.

Finally, my warmest thanks to my wife, Jane—to whom this book is dedicated—for her unflagging support and encouragement.

I

Introduction

I have had the pleasure, and the pain, of teaching a course on Federal Jurisdiction with some regularity for about twenty years. Teaching in that esoteric and difficult corner of the law, and then spending several years in the Department of Justice,[1] have given me an opportunity to learn more than most people want to know about judicial federalism, and especially about the relationships between federal and state court jurisdiction and the roles played by those courts in the administration of our federal system.

My focus on judicial federalism—with a heavy jurisdictional tinge—left me convinced that the federal system was alive and well, and that indeed the important role of the states in the functioning of that system was established beyond dispute. The examples are numerous and familiar to all students of the subject, as well as to lawyers who labor in the vineyards of federal and Supreme Court practice. They include, just to mention a few of the most prominent cases and doctrines:

- The rule of *Murdock v. Memphis*,[2] establishing that the state courts are the final arbiters of questions of state law (so long as that law passes federal constitutional and statutory muster), even if a question of state law arises in a case that falls within federal appellate jurisdiction because it is one "arising under" federal law.[3]
- The *Erie*[4] decision, interpreting the Rules of Decision Act[5] to require

---

1. I served as Deputy Solicitor General from late 1988 to the spring of 1991.

2. 87 U.S. (20 Wall.) 590 (1875).

3. The Court in *Murdock* avoided the constitutional issue (of federal authority to review state court decisions of purely state law issues) by holding that the amended version of the statute authorizing Supreme Court review of state court decisions did not contemplate or require review of questions of state law in such cases.

4. Erie R.R. v. Tompkins, 304 U.S. 64 (1938).

5. Originally § 34 of the Judiciary Act of 1789, now 28 U.S.C. § 1652.

the application in the federal courts of state common as well as statutory law, except when federal law otherwise requires.

• The judicially developed rules exemplified by *Younger v. Harris,*[6] which require federal courts in many instances to yield jurisdiction to state courts even with respect to decisions of federal questions,[7] as well as a number of federal statutes that deny lower federal court jurisdiction in even stricter terms.[8]

• The growing willingness of the Supreme Court in recent years to limit the availability of federal habeas corpus for state prisoners complaining of violations of their federal rights in the state proceedings leading to their convictions.[9]

• The continuing insistence of the Supreme Court, despite heavy fire both from academics and from a minority of the Justices, on giving the Eleventh Amendment an interpretation that severely limits the availability of federal court actions seeking monetary relief for state violations of federal law.[10]

6. 401 U.S. 37 (1971). For discussion of the antecedents and descendants of the *Younger* decision, as well as a bibliography of analyses and criticisms of the *Younger* doctrine, see P. Bator, D. Meltzer, P. Mishkin, & D. Shapiro, *Hart & Wechsler's The Federal Courts and the Federal System* 1392–1405, 1420–38 (3d ed. 1988) (hereafter referred to as *Hart & Wechsler*) and the 1993 Supplement thereto at 203–14 (hereafter referred to as *Hart & Wechsler* 1993 Supp.).

7. Subsequent state court decisions are subject only to direct Supreme Court review or to possible federal habeas corpus review in criminal cases.

Other judicially developed doctrines require federal court abstention in certain cases involving questions of *state* law. *See, e.g.,* Railroad Commission v. Pullman Co., 312 U.S. 496 (1941); *Hart & Wechsler* 1356–74.

8. *See, e.g.,* 28 U.S.C. §§ 1341 (the Tax Injunction Act), 1342 (the Johnson Act, relating to challenges to state public utility rate orders), 2283 (the Anti-Injunction Act). *See generally Hart & Wechsler* at 1309–45.

9. *See, e.g.,* Stone v. Powell, 428 U.S. 465 (1976) (limiting availability of federal habeas corpus in cases involving challenges to state court use of evidence allegedly obtained in violation of the Constitution); Wainwright v. Sykes, 433 U.S. 72 (1977) (limiting availability of federal habeas corpus for state court prisoners who failed to raise their claims properly in state court); Teague v. Lane, 489 U.S. 288 (1989) (limiting availability of federal habeas corpus for prisoners whose federal claim depended on application of a "new rule"); McCleskey v. Zant, 499 U.S. 467 (1991) (limiting ability of state prisoners to pursue successive federal habeas corpus petitions).

10. Among the most significant decisions since 1970 in this area are Edelman v. Jordan, 415 U.S. 651 (1974); Atascadero State Hospital v. Scanlon, 473 U.S. 234 (1985); and Dellmuth v. Muth, 491 U.S. 223 (1989). At the same time, the Court has upheld the power of Congress to abrogate state Eleventh Amendment immunity in the exercise of national legislative power under § 5 of the Fourteenth Amendment (*see* Fitzpatrick v. Bitzer, 427 U.S. 445 (1976)), and under the Commerce Clause (*see* Pennsylvania v. Union Gas Co., 491 U.S. 1 (1989)).

• The position of the Supreme Court that—although Congress has considerable power to preempt state law, and although some state laws are preempted by the Commerce Clause and other provisions of the Constitution itself[11]—national statutory preemption of state law will not be found in the absence of a direct federal-state conflict or a sufficiently "clear statement" of preemptive effect in the relevant Act of Congress.[12]

These and other doctrines[13] emphasize the important role of the state courts, and of state law, in our constitutional system. There are, of course, other doctrines that underscore the ultimate supremacy of national authority when properly asserted—doctrines rooted in the Supremacy Clause, in the broad powers conferred on Congress by Article I and on the federal courts by Article III, and in the statutes enacted pursuant to those Articles.[14] Indeed, some of those doctrines may well

---

For further discussion of the issues raised by the Court's interpretation of the Eleventh Amendment, see *Hart & Wechsler* at 1159–73, 1179–82, 1191–1204, 1213–21; *Hart & Wechsler* 1993 Supp. at 148–52, 170–71.

11. On the history and significance of Commerce Clause preemption (often referred to as the "negative" or "dormant" Commerce Clause doctrine), see L. Tribe, *American Constitutional Law* ch. 6 (2d ed. 1988). As Tribe summarizes the principal impact of the doctrine, "[t]he validity of state action affecting interstate commerce must be judged in light of the desirability of permitting diverse responses to local needs and the undesirability of permitting local interference with such uniformity as the unimpeded flow of interstate commerce may require." *Id.* at 407.

12. For a case putting extraordinary emphasis on the necessity of a "clear" legislative statement before national preemption of state law will be found, see Gregory v. Ashcroft, 501 U.S. 452 (1991) (holding that the federal Age Discrimination in Employment Act does not preempt state law requiring mandatory retirement of appointed state judges at age 70). For discussion of the case, see W. Eskridge & P. Frickey, Quasi-Constitutional Law: Clear Statement Rules as Constitutional Lawmaking, 45 Vand. L. Rev. 593, 623–24, 633–36 (1992); D. Shapiro, Continuity and Change in Statutory Interpretation, 67 N.Y.U. L. Rev. 921, 947 (1992).

Many Supreme Court decisions apply a milder but still significant presumption against construing an act of Congress to preempt state regulatory law governing *private* conduct. *See, e.g.,* Cipollone v. Liggett Group, Inc., 112 S. Ct. 2608 (1992).

13. *See, e.g.,* Claflin v. Houseman, 93 U.S. 130 (1876) (establishing presumption of state court concurrent jurisdiction of claims arising under federal law); Northern Pipeline Constr. Co. v. Marathon Pipe Line Co., 458 U.S. 50 (1982) (holding unconstitutional—as exceeding limited federal jurisdiction authorized by Article III—Act of Congress assigning to federal court bankruptcy judges jurisdiction over certain state law claims involving a bankrupt); Merrell Dow Pharmaceuticals Inc. v. Thompson, 478 U.S. 804 (1986) (holding that state law claim depending in significant part on a question of federal law did not fall within the statutory jurisdiction of the federal district courts).

14. Among the most prominent examples of decisions asserting federal supremacy are Martin v. Hunter's Lessee, 14 U.S. (1 Wheat.) 304 (1816) (upholding Supreme Court's statutory and constitutional authority to review and reverse state court judgments); Testa

go a step too far—excluding the states from playing a role they should be empowered to play in the judicial enforcement of national law.[15] But in general, and despite the vigorous debates among academics and judges about where to draw the line, federalism seemed to me to be secure and healthy—perhaps too healthy for those who seek more vigorous assertions of national supremacy and greater federal court authority to ensure the vindication of national rights.[16]

Yet all the while, I had a sense that there was some rumbling in the distance. Not too far from my own corner of academic study, the Supreme Court had made a number of false starts in attempting to protect the states from federal intrusion—most notably in the ill-starred decision in *National League of Cities v. Usery*.[17] And though the latest of these efforts—*New York v. United States*[18]—is still with us, and may prove more durable than its predecessors, the states do not appear to be doing as well on the substantive front as my focus on the niceties of federal and state court jurisdiction would suggest. Indeed, even in the closely related area of a state's ability to serve judicial process on out-of-staters, the trend for a number of years has been in the direction of limiting state power under the Fourteenth Amendment—a trend that has suffered what may be only a passing blip when state territorial

---

v. Katt. 330 U.S. 386 (1947) (requiring state court to entertain federal claim for treble damages for violation of the Emergency Price Control Act); Ward v. Board of County Commissioners of Love County, 253 U.S. 17 (1920) (holding that state court must afford remedy in action seeking refund of state taxes coercively collected in violation of federal law); General Oil Co. v. Crain, 209 U.S. 211 (1918) (holding that state court may not rely on state sovereign immunity doctrine to bar assertion of federal claim).

15. Tarble's Case, 80 U.S. (13 Wall.) 397 (1872) (holding that state court may not entertain habeas corpus petition on behalf of one allegedly held in custody unlawfully by U.S. Army) is a leading example. For criticism of the decision, see *Hart & Wechsler* at 488–92.

16. As an example of the debate, see the materials on federal habeas corpus in *Hart & Wechsler* at 1487–1505, 1518–24, 1539–52, and *Hart & Wechsler* 1993 Supp. at 238–55. Congress in recent years has considered many bills designed to alter the scope of federal habeas corpus. *See, e.g.,* S. 1241, 102d Cong., 1st Sess. (1991); S. 1356, 103d Cong., 1st Sess. (1993): S. 1441, 103d Cong. 1st Sess. (1993). For discussion of efforts at legislative change in the 101st and 102d Congresses, see L. Yackle, The Habeas Hagioscope, 66 S. Cal. L. Rev. 2331, 2357–73 (1993). For discussion of more recent, and still pending, efforts, see N.Y. Times, Feb. 10, 1995, at A29, col. 1.

For a perceptive essay linking the debates over federal court jurisdictional issues to broader issues of nationalist and federalist conceptions of our political structure, see R. Fallon, The Ideologies of Federal Courts Law, 74 Va. L. Rev. 1141 (1988).

17. 426 U.S. 833 (1976), overruled by Garcia v. San Antonio Metropolitan Transit Auth., 469 U.S. 528 (1985).

18. 112 S. Ct. 2408 (1992). The case is fully discussed in ch. 3, sec. A, and ch. 4, sec. A.

jurisdiction based solely on temporary physical presence (coupled with service of process) was upheld by the Supreme Court in the *Burnham* case.[19] And when it came to the everyday operations of government, national power seemed to be on the march even during the Republican years (from 1980 to 1992) when the notion of a "new federalism" was much heralded in theory but, in the view of many, not implemented in practice.[20] Moreover, state governments often complained bitterly about the costs of complying with nationally imposed requirements that did not carry with them the funds needed for implementation.[21]

The honor of being invited to give the Rosenthal Lectures at Northwestern University Law School in 1994 struck me as affording a fine occasion to step back from my corner of academic study and to take a broader look at the federal system as originally established, as it has existed for the past two centuries, and as it exists today. Moreover, I was excited by the opportunity to think more deeply, and to read more broadly, about the stimulating questions asked by Gerald Gunther

19. *See* Burnham v. Superior Court, 495 U.S. 604 (1990). Important decisions prior to *Burnham* in which the Supreme Court struck down state efforts to assert territorial jurisdiction include Hanson v. Denckla, 357 U.S. 235 (1958); Shaffer v. Heitner, 433 U.S. 186 (1977); Kulko v. Superior Court, 436 U.S. 84 (1978); and World-Wide Volkswagen Corp. v. Woodson, 444 U.S. 286 (1980). Indeed, prior to *Burnham*, the high-water mark of the Court's recognition of state power in this area may have been McGee v. International Life Ins. Co., 355 U.S. 220 (1957).

20. A prominent example of the assertion of national authority during the Reagan years was the act of Congress conditioning significant federal highway aid to a state on the state's adoption of a minimum drinking age of 21. *See* 23 U.S.C. § 158. (The constitutionality of this condition was upheld in South Dakota v. Dole, 483 U.S. 203 (1987).)

For a description of the gradual, relatively recent, and continuing transition from industry-specific regulation at the national level to such "cross-cutting" (or cross-industry) national laws as those governing the environment and occupational safety, see the comments of Murray Weidenbaum in *Regulation, Federalism, and Interstate Commerce* 83 (A. D. Tarlock ed., 1981).

It remains to be seen whether the 104th Congress will be more successful in its efforts to reallocate substantial authority to the states.

21. For example, proposals for national health care reform led to complaints in New York and other states that they would be expected to shoulder a disproportionate share of the costs associated with health reform. *See, e.g.*, K. Sack, Clinton's Health Plan: The Region, N.Y. Times, Sept. 23, 1993, at A23; R. Pear, Clinton's Health Plan: What the States Must Do, N.Y. Times, Sept. 23, 1993, at A23. On the costs of dealing with environmental pollution, see Hard Times [in California] Dilute Enthusiasm for [National] Air Laws, N.Y. Times, Nov. 24, 1993, at A1, A30. In response to these and similar complaints, Congress recently enacted significant limitations on its power to impose "unfunded mandates" on the states. *See* N.Y. Times, Feb. 2, 1995, at A1.

in his coursebook on constitutional law.[22] Loosely paraphrased, those questions include such redoubtable issues as whether and to what extent we are constitutionally bound to a scheme of government in which power is allocated in some significant ways between the central government and the states, and, perhaps most interesting of all, whether a truly federal system—in which power is shared and in which adequate protections are afforded to ensure the autonomy and survival of different levels of government—serves any useful purposes as we approach the end of the century. In other words, if we were writing on a clean slate (and perhaps in a constitutional sense the slate is almost clean or could be made so by a few simple Amendments), how federal a system of government would we want?

When I began to read more broadly in the law—looking not simply at the jurisdictional aspects of federalism but at all of its constitutional and statutory aspects as well—and to delve as much as time and my own expertise permitted into the historical, economic, and political science materials relating to federalism, I made some discoveries that surprised me. First, I found that the extent of published material germane to these issues is vast and—perhaps because of the increasing worldwide interest in federalism as a possible method of bringing disparate factions together into a governable society—growing at what seems an exponential rate.[23] Indeed, I could not hope to read all of the relevant literature in one lifetime (at least, starting at the onset of my twilight years); I could barely keep up with the significant new studies if at the same time I was going to secure a respectable grounding in the important learning and research of earlier scholars.

Second, I became aware that there was virtually no important issue of federalism on which a particular point of view commanded a clear consensus of the scholars in the field. Thus, on the historical side, some were convinced—and convincing in their arguments—that the entire impetus behind our system of government was essentially centripetal, while others argued with equal persuasiveness that a healthy federalism

---

22. See G. Gunther, *Constitutional Law* 66–67 (12th ed. 1991).

23. These works include not only a wealth of books on the legal, political, social, and economic aspects of American and international federalism but also innumerable articles, anthologies of essays, and intensive monographs on specific issues. For example, in a recent volume exploring federalism issues primarily in the context of the regulation of pollution control (W. Lowry, *The Dimensions of Federalism: State Governments and Pollution Control Policies* (1992)), the bibliography appearing at the end of the volume, which consists primarily of works by nonlawyers, takes up some eighteen pages of small print. See *id.* at 147–64.

lay at the heart of our constitutional structure. On the economic side, some argued that only through greater centralization could the country keep up with the demands of the modern world, while others argued that modern theories of competition demonstrated the value of a strong federal system. And when it came to issues of morality, republicanism, and the safeguarding of individual and group rights, opinions seemed to cover so broad a range that they almost defied categorization.[24]

Finally, and despite the wealth of literature in the field, I found some impressive scholarship urging that the subject was simply not worth taking seriously. Arguments about federalism values, these scholars hinted (or said more bluntly), resembled what some critics thought about appeals to patriotism; they were little more than the last refuge of a scoundrel.[25] Virtually no one who thought rationally about important issues would take federalism seriously, they suggested. Instead, an appeal to federalism values—to the virtues of diffused governmental authority—was likely to come from those who opposed any governmental action and who were, at the moment, fighting against action at the national level; conversely, those who were truly concerned about a problem tended not to hesitate advocating a national solution because they knew that solutions at the state level would simply not be adequate to the task.[26] No one really cared (or should care), these people

24. The quantity of writings in all these areas is so vast that a footnote attempting to present even a representative sample would be unjustifiably long. Many of the relevant works in the areas of history, economics, political science, social theory, and law will be cited throughout the materials that follow, and a working bibliography appears at the close of this essay.

25. An article appearing after these lectures were delivered has perhaps put the case most forcefully, describing federalism as "a neurosis, a dysfunctional belief to which we cling despite its irrelevance to present circumstances," and suggesting that "claims of federalism are often nothing more than strategies to advance substantive positions." E. Rubin & M. Feeley, Federalism: Some Notes on a National Neurosis, 41 UCLA L. Rev. 903, 950, 948 (1994). See also A. Anderson, The Meaning of Federalism: Interpreting the Securities Exchange Act of 1934, 70 Va. L. Rev. 813 (1984).

Essays on Supreme Court Justices have suggested that at least some of them resorted to federalism arguments only when those arguments served the cause of another, more substantive agenda. See, e.g., the analysis of Justice Fortas's approach to federalism in L. Kalman, Abe Fortas and Strategic Federalism in Law and Politics, in Federalism and the Judicial Mind: Essays on American Constitutional Law and Politics 109 (H. Scheiber ed., 1992).

26. See E. Rubin & M. Feeley, Federalism: Some Notes on a National Neurosis, 41 UCLA L. Rev. 903, 935, 948 (1994). The point is also wryly expressed (though not endorsed) by Lino Graglia in his brief essay, From Federal Union to National Monolith: Mileposts in the Demise of American Federalism, 16 Harv. J.L. & Pub. Pol'y 129, 135 (1993).

suggested, about federalism per se. As examples, they brought forward such eminent jurists as Oliver Wendell Holmes, who manifested relatively little interest in issues of federalism throughout his career,[27] and William Brennan, who has been described as a committed nationalist until the Supreme Court decided to pull back on the scope of individual rights—at which point he declared his allegiance to federalism principles, evidently in the interest of retaining as much as possible (or even extending) at the state level the ground that the Supreme Court had given up.[28]

This exposure to such a wide variety of views left me in a quandary. What could I, as one not immersed in the disciplines of history, economics, or political science, add to the debate? Regrouping, I reflected that as a law teacher and practitioner I had learned a great deal about some aspects of American federalism, had seen those aspects at work in the courts, and had debated their merits in the classroom. Moreover, my professional career had afforded me intense exposure to the dialectical approach of the adversary system, and the luxury of three lectures in which to develop my ideas seemed ideally suited to approaching the problems of federalism through a dialogue—a dialogue with myself. In the first lecture, I would try to set forth as forcefully as I could, and from several viewpoints, the case for a strong central government unhampered by the restraints of a system in which the states play a crucial policy-making role. Having persuaded my listeners (or readers) that centripetal forces are both desirable and irresistible, I would then attempt in the second lecture to persuade that same audience of the opposite—that a healthy federal system (one that emphasized the significance of state autonomy) was in every sense essential to the existence of a vigorous

---

27. For discussion of Holmes's view of federalism, see S. Krislov, Oliver Wendell Holmes and the Federal Idea, in *Federalism and the Judicial Mind: Essays on American Constitutional Law and Politics* 37 (H. Scheiber ed., 1992).

There is no doubt, however, that other renowned Justices, including Black, Frankfurter, Brandeis, and (the second) Harlan, valued federalism as an end in itself, not simply as a pretext or an excuse for a hidden agenda. The contribution of some of these Justices will be discussed in the chapters that follow. (For a recent, and highly critical, analysis of the approach of Justice Frankfurter to problems of federalism—an approach that the author regards as far too deferential to the states—see M. McManamon, Felix Frankfurter: The Architect of "Our Federalism," 27 Ga. L. Rev. 697 (1993).)

28. For discussion of Justice Brennan's views, see R. Post, Justice Brennan and Federalism, in *Federalism: Studies in History, Law, and Policy* 37 (H. Scheiber ed., 1988). *See also* the discussion of Justice Fortas's "strategic" use of federalism in the essay by Kalman cited at note 25, *supra*.

and prosperous democracy.[29] And in the third and final lecture, I would attempt a synthesis—one that sought to draw from the arguments some conclusions about the legal, practical, and moral virtues and defects of a federal system.[30]

Lawyers may not have invented the process of dialogue, though they and the judges selected from their ranks depend heavily on that process for the development and assessment of ideas as well as evidence. But many other disciplines thrive on dialogue too. Among those who never tried a case for a client, Socrates was a master of the process—though more as a method of instructing his students than of engaging in true debate. And Marx, like Hegel, built a theory of history on its frame. On a more mundane level, the great calypso singers Lord Invader and Lord Beginner conducted a famous dialogue on the proper approach to marriage, and closer to home, some of the most challenging and enduring works of legal scholarship have been written in dialectical form.[31] So I had ample precedent for my approach, and I suspected that, like some of the models I hoped to emulate, the process of presenting the thesis and antithesis could be at least as useful as the synthesis. As a strong believer in the virtue of process as an end in itself, I was encouraged by that thought.[32]

Before embarking on this enterprise, I should underscore a few points about my approach and about the work I have done in preparation for it.

29. In these two lectures, I would not purport to embrace every argument made, any more than a vigorous advocate would necessarily adopt every argument made in a brief to a court if he were suddenly to change roles and become the judge in the case. But I would undertake to present only those arguments that I viewed as worthy of respectful presentation and consideration.

30. In this final lecture, I would not attempt to tie up every loose end resulting from the opposing arguments in the earlier lectures—any more than a court would do in attempting to resolve the core of an adversary dispute. But I would try to present my own approach to the problems of federalism, and would be prepared to defend all the views expressed as reflecting my personal convictions—convictions largely derived from and dependent upon the preceding dialogue.

31. *See, e.g.,* H. M. Hart, The Power of Congress to Limit the Jurisdiction of Federal Courts: An Exercise in Dialectic, 66 Harv. L. Rev. 1362 (1953); *cf.* L. Fuller, The Case of the Speluncean Explorers, 62 Harv. L. Rev. 616 (1949).

32. Dialogues, of course, can take many forms, ranging, for example, from the Q and A of Henry Hart's dialectic (note 31, *supra*), to the full and reasoned presentation of a series of contrasting views in Lon Fuller's series of judicial opinions in the Case of the Speluncean Explorers (note 31, *supra*). My own choice, having just completed several years as a litigator, is to present contrasting views in the form of adversarial briefs and then to attempt at least a limited synthesis in the final lecture.

First, the subject is so vast, and the materials so extensive, that although I have not limited myself to secondary sources, I have benefited immensely from them in my research. Of course, no one could presume to think seriously about this subject without reading substantial portions of *The Federalist Papers, The Anti-Federalist Papers,* and other primary materials relating to the Constitutional Convention and the ratification debates. Indeed, many of the crucial judicial opinions, starting with cases like *Chisholm v. Georgia*[33] (which predates John Marshall's service on the Court) and extending to the present day, are themselves primary materials on the operation and nature of the federal system. Some rereading of such philosophers and political scientists as Locke, Hume, and Montesquieu, whose works were familiar to the Framers, was also essential. But I lay no claim to original archaeological findings, either in primary documents buried in state or federal archives or in lesser known writings of scholars whose work predated the Constitutional Convention.[34] My contribution, I believe, lies in the effort to extract from the mass of available material the strongest competing arguments and to develop some conclusions and suggestions based on those arguments.

Second, the process of dialectic is not so airtight that an opening argument can ignore completely the competing arguments that the advocate knows are waiting in the wings. Especially since I have left myself no formal opportunity to submit a reply brief in the three lectures that structure my approach, I will inevitably anticipate and attempt to refute some of the more salient arguments for state autonomy in making the best case I can for national authority unrestrained by state power. Thus, the technique I have chosen may lead to some degree of repetition, but I hope that discussion of similar ideas from the very different perspectives of the advocates of national authority on the one hand, and of diffusion of power on the other, will help illuminate those ideas and put them in better perspective.

Third, a note on terminology is called for before the debate begins in earnest. Part of the genius of those most responsible for the framing and adoption of the Constitution was that they preempted the term "federalist," thus forcing the true federalists—those who favored some change (but not too much) in the alliance that formed the Articles

---

33. 2 U.S. (2 Dall.) 419 (1793), discussed in ch. 2, sec. A.1.

34. As an example of the latter, see Samuel Beer's recent study of federalism, in which he points to the influence of the Utopian writings of the prerevolutionary scholar James Harrington. S. Beer, *To Make a Nation: The Rediscovery of American Federalism* xv, 84–131, 216, 229–30, 245, 265–66 (1993).

of Confederation—to call themselves "anti-federalists."[35] Many battles have been won, at least in part, by the ability of one side or the other to march under the proper linguistic banner—surely, Margaret Sanger's distaste for the phrase notwithstanding,[36] the birth control movement received a gigantic boost when its supporters began to describe themselves as advocates of "planned parenthood." Indeed, those who can refer to themselves as "for" something, especially something that sounds inherently reasonable—are well ahead of the game if their opponents must admit that they simply stand against it.

Putting the best and least cynical face on it, the term "federalist" may have undergone a sea change in the last two centuries so that, whether or not the advocates of Union in 1789 picked the proper word to describe themselves at the time, those who view themselves as committed federalists today are not advocates of a strong central government at the expense of the states.[37] I have therefore chosen—doubtless with an occasional lapse—to describe those who advocate strong central authority as "nationalists," and those who advocate substantial diffusion of authority between the national government and the states as "federalists." Perhaps this too will cause confusion, but it is surely more attuned to contemporary discussion and debate.[38]

35. Garry Wills, in his introduction to the 1982 Bantam Edition of *The Federalist* at xii, notes the cleverness of the nationalists in co-opting the "Federalist" label and also notes that Elbridge Gerry, a frustrated opponent of ratification who understood the disadvantage of being labeled as "anti-federalist," suggested that the adversaries should instead be labeled "rats" and "anti-rats." *Id.*

36. *See* J. Reed, *From Private Vices to Public Virtue* 112 (1978).

37. Indeed, an important recent study of the period from 1788 to 1800 suggests that the concept of federalism underwent a significant transformation even during those early years. *See* S. Elkins & E. McKitrick, *The Age of Federalism* (1993). This transformation may help explain the fact that James Madison—originally one of the leading advocates of a strong central government (see ch. 2)—later became a supporter of the right of the states to nullify federal legislation on constitutional grounds (see ch. 3, note 139).

38. I recognize that even among those who regard themselves as "federalists"—as advocates of diffusion of power among several tiers of government—there are wide differences of opinion about the degree of state autonomy that is appropriate in general and in particular contexts. (Indeed, there is a growing body of thought that no two problems of federalism are sufficiently similar that generalizations on the subject are likely to have much value.)

I do not mean to slight these differences, and I hope several of them will emerge in the discussion. Some scholars have labored hard to develop a full vocabulary of expressions to cover the range of federations that can and do exist in different forms in the world today. *See, e.g., Federal Systems of the World* xvi (D. Elazar ed., 1991). Even within the United States, there are significant differences in the relationship between the central government on the one hand and the states, the Indian tribes, Puerto Rico, Guam, the Virgin Islands, and other assorted territories and possessions on the other. *See id.* at 304–38.

Fourth, I am aware that in presenting the case for national power (in chapter 2), and for state autonomy (in chapter 3), I am undoubtedly suggesting a more extreme approach on both sides than any serious participant in the current debates is likely to advocate. Thus among those who favor substantial expansion of national power, there are probably none who would seriously consider abolishing the states as significant political entities, or even taking away the bulk of their existing powers over such intrinsically local matters as snow removal, pothole filling, elementary education, vandalism, and a whole range of similar regulations governing human conduct. And among the advocates of substantially increased state and local power, there are few who would reduce the federal government to the role of a pure "night watchman" state safeguarding only defense and foreign policy (at least not if the alternative were to vest all remaining governmental powers in state and local authorities).

But the debate between current-day federalists and nationalists has developed many points of friction, and the presentation here is designed to cast some light on those points of disagreement by digging deeper than the participants are wont to do—by taking as little for granted at the outset as it seems possible to take, given whatever consensus may be found about the origins and purposes of American society. In that sense, then, the briefs that follow may shed some light, but they are not intended to reflect the fully rounded views of any current participant in the debate over the allocation of governmental authority.[39]

Finally, although I recognize that works of scholarship should ordinarily avoid the mystery writer's tactic of holding back the identity of the culprit until the end, I am reluctant to set forth the heart of my conclusions at the outset. I confess that the dialogue is one whose outcome (for myself) is preordained, at least in the sense that I have tried to work the problems through in the large before sitting down to draft these lectures. But if the dialogue itself is to be of value for the listener or reader, and if many aspects of the synthesis remain to be worked out in my own mind as I write this introduction, I think it would be a mistake to try to summarize my conclusions now.[40]

---

39. More will be said about the actual areas of agreement, and their significance, in the final chapter.

40. I note that in Henry Hart's renowned dialogue on the power of Congress over the federal courts, what one of my colleagues described as the "deus ex machina" of the dialogue (i.e., the availability of state courts of general jurisdiction to vindicate federal

There is one aspect of my thinking, however, that I am happy to flag at this early stage, because doing so may be useful to the reader (or listener) while considering the various arguments in the chapters that follow. As I hope to show, state lines—arbitrary as they may be—have certain virtues that arise in part from their very arbitrariness. At the same time, many problems may yield best to regional, that is, multistate treatment, and the values of a kind of "regional" or "intermediate" federalism, aided by the power of Congress to approve interstate compacts, have in my view received insufficient attention in the debate. Part of my effort at synthesis, then, will focus on this issue of regional problem solving as one of the potential virtues of our system of governance.

---

rights even when federal courts were unavailable) was not revealed, or at least was not highlighted, until the very end. *See* H. M. Hart, The Power of Congress to Limit the Jurisdiction of Federal Courts: An Exercise in Dialectic, 66 Harv. L. Rev. 1362, 1401–2 (1953).

2

The Case for Strong National Authority

A. Concepts of Federalism Impose No Significant Constitutional Limits on the Exercise of National Authority or on the Displacement of State Law and Regulation by National Law

1. The Constitution Is Not a Compact: The National Government Derives Its Authority from the People, Not from the States

Although some have suggested that the national government formed by the Constitution was essentially the product of a compact among sovereign states,[1] this description does not aptly characterize either the preconvention or the postratification nature of the systems of government then in effect. Lincoln was much closer to the mark when (admittedly under the political pressure of defending the Union against the principle of secession) he said that the Union was older than any of the states—suggesting that the states derived their existence, and whatever

---

1. Those who led or supported secession in 1861 were, of course, among the most passionate advocates of this view. *See, e.g.,* Speech on the Harbors and Rivers Bill, included in 2 *The Papers of Jefferson Davis: 1841–1846,* at 500–501 (J. McIntosh ed., 1974). But the view also finds support among both supporters and opponents of the original Constitution. Madison himself, in his later years, spoke of the Constitution as a "compact"; *see* S. Beer, *To Make a Nation: The Rediscovery of American Federalism* 318 (1993), and references to Madison's writings in authorities cited *id.* at 434 nn. 21–23. For a statement of the views of the anti-federalist Luther Martin, see 3 *The Records of the Federal Convention of 1787,* at 172–232 (M. Farrand ed., 1911). Martin argued that "*States, when once formed,* are considered, *with respect* to each other, as *individuals* in a state of nature," and that "a *federal government* is formed by the *States* . . . in their *sovereign* capacities, in the same manner as *treaties* and *alliances* are formed." *Id.* at 183, 192.

As a footnote to this footnote, Woodrow Wilson evidently believed that as an original matter, the South was right in its constitutional views about secession, but that later historical developments had forged a Nation that justified the North's refusal to permit secession. *See* A. Heckscher, *Woodrow Wilson* 11 (1991).

privileges or rights they may have, from the Constitution itself and not from any preexisting pattern or understanding.[2]

To begin, the original states were, of course, colonies of Great Britain, and as such had no true autonomy or "sovereignty." Indeed, the notion of sovereignty prevailing at that time did not admit of division, and was viewed in prevailing political theory as residing in the King (acting in Parliament). The colonies' first steps toward independence from Great Britain lay in the creation of a Continental Congress, a body that regarded itself as more of a political entity (a kind of popular convention, perhaps) than a gathering of governments.[3] And, of critical importance, no colony declared itself independent of Great Britain until authorized (or perhaps mandated) to do so by the Continental Congress itself.[4]

Thus from the beginning of the movement for independence, Americans acted as a "nation" rather than as a loose alliance of separate political entities. To be sure, the government that came into existence with the Articles of Confederation was a government with virtually no direct power to act on the people themselves. The central government's ability to raise funds and troops was dependent on the former colonies (now states), and it was dissatisfaction with this weak central government that led to the call for a convention originally designed to amend the Articles. Thus, the government that existed under the Articles may have had the appearance—supported by language in the Articles themselves—of a league or alliance of sovereign states. But given the background of nationhood from which that government sprang, it is more appropriately viewed as the product of a widespread popular reluctance to establish a central authority with too much power—a reluctance that was hardly surprising in the aftermath of the break with Great Britain.

The unacceptability of a "Compact Theory," or indeed any theory that sees the national government as deriving its power from sovereign states, is confirmed by the background and circumstances of the Constitutional Convention, the nature of the ratification process, and most significantly by the text and structure of the Constitution itself.

The Constitutional Convention, as originally established, was made

2. See A. Lincoln, Message to Congress in Special Session, July 4, 1861, in 4 *The Collected Works of Abraham Lincoln* 434–35 (R. Basler ed., 1953).

3. See S. Beer, *To Make a Nation: The Rediscovery of American Federalism* 197 (1993).

4. See *id.* at 200; authorities cited and quoted *id.* at 419 n. 13.

up of representatives of the states, who voted by state, and who came together (as noted above) for the limited purpose of amending the Articles of Confederation. But it soon became apparent to the participants— the secrecy and isolation of the process was such that the general public knew little of what was going on until the final product emerged[5]—that a very different kind of national government would be established by the new document and that this government would have a significant range of direct powers. Moreover, the key players in the Convention were nationalist to the core: Madison originally favored a national veto over all state laws,[6] Washington explicitly rejected the claim that the thirteen colonies were at any period sovereign entities,[7] while Pinckney ridiculed as a "species of political heresy" the idea that each state was separately and individually independent.[8] And Hamilton—perhaps the strongest nationalist of all—evidently had serious doubts whether the states should even be permitted to exist as political entities when the new Union came into existence.[9]

Further rebuttal of the compact theory is furnished by the method of ratification that was agreed on at the Convention and recognized as valid in the course of the ratification debates. Approval of every state was not required for the new Union to come into existence; rather ratification by two-thirds (i.e., nine) of the states would be sufficient. Thus, no one state could block creation of the Union,[10] and, interestingly enough,

5. See J. Rakove, *The Beginnings of National Politics* 396–99 (1979).

6. See G. Wood, *The Creation of the American Republic 1776–1787*, at 473 (1969). Madison's later drift toward the views of Jefferson on questions of state sovereignty and authority is described in H. Scheiber, Federalism and the Constitution: The Original Understanding, in *American Law and the Constitutional Order* 85, 97 (L. Friedman & H. Scheiber eds., 1988). Scheiber also notes that from the beginning, Hamilton was more nationalist in his views than Madison. *See, e.g., id.* at 87–91. But as Scheiber and others have observed, Madison's nationalism was itself a potent force at the Convention and his statement of the basis for a strong national government in *The Federalist* No. 10 was one of the most powerful arguments for an "extended republic."

7. See H. J. Powell, The Modern Misunderstanding of Original Intent, 54 U. Chi. L. Rev. 1513, 1517 (1987). (This article is a critical review of R. Berger, *Federalism: The Founders' Design* (1987).)

8. See H. J. Powell, The Modern Misunderstanding of Original Intent, 54 U. Chi. L. Rev. 1513, 1519 (1987).

9. See H. Scheiber, Federalism and the Constitution: The Original Understanding, in *American Law and the Constitutional Order* 85, 87 (L. Friedman & H. Scheiber eds., 1988).

10. Compare the terms of the Maastricht treaty relating to the European Community— a treaty that reflects a true coming together of sovereign entities and that requires unanimous approval in order go into effect. Indeed, Denmark's original refusal to ratify (as a

ratification by nine states could not be achieved without the support of states representing a majority of the population of the new Union.[11] True, the nationalist theory would seem even more forceful had ratification been authorized on the basis of a single nationwide convention, and had the ratification provision not referred to "this Constitution between the States." But the logistical and practical difficulties, as well as the political necessities of the time, help to explain why no such convention was contemplated. Of perhaps greatest significance in the ratification process, the procedure called for action *not* by the legislature of each state—the generally recognized repository of state sovereignty to the extent that such sovereignty existed at all—but rather by separate state conventions.[12] Thus the method chosen underscored what the document itself made even clearer—that the new Union was being created not by the states but by the people.[13]

The strongest evidence of the nationalist thesis, as suggested above, is to be found in the Constitution itself. As Jefferson Powell has noted, "the Constitution contained no explicit guarantee of state sovereignty."[14] Nor is the guarantee implicit. Indeed, any notion of state sovereignty would have been blatantly at odds with prevailing legal thought, which refused to accept the notion of divided sovereignty,[15] and with the firm philosophical foundation underlying the Constitution—a foundation consisting of the ultimate sovereignty of the people of the United States.

The starting point of analysis is the Preamble, which declares that "We the People of the United States, in Order to form a more perfect Union, . . . do ordain and establish this Constitution for the United States of America." The emphasis on "the People," which has been observed

---

result of a popular referendum) caused considerable commotion and necessitated a good deal of negotiation in order to persuade Denmark (and other nations in doubt) to join in. See As Goes Denmark, Washington Post, May 20, 1993, at 22.

11. See S. Beer, To Make a Nation: The Rediscovery of American Federalism 335 (1993).

12. The Constitution did not specify how these conventions were to be selected or organized. It simply stated, in Article VII, that "The Ratification of the Conventions of nine States shall be sufficient for the Establishment of this Constitution between the States so ratifying the Same."

13. The argument is fully developed in S. Beer, To Make a Nation: The Rediscovery of American Federalism ch. 10, especially at 330–36.

14. H. J. Powell, The Compleat Jeffersonian: Justice Rehnquist and Federalism, 91 Yale L.J. 1317, 1367 (1982).

15. For discussion of the widely accepted notion of the era that sovereignty was single and indivisible, see H. J. Powell, The Modern Misunderstanding of Original Intent, 54 U. Chi. L. Rev. 1513, 1524–26 (1987).

by eminent historians and political scientists in our own century,[16] did not escape notice at the time. That the Union derived its authority from the people as sovereign was the centerpiece of the arguments of James Wilson, one of the leaders of the campaign for ratification,[17] and moved Patrick Henry—one of the most eloquent anti-federalists—to complain that the document should properly begin "We the states. . . ."[18] Not only did the Preamble begin by stressing establishment of the Union by the people, it continued by invoking the need for a "more perfect Union"—a phrase that is not quite the solecism it may seem but is instead a strong reminder that the people have already come together in a Union under the Articles of Confederation.

The first three Articles that follow the Preamble proceed to establish the three branches of the national government and to endow each with specific powers. One need not accept the ultranationalist views of Professor Crosskey and his followers—that the specification of legislative powers in the Constitution served principally to secure those powers against the federal Executive rather than against the states[19]—in order to recognize that the first three Articles do little or nothing to guarantee any measure of sovereignty or general authority to the states. Thus, such references to the states as do appear in Article I (the Article dealing principally with the powers of the legislative branch) fall into essentially three categories. First, certain provisions recognize the states as structural participants in the federal government—a point that has been well noted by such scholars as Herbert Wechsler and Martin Diamond.[20] For example, the electors of members of the House of Representatives are

16. *See, e.g.,* S. Beer, *To Make a Nation: The Rediscovery of American Federalism* 254 (1993); H. J. Powell, The Compleat Jeffersonian: Justice Rehnquist and Federalism, 91 Yale L.J. 1317, 1363–69 (1982).

17. *See* J. McMaster & F. Stone, *Pennsylvania and the Federal Constitution* 229, 302, 316, 389 (1888); S. Beer, *To Make a Nation: The Rediscovery of American Federalism* 323–25 (1993).

18. 3 *The Debates in the Several State Conventions on the Adoption of the Federal Constitution* 22, 44 (J. Elliot ed., 2d ed. 1901).

19. This view is advanced by William Jeffrey, Jr. (a scholar who draws in part on William Crosskey's extraordinary two-volume study, *Politics and the Constitution in the History of the United States* (1953)) in Jeffrey's essay, The Constitution: "A Firm National Government," in *How Federal Is the Constitution?* 16, 17 (R. Goldwin & W. Schambra eds., 1987).

20. *See* M. Diamond, *The Federalist* on Federalism: "Neither a National nor a Federal Constitution but a Composition of Both," 86 Yale L.J. 1273 (1977); H. Wechsler, The Political Safeguards of Federalism: The Role of the States in the Composition and Selection of the National Government, 54 Colum. L. Rev. 543 (1954).

to have the same qualifications as the voters for the largest branch of the state legislature,[21] and each state is guaranteed at least one representative. Perhaps best known among these structural provisions, the "Connecticut Compromise" provides that every state shall have two senators chosen by the state legislature (although the senators are each to have one vote—clearly not required to be cast by state).[22]

The second category consists primarily of *prohibitions* on the states. Article I, § 10 prohibits the states from engaging in a wide range of activities, some of which are altogether foreclosed and others allowed only with the explicit consent of Congress. These prohibitions are of sufficient significance to belie in themselves the notion that the states participated in the Union as sovereign entities, at least as the term was then understood. As an example, the states are precluded by this section from entering treaties, coining money, or (without the consent of Congress) imposing any duties or tariffs on imports or exports—one of the principal sources of revenue at the time.

The third category—a narrow one at best—does reserve certain powers to the states and prohibit Congress from acting against the states in certain ways. Thus, the training of the militias and the appointment of officers are reserved to the states (although Congress is expressly given the authority to prescribe the appropriate discipline, and also—in separate clauses of Article I, § 8—to establish a national army and navy, to call forth the militia, and to declare war).[23] And in Article I, § 9, Congress is precluded from preventing "migration or importation" of persons into the states until 1808 (the infamous provision that authorized continued importation of slaves but that notably permitted Congress to stop all such immigration in less than 20 years), and is also precluded, inter alia, from taxing exports from any state.

This last narrow category can hardly be considered to be the basis of a significant protection of a federal system of government, nor can

21. U.S. Const. Art. I, § 1, cl. 1.

22. For discussion of the Connecticut Compromise, see G. Wood, *The Making of the Constitution* 25–30 (1987).

23. Thus, Article I, § 8 provides that Congress may call forth the "Militia" to "execute the Laws of the Union, suppress Insurrections and repel Invasions," and further states that Congress may "provide for organizing, arming, and disciplining, the Militia, and for governing such part of them as may be employed in the Service of the United States, reserving to the States respectively, the Appointment of the Officers, and the Authority of training the Militia according to the discipline prescribed by Congress." For a recent decision affirming the breadth of national power under these provisions, see Perpich v. Department of Defense, 496 U.S. 334 (1990).

the second category—the prohibitions against the states. The most that can be said of the structural elements in the first category is that they increase the likelihood that representatives selected from the separate states will have some say in the determination of national policy and that the voices of representatives from the smaller states will be disproportionately greater than those from the more populous states.

As to the "limited" powers granted to Congress in Article I, and especially in the enumeration of powers in § 8, much is made of these limitations in some of *The Federalist* essays,[24] but little is said in those essays or elsewhere, on a specific level, to warrant the conclusion by a careful reader that the powers conferred are either few or narrow. Indeed the reference in § 8 to the general welfare was recognized by the anti-federalists to be a time bomb, as was the "Necessary and Proper" Clause. And although Hamilton and Madison may not have been at one on the authority conferred by this latter clause, the Hamiltonian view plainly prevailed at an early stage, in John Marshall's justly renowned opinion in the *McCulloch* case.[25]

Article I, then, affords little if any comfort to those who would find in the Constitution a guarantee of state sovereignty or even of significant state authority or autonomy. Of course, even less comfort can be found in Article II, the provision dealing with the executive branch, since in this Article the only reference to the states is to give them a structural role in the selection of the President through two mechanisms: (1) the Electoral College, and (2) the provisions for turning over to the House of Representatives (for voting on a state-by-state basis) cases in which the Electoral College cannot muster the necessary majorities to select a President or Vice President.[26]

---

24. E.g., *The Federalist* Nos. 39 (Madison) and 45 (Madison).

25. The authority of Congress, acting under the Necessary and Proper Clause, to create the Bank of the United States was upheld in McCulloch v. Maryland, 17 U.S. (4 Wheat.) 316 (1819). For discussion of the close relationship between Marshall's opinion in *McCulloch* and Hamilton's broad construction of the Necessary and Proper Clause, see S. Beer, *To Make a Nation: The Rediscovery of American Federalism* 5–6 (1993).

26. *See* U.S. Const. Art. II, § 1, para. 3. As modified by the Twelfth Amendment, the Constitution requires electors to cast distinct votes for President and Vice President; it does not require the electors in any state to cast their individual votes for the candidate receiving the largest number of popular votes in their state. The "unit vote," under which the entire delegation of electors in a state is delivered to the winner of the state's popular vote, has been voluntarily chosen by every state but one. *See* W. Elliott, Electoral College, in 2 *The Encyclopedia of the American Constitution* 617 (1986). And in Ray v. Blair, 343 U.S. 214 (1952), the Supreme Court held that a state may constitutionally require those

As for Article III (relating to the judicial power), this Article does provide for limited federal court jurisdiction and does not itself ensure that there will be any inferior federal courts. But the jurisdictional limits are potentially as broad as the power of Congress (in view of the "Arising Under" Clause), and in some ways even broader, since those limits extend not only to cases arising under the Constitution, federal laws, and treaties but also to controversies between a state and a citizen of another state, and between citizens of different states—even though those controversies do not raise (and to some extent perhaps could not raise) any question of federal law. These latter jurisdictional provisions underscore once again the nationalist theme. The Constitution in Article III does not guarantee sovereignty to the states so much as it protects the states from each other (in providing for jurisdiction over interstate disputes) and (in authorizing diversity jurisdiction) protects citizens from having to litigate in state courts in states in which they do not reside.

If any basis for state sovereignty—or autonomy—is to be found in the Constitution (putting aside the Amendments for the moment), it lies in Article IV. Yet that Article too seems essentially designed to protect the states from each other (and to provide for common defense): in the Full Faith and Credit Clause, the obligation of each state to extradite persons wanted for crimes in other states, the Privileges and Immunities Clause, and the requirement that the United States protect every state against invasion and (on application) from domestic violence.[27]

Two provisions of Article IV might support a more forceful argument that the Constitution is a compact among the states that both contemplates and demands a strong federal system: (1) the requirement that the United States "guarantee to every State in this Union a Republican Form of Government," and (2) the provision that no state can be subdivided into several states, or joined with any other state, without the consent of

---

chosen by a political party as Presidential Electors to take a pledge to support that party's nominees for President and Vice President. (In a powerful dissent, Justice Jackson argued that, regardless of the prevailing custom, the Constitution contemplated that the Electors would be free agents and could not be legally bound to vote for particular persons.)

27. Article IV, in the last paragraph of § 2, also states: "No Person held to Service or Labour in one State, under the laws thereof, escaping into another, shall, in consequence of any Law or Regulation therein, be discharged from such Service or Labour, but shall be delivered up on Claim of the Party to whom such Service or Labour may be due." This "fugitive slave" provision can hardly be seen as a protection of states' rights; it is rather a limitation on each state's power to govern within its borders—a limitation that builds into the Constitution an interstate protection of the property rights of individual slave owners.

Congress *and* of the states involved.[28] These provisions are more fully discussed in the next chapter, but suffice it to say here that they are not without ambiguity, and, at the very least, it takes a considerable stretch to read into them a constitutional requirement of a vigorous federal system consisting of both a national government and of states with significant governmental powers.

The first of these provisions—the "Guarantee" Clause—may fairly be read as essentially a *limitation* on the states, and one that Congress is specifically authorized to enforce. The provision, in other words, may be viewed as guaranteeing to the *people* of every state that the central government will come to their aid if the state in which they live threatens to abandon the essentials of republican government. And the second provision, while it does ensure to each state the security of its boundaries, may be seen as more of a protection against incursions by other states (or intrastate efforts at secession) than as an affirmation of sovereignty or autonomy in any broader sense. Surely there is nothing in this provision guaranteeing the states any specific powers within their guaranteed borders.

Article V, dealing with the amending process, does give the states and their legislatures an important role, but like other provisions already discussed, this Article may fairly be read simply as affording the states a structural role in the operation of the Union, a status that is underscored by the prohibition on any Amendment of the provision guaranteeing the states "equal Suffrage" in the Senate.[29] And Article VI, the final provision of the original document (not including the method of ratification already mentioned), is in several respects the culminating affirmation of national power. It not only requires state as well as federal officers to take an oath to support the Constitution but also provides that the Constitution, and laws and treaties adopted pursuant to it, shall be "the supreme Law of the Land, and the Judges in every State shall be bound thereby," thus leaving no doubt whatever that in the event of any conflict between federal and state authority, federal authority (if valid and properly exercised) will prevail.

The Bill of Rights incorporated in the first ten Amendments was not,

28. The "Republican Form of Government" Clause appears in U.S. Const. Art. IV, § 4; the other provisions referred to in text appear in Art. IV, § 3.

29. For the view that Article V is not "the exclusive mechanism of lawful constitutional amendment," and that other "majoritarian" methods are available to the people, see A. Amar, The Consent of the Governed: Constitutional Amendment outside Article V, 94 Colum. L. Rev. 457, 457–58 (1994).

of course, part of the original Constitution, and Hamilton (somewhat disingenuously, perhaps) made an argument that no such guarantees were required in view of the limited powers conferred on the national government.[30] But the Bill was adopted, and is regarded by many as "the major legacy" of the concerns expressed by the anti-federalists in the ratification debates.[31] Indeed, the advocates of the Constitution may well have recognized that the Bill would serve nationalist purposes by effectively affirming the breadth of national power with respect to actions not limited or prohibited by the Amendments. Madison even thought it worthwhile to make an effort (eventually abandoned) to have the principal guarantees of the Bill made applicable to the states as well.[32] Thus, as Gordon Wood has pointed out, even adoption of the Bill of Rights was in one respect a victory for the nationalists, and in the main, the rights guaranteed by these Amendments are guarantees to *individuals* that national power will not be misused to their detriment.[33] Apart from the ambiguous terms of the Second Amendment, which uses the word "State" in a preliminary clause but which purports to confer a right directly on "the people," and the Sixth Amendment's guarantee that in criminal cases, the accused is entitled to a jury of "the State and district wherein the crime shall have been committed," the only reference to the states, and the only provision purporting directly to protect their interests, is the Tenth Amendment, which explicitly preserves to the states "or to the people" all powers not prohibited to the states or delegated to the United States by the remainder of the Constitution. This provision, scholars and judges generally (but not universally) agree, is at most an effort to emphasize that the national government is not one of absolute power. Indeed, as the Supreme Court indicated in the *Darby* case,[34] the Amendment is at bottom a tautology since it can be paraphrased as providing that the powers not vested in the national government are

---

30. *The Federalist* No. 84 (Hamilton).

31. *See* 1 H. Storing, *The Complete Anti-Federalist* 64 (1981).

32. *See* S. Beer, *To Make a Nation: The Rediscovery of American Federalism* 291 (1993).

33. *See* G. Wood, *The Making of the Constitution* 35–36 (1987). Wood concludes his discussion of this issue by observing, a bit wryly, that even the Bill of Rights "ended up in the Federalists' hands." *Id.* at 36. Akhil Amar, however, has stressed the structural elements (including the protection of state and local interests) that have often been neglected in interpreting the Bill of Rights. *See* A. Amar, The Bill of Rights as a Constitution, 100 Yale L.J. 1131 (1991), discussed in ch. 3, sec. A.

34. United States v. Darby, 312 U.S. 100, 124 (1941) (referring to the Tenth Amendment as a "truism").

not vested in the national government. Thus it appears to add nothing to the authority of the states that they did not already have under the original charter.[35]

During the ratification debates, the anti-federalists protested that entry into such a Union would mean the ultimate destruction of the states as polities of any importance in our government.[36] Moreover, they referred to a number of specific provisions in support of their arguments—provisions that have indeed turned out to confer substantial powers on the central government.[37] Reliance on the opponents of a document for its interpretation is always questionable, and the authors of *The Federalist* did make a serious effort to dispel the fears of those opponents. Madison, for example, said that the powers conferred on the federal government were "few,"[38] noted that the people would be the ultimate arbiters of conflicts between the central authority and the states and were not likely to favor central power when disputes arose,[39] and referred on several occasions to the sovereignty of the states—a sovereignty that they would retain in significant part.[40] Even Hamilton, less willing to concede significant limitations on federal power, spoke of "the sovereign power" of the states.[41]

But *The Federalist*, it must be recalled, was not an abstract work of political theory; it was a powerful work of advocacy that was in large part a massive attack on the weakness of the central government under the Articles of Confederation and that was at the same time designed to make the new Constitution palatable to a broad audience. Some greater deference to state rights and interests in this document than in the

---

35. The *Darby* decision was cited approvingly, and the point made that the Tenth Amendment is "essentially a tautology" in New York v. United States, 112 S. Ct. 2408, 2418 (1992)—the Court's most recent effort to impose significant constitutional limits on national power to intrude on state authority. The *New York* case is discussed in more detail in ch. 3, sec. A., and ch. 4, sec. B.

36. *See* H. J. Powell, The Compleat Jeffersonian: Justice Rehnquist and Federalism, 91 Yale L.J. 1317, 1366–68, and authorities cited at nn. 296, 302, 307 (1982).

37. For example, particular objection was raised to the potential reach of the broad grants of power (especially over commerce), coupled with the power conferred under the Necessary and Proper Clause—powers whose exercise would bind the states under the Supremacy Clause. *See* 1 H. Storing, *The Complete Anti-Federalist* 24–26 (1981). The anti-federalist view was that national power should properly be limited to the *facilitation* of such matters as commercial intercourse among the states. *Id.* at 25.

38. *The Federalist* No. 45 (Madison).

39. *The Federalist* No. 46 (Madison).

40. *E.g., The Federalist* Nos. 39 (Madison) and 45 (Madison).

41. *E.g., The Federalist* No. 9 (Hamilton).

Constitution itself is thus not surprising.[42] Yet even in the heat of debate, there are critical passages in *The Federalist* emphasizing that the ultimate authority on which the Constitution rests is "the people alone,"[43] that the states are "constituent parts of a national society,"[44] and that the proposed Constitution derives from the need for "one nation, under one foederal government" which adequately reflects the fact that we are "one connected country" and "one united people."[45] It is interesting to note that John Jay, one of the authors of *The Federalist*, vigorously attacked the notion of state sovereign immunity (when he served as Chief Justice) in his opinion in *Chisholm v. Georgia*.[46] To be sure,

42. This aspect of *The Federalist Papers* is discussed by Garry Wills in his introduction to the Bantam edition (1982) at xii–xv, and in D. Kennedy, Federalism and the Force of History, in *How Federal Is the Constitution?* 67, 70–71 (R. Goldwin & W. Schambra eds., 1987). *See also* H. Scheiber, Constitutional Structure and the Protection of Rights: Federalism and the Separation of Powers, in *Power Divided: Essays in the History and Practice of Federalism* 17 (H. Scheiber & M. Feeley eds., 1989) (arguing that while federalism was a concept manufactured out of the necessity of obtaining support for ratification, separation of powers within the federal government stemmed from a recognized and principled theory whose impact on the protection of liberty in our society has been more pervasive and impressive).

43. *The Federalist* No. 46 (Madison). Madison also states in this paper that while the "natural attachment" of the people was to "the governments of their respective States," they might in the future "become more partial to the foederal than to the State governments." Surely, he argued, the people could not, in such a case, be "precluded from giving most of their confidence where they may discover it to be most due." But after this ringing affirmation of the significance of the people's choice, Madison does attempt to allay fears of overcentralization by reminding his readers that "it is only within a certain sphere, that the foederal power can, in the nature of things, be advantageously administered." (Note that this last passage seems addressed more to practical than to legal limits on federal power.)

44. *The Federalist* No. 9 (Hamilton). As Garry Wills emphasizes in his introduction to the Bantam edition (1982) at xiii, Hamilton in this paper draws an analogy between the new Union and the solar system, comparing the federal government to the sun. "[T]his very illustration," Wills points out, "enforces the idea of a single sovereignty: there can be only one force of gravity if the system is to cohere." Moreover, he argues, the concept of multiple sovereignty in the same territory *(imperium in imperio)* was generally viewed as a solecism. There could be no "realm within a realm." *Id.* Thus, in Wills's view, the occasional references to state "sovereignty" in *The Federalist Papers* were "dictated by the campaign to ratify," *id.* at xv, and the word when so used was being employed in a far weaker sense than when the concept was used to predicate the existence of ultimate sovereignty in the people who ordained the Constitution.

45. *The Federalist* No. 2 (Jay).

46. 2 U.S. (2 Dall.) 419 (1793). Jay argued that the "feudal" doctrine of sovereign immunity—at least as it related to the position of the states in the federal union and to a suit brought against a state by a citizen of another state—was incompatible with popular sovereignty. Justice Iredell, the sole dissenter, did support the defendant state's invocation

the *Chisholm* decision led in remarkably short order to the Eleventh Amendment, which many have seen as a reaffirmation of the role of the states as sovereign entities. But recent historical scholarship, together with the text of the Amendment itself, combine to make a powerful case for a more limited interpretation of the first Amendment to follow ratification of the Bill of Rights—an interpretation that simply removes one category of cases based on party identity (those in which a state is the defendant) from federal jurisdiction, but does not in any way affect the power of the national legislature to subject a state to federal court suits as well as to national law.[47] Indeed, the need for such an Amendment to accomplish even this limited result is strong evidence that the original document did not itself afford significant protection to state sovereignty, autonomy, or immunity.

2. Whatever Elements of State Authority May Have Been Incorporated or Preserved in the Original Constitution Have Been Eroded by Subsequent Amendments, Evolving Constitutional Doctrine, and Historical Practice

Even if one assumes that the Constitution, as originally conceived, contained important legal protections of state power and authority against federal intrusion, subsequent events have all but eroded any such protections, so that the states today stand legally naked against the potential onslaught of federal power.

The process began with the earliest interpretations of the Constitution by the Supreme Court—led by John Marshall, one of the strongest

---

of sovereign immunity in a federal court, but ultimately rested his decision on statutory interpretation, rather than on the Constitution itself.

47. The seminal study in recent years is probably J. Gibbons, The Eleventh Amendment and State Sovereign Immunity: A Reinterpretation, 83 Colum. L. Rev. 1889 (1983). *See also, e.g.,* A. Amar, Of Sovereignty and Federalism, 96 Yale L.J. 1425 (1987); W. Fletcher, A Historical Interpretation of the Eleventh Amendment: A Narrow Construction of an Affirmative Grant of Jurisdiction rather than a Prohibition against Jurisdiction, 35 Stan. L. Rev. 1033 (1983); J. Orth, *The Judicial Power of the United States: The Eleventh Amendment in American History* (1987). As Gibbons notes, the view that the Constitution abrogated sovereign immunity was, at the time of the ratification debates, advanced by both pro- and antiratification forces. Gibbons, *supra,* at 1902–8.

For contrasting views of the virtues of state sovereign immunity and the proper scope of the Eleventh Amendment, see, e.g., A. Althouse, When to Believe a Legal Fiction: Federal Interests and the Eleventh Amendment, 40 Hastings L.J. 1123 (1989); G. Brown, Has the Supreme Court Confessed Error on the Eleventh Amendment? Revisionist Scholarship and State Immunity, 68 N.C. L. Rev. 867 (1990).

nationalists of the Republic's early years.[48] Perhaps the most significant of the nationalizing decisions was *McCulloch v. Maryland,* which adopted Hamilton's broad view of the authority of Congress under the Necessary and Proper Clause of Article I.[49] But there were other important decisions as well, including Chief Justice Story's ringing affirmation of Supreme Court authority to reverse state court decisions,[50] Chief Justice Marshall's application of that power (in the face of the Eleventh Amendment) to cases in which a state itself was the appellee in an appeal from a state supreme court decision,[51] and a variety of decisions asserting the reach of federal power in other important respects.[52] Of course, the trend was not entirely one directional: the Bill of Rights was held inapplicable to the states;[53] thus, the states remained free (as far as federal law was concerned), even to abridge speech or to establish a religion (as some did), so long as they did not violate the specific prohibitions of the original Constitution. And the ability of the states to regulate activity that was also subject to regulation under Congress's Article I commerce power was recognized, although the nature and extent of this state power were subject to varying interpretations during the nineteenth century.[54] Yet it was also made clear during this period not only that Congress

48. Jefferson Powell has argued forcefully that the concept of "intent," as understood at the time the Constitution itself was originally drafted and ratified, was heavily dependent in people's minds not only on the language and historical setting of the document but on the authoritative interpretations of the document by those (especially the Supreme Court) duly authorized to interpret it. *See* H. J. Powell, The Modern Misunderstanding of Original Intent, 54 U. Chi. L. Rev. 1513, 1533–38 (1987).

49. *See* note 25, *supra,* and accompanying text.

50. *See* Martin v. Hunter's Lessee, 14 U.S. (1 Wheat.) 304 (1816).

51. *See* Cohens v. Virginia, 19 U.S. (6 Wheat.) 264 (1821). The rationale of *Cohens* was recently unanimously reaffirmed by the Supreme Court in reviewing a state court judgment in an action against a state agency for monetary relief. McKesson Corp. v. Division of ABT, 496 U.S. 18, 31 (1990).

52. *E.g.,* Gibbons v. Ogden, 22 U.S. (9 Wheat.) 1 (1824) (dealing with the national commerce power). For the suggestion that neither the *Gibbons* nor the *McCulloch* decisions purported to give Congress carte blanche, see G. Gunther, *Constitutional Law* 97 (12th ed. 1991).

53. *See* Barron v. Mayor and City Council of Baltimore, 32 U.S. (7 Pet.) 243 (1833).

54. In his opinion in *Gibbons,* Chief Justice Marshall indicated that the states, in pursuance of legitimate state purposes, could impinge on commerce among the states. In The License Cases, 46 U.S. (5 How.) 504, 573 (1847), Chief Justice Taney, in a separate opinion, argued that the states could regulate interstate commerce so long as the regulation did not conflict with any act of Congress. Then in Cooley v. Board of Wardens, 53 U.S. (12 How.) 299 (1851), the Court struck the balance by allowing state regulation in areas where the need for national uniformity was not so urgent that state action was precluded even in the absence of an Act of Congress.

could exercise its Commerce Clause power by preempting a particular field of regulation but also that (absent congressional authorization) some kinds of state interference with interstate and foreign commerce were precluded by the very existence of the federal commerce power—the famous "dormant" or "negative" Commerce Clause theory that has been both attacked and defended ever since.[55]

The outcome of the Civil War settled on the battlefield the theoretical debates over the asserted rights of state nullification and secession—rights that, in the view of many, were plainly inconsistent with the Union as originally established. And in the wake of the Civil War, extending into the present century, a series of constitutional Amendments went even farther to solidify federal power and to reduce the "structural" role of the states in the operation of the federal government. The Fourteenth Amendment (and, of course, the Thirteenth) imposed significant federal limitations on state power, and these limitations were gradually extended in the present century to cover many of the guarantees of the Bill of Rights. The Fifteenth, Nineteenth, Twenty-fourth, and Twenty-sixth Amendments severely curtailed the power of the states to limit the right to vote.[56] The Sixteenth Amendment—overruling a Supreme

55. For discussion of the doctrine as it has developed since the *Cooley* case in 1851, see L. Tribe, *American Constitutional Law* ch. 6, especially §§ 6–4 to 6–14 (2d ed. 1988).

For further contributions to the ongoing debate, see, e.g., CTS Corp. v. Dynamics Corp., 481 U.S. 69, 94, 95 (1987) (Scalia, J., concurring in part and arguing that, in the absence of congressional preemption, the Court should strike down a state law on *"Cooley"* grounds only if it "discriminates against interstate commerce" or "create[s] an impermissible risk of inconsistent regulation by different States," but normally not on the ground that the burden on commerce "is clearly excessive in relation to the putative local benefits") (internal quotes omitted); R. Collins, Economic Union as a Constitutional Value, 63 N.Y.U. L. Rev. 43 (1988) (*Cooley* doctrine, as it has evolved, has succeeded in promoting interstate harmony); E. Kitch, Regulation, the American Common Market and Public Choice, 6 Harv. J. L. & Pub. Pol'y 119 (1982) (application of dormant Commerce Clause by Supreme Court is undesirable because it encourages the enactment of intrusive and counterproductive federal statutory regulation).

As this book was going to press, another voice was added to the criticism of the dormant Commerce Clause theory and an eloquent plea made for its abandonment as a limitation on state power. See M. Redish, *The Constitution as Political Struture* 63–98 (1995). In this work, Professor Redish also argues more generally for increased Supreme Court enforcement of constitutional limits on *federal* power.

56. The Fifteenth Amendment prohibits the states from abridging the right to vote on the basis of race, color, or previous condition of servitude; the Nineteenth guarantees women's suffrage; the Twenty-fourth prohibits the states from denying or abridging the right to vote in federal elections by reason of failure to pay "any poll tax or any other tax"; and the Twenty-sixth provides that the right to vote shall not be denied or abridged on account of age in the case of any citizen who is eighteen years of age or older.

Court decision[57] and affirming the power of Congress to levy a direct tax on income from property without apportioning the tax among the states according to population—greatly enhanced federal power to raise revenue. And the Seventeenth, in providing for direct election of Senators, eliminated the participation of the state legislatures in the electoral process and thus reduced significantly the structural role played by state authority in determining the composition of the national legislature. Indeed, the only post–Civil War Amendment to increase state power in any respect is the Twenty-first, which allowed a state to prohibit the transportation or possession of "intoxicating liquors" "for delivery or use therein . . . in violation of the laws thereof."

While these specific alterations of the text (with the notable exception of the Twenty-first Amendment)[58] were diminishing whatever state authority existed prior to their adoption, the Supreme Court followed a jagged course of interpretation that ultimately ceded a vast range of substantive regulatory authority to the national government. There was, of course, a period of renown (and, in the view of many, of infamy) in which the Court precluded the federal government from enacting and implementing a wide range of social and economic legislation on the grounds (among others) that the commerce or the taxing power did not reach that far, or that the state police power guaranteed by the Tenth Amendment stood in the way.[59] But a number of these decisions rested

---

Recent years have seen extensive federal regulation, both constitutional and statutory, relating to state power over voting and over the drawing of electoral lines for state as well as federal elections. In the former (constitutional) category, see, e.g., Reynolds v. Sims, 377 U.S. 533 (1964); Shaw v. Reno, 113 S. Ct. 2816 (1993). In the latter (statutory) category, see the Voting Rights Act of 1965, as amended, 42 U.S.C. § 1972 et seq.

57. Pollock v. Farmers' Loan & Trust Co., 157 U.S. 429 (1895).

58. The Twenty-first Amendment, it should be recalled, came in the aftermath of the nationwide prohibition decreed by the Eighteenth; as a measure of political compromise, it substituted for that national prohibition a system of state options in the matter of the regulation of alcoholic beverages.

In any event, the guarantee of state authority over alcoholic beverages in this Amendment serves to underscore the *absence* of comparable guarantees in other areas.

59. Among the decisions dating from the late nineteenth century to the fourth decade of the twentieth that significantly limited national regulatory power were: United States v. E.C. Knight Co., 156 U.S. 1 (1895) (holding that "manufacture" was not commerce within the meaning of the Commerce Clause); Adair v. United States, 208 U.S. 161 (1908) (striking down, on substantive due process grounds, federal statute prohibiting "yellow dog" contracts—contracts that made nonmembership in a trade union a condition of employment—in the railroad industry); Hammer v. Dagenhart, 247 U.S. 251, 276 (1918) (invalidating federal statute prohibiting transportation in commerce of goods produced by certain kinds of child labor—statute held (1) to exceed the authority delegated to Congress

far less on the perceived virtues of federalism than on the notion that any government, state or federal, was disabled from interfering with private freedom to contract or indeed to engage in economic activity in almost any manner short of mayhem (or certain conspiracies in restraint of trade).[60]

In any event, the edifice collapsed in the famous "switch in time that saved nine" in 1937 and the decisions that came in its wake—decisions that gave the judicial seal of approval to many of the nationwide changes wrought by the New Deal.[61] Today, the power of Congress to regulate commerce is so broad that since 1937, only in *New York v. United States*[62] has a congressional effort to regulate commerce been invalidated by the Supreme Court as exceeding the grant of constitutional authority.[63] The existence of the states' "police power"

---

over commerce, and (2) to apply to a "purely local matter to which the federal authority does not extend"); United States v. Butler, 297 U.S. 1, 68 (1936) (striking down the Agricultural Adjustment Act of 1933 because Congress's attempt, through exercise of its power to tax, to "regulate and control agricultural production . . . [exceeded] the powers delegated to the federal government").

60. The notion of substantive due process (and particularly its manifestation in theories of freedom of contract) also led the Court during this period to strike down many state efforts to regulate business activity. The most notable example was Lochner v. New York, 198 U.S. 45 (1905) (invalidating state law prohibiting the employment of bakery workers for more than ten hours per day or sixty hours per week). Of particular interest here is Coppage v. Kansas, 236 U.S. 1 (1915), which struck down a state law virtually identical to the federal law invalidated only a few years earlier in Adair v. United States, 208 U.S. 161 (1908).

On the other hand, even during this period, states could exercise regulatory power that the federal government could not in matters such as the permissible limits of child labor in the manufacturing process. *See* Hammer v. Dagenhart, 247 U.S. 251, 275 (1918) (discussing the legitimacy of regulation of child labor by "every State in the Union").

61. Among the most significant decisions were NLRB v. Jones & Laughlin Steel Corp., 301 U.S. 1 (1937) (upholding the constitutionality of the National Labor Relations Act); and (several years later) Wickard v. Filburn, 317 U.S. 111 (1942) (upholding as a valid regulation of interstate commerce the marketing quota provisions of the Agricultural Adjustment Act of 1938). The demise of substantive due process as a basis for invalidating regulation of economic activity was marked in West Coast Hotel Co. v. Parrish, 300 U.S. 379 (1937) (sustaining state minimum wage law for women). (Since the state law in the *Parrish* case was limited to women, it might not survive a challenge under modern equal protection analysis.)

62. 112 S. Ct. 2408 (1992).

63. For a brief period, National League of Cities v. Usery, 426 U.S. 833 (1976) (since overruled), stood as an "island in the stream" protecting the states against certain exercises of congressional power over commerce that would be valid as against private entities. Chief Justice Rehnquist, the author of the Court's *National League of Cities* opinion, has called

has been held not to preclude federal preemption of state law in areas in which Congress is properly exercising its authority under Article I.[64] The grant of authority to Congress in § 5 of the Fourteenth Amendment has been held, in effect, to include the authority to give that Amendment a more expansive interpretation than the Supreme Court had given, or would otherwise give it.[65] And the ability of Congress to use its power of the purse—its power to condition a grant to a state on the

---

it a "mistake to conclude that Congress' power to regulate pursuant to the Commerce Clause is unlimited." Hodel v. Virginia Surface Mining & Reclamation Assn, Inc., 452 U.S. 264, 310 (1981) (concurring separately in the judgment). But as Professor Tribe notes, "none of [Chief Justice Rehnquist's] fellow Justices have shown any inclination to plow with him territory that the Court tilled so fruitlessly from 1887 to 1937." L. Tribe, *American Constitutional Law* 310–11 n. 6 (2d ed. 1988).

With respect to the *New York* case, referred to in text, the Court did strike down one of three "incentives" enacted by Congress to encourage state provisions for the dumping of low-level radioactive waste, and it did so on the grounds that the particular action exceeded Congress's power under the Commerce Clause. But it is noteworthy that (1) the Court was dealing not with congressional regulation of private activity but with a national effort to compel action by state governing authorities; (2) the Court's real concern seemed to focus not on the objective of Congress but on the particular means chosen—the effort to "coerce" state legislators into taking regulatory action for which they would be accountable to their own electorates; and (3) the Court specifically equated the question of the limits of Congress's enumerated powers with that of "discerning the core of sovereignty retained by the States under the Tenth Amendment." 112 S. Ct. at 2419. This important decision is more fully discussed in succeeding chapters.

One interesting recent lower court decision that seems more directly in point in drawing a limit to the national commerce power is United States v. Lopez, 2 F.3d 1342 (5th Cir. 1993) (invalidating, as exceeding Congress's power under the Commerce Clause, a federal statute making it illegal to possess a firearm on or within one thousand feet of any school grounds). The court of appeals indicated that the result might be different had Congress made "adequate" findings to support federal regulation. (The decision is squarely in conflict with the decision of the Ninth Circuit in United States v. Edwards, 13 F.3d 291 (1993), and the Supreme Court has granted certiorari in *Lopez* in order to resolve the conflict. 114 S. Ct. 1536 (1994).) [See postscript, p. 141, *infra*.]

64. *See, e.g.,* Hodel v. Virginia Surface Mining & Reclamation Assn, 452 U.S. 264, 289–97 (1981).

In a recent article, Professor Gardbaum argues that the United States (unlike Canada and the European Community) has moved to a form of federalism that, as a constitutional matter, rests largely if not entirely in the discretion of the national government, not only because of the expansive definition of Congress's substantive powers under Article I but because of the Supreme Court's willingness to uphold Congress's power to preempt state law even in the absence of a conflict with federal law. S. Gardbaum, The Nature of Preemption, 79 Cornell L. Rev. 767, 813 & n. 218 (1994). Preemption in the absence of a conflict, he contends, is not properly within the scope of the Supremacy Clause. *See id.* at 773–77.

65. *See* Katzenbach v. Morgan, 384 U.S. 641 (1966).

state's willingness to comply with specified federal conditions—has been broadly sustained.[66] On the judicial front, the ability of Congress and of the federal courts to mandate state court enforcement of federal law, whether those courts want to or not, and in ways that they may properly reject for the enforcement of their own laws, has been consistently upheld, even before the famous about-face in 1937.[67]

Again, it would be a grave mistake to conclude that state interests have gone unrecognized during this era. But it would be an even graver mistake to overestimate the significance of that recognition. Thus, the *Erie* decision, noted above,[68] requires the application of state law in the federal courts only when federal law (*including* federal common law)[69] does not require otherwise. The rule of *Younger v. Harris* and

66. Congress's power to spend in pursuit of the general welfare (without regard to whether exercise of the power is tied to some other power enumerated in Article I) was first clearly articulated in United States v. Butler, 297 U.S. 1 (1936) (see note 59, *supra*). In cases since *Butler*, the Court has never invalidated any congressionally imposed condition on the receipt of federal funds by the states. (For the most recent decision in this area, see South Dakota v. Dole, 483 U.S. 203 (1987).) Although the possibility remains that such a condition might be invalid as bearing an insufficient relation to the purpose of the spending program, or might be invalid as imposing an "unconstitutional condition" (by limiting freedom of speech, for example), it is noteworthy that the *Dole* case itself involved a condition (minimum drinking age) that—the Court assumed for purposes of the case—Congress could not have imposed directly on the states in view of the Twenty-first Amendment.

67. Notable examples (both before and since 1937) include Ward v. Board of County Commissioners of Love County, 353 U.S. 17 (1920); General Oil Co. v. Crain, 209 U.S. 211 (1908); Testa v. Katt, 330 U.S. 386 (1947); Felder v. Casey, 487 U.S. 131 (1988); Howlett v. Rose, 496 U.S. 356 (1990); and McKesson Corp. v. Division of ABT, 496 U.S. 18 (1990).

See also FERC v. Mississippi, 456 U.S. 742 (1982) (upholding validity of congressional directive to state regulatory authorities to "consider" certain regulatory standards and to follow certain procedures in considering those standards). Whether the *FERC* decision survives in full after New York v. United States, 112 S. Ct. 2408 (1992) (more fully discussed below), is not entirely clear.

68. *See* ch. 1.

69. There has been a vigorous debate over the question whether the Rules of Decision Act, 28 U.S.C. § 1652, precludes the development of federal common law in the absence of authority to do so provided by the federal Constitution, or by a federal treaty or statute. For leading examples of the positions taken in this debate, compare M. Redish, Federal Common Law, Political Legitimacy, and the Interpretive Process: An Institutional Perspective, 83 Nw. U. L. Rev. 761 (1989), with L. Weinberg, Federal Common Law, id. at 805. *See also* M. Redish, *The Federal Courts in the Political Order* 29–46 (1991); Symposium, Federal Courts, 12 Pace L. Rev. 227–357 (1992). Although the Supreme Court has been reluctant in recent years to exercise federal common law authority, it has never suggested that the Rules of Decision Act bars it from doing so. *See Hart & Wechsler* 1993 Supp. at 113.

its progeny, also referred to above,[70] is plainly subject to congressional alteration, as are the judicial limits recently imposed on the availability of federal habeas corpus. And the *National League of Cities* case[71]— the major effort in recent decades to declare a sphere of constitutional protection for the states against federal incursion—died, first by degrees in a series of cases distinguishing it,[72] and then by official pronouncement in the Court's decision in *Garcia v. San Antonio Metropolitan Trans. Auth..*[73] True, one more interesting and impressive effort to afford constitutional protection has been made in *New York v. United States,*[74] but whatever that case means (a question discussed in more detail in the next chapter), two points should be recognized. First, it is hard to imagine an intelligent drafter of federal legislation who could not achieve the desired goal by working around the Court's decision in the *New York* case (through resort to the power of the purse, for example), and second, the reach and durability of the decision itself is thus far essentially untested.

In sum, one wise commentator was undoubtedly correct when he summarized the present state of the law by the formula $P = C$ (Federal power (P) is as broad as Congress (C) wishes it to be).[75] Indeed, in view of the power of the Executive to issue regulations, to call up the

---

70. *See* ch. 1.

71. National League of Cities v. Usery, 426 U.S. 833 (1976) (holding unconstitutional, as violative of limitations imposed on the scope of the federal commerce power by the Tenth Amendment, national legislation making the Fair Labor Standards Act provisions for overtime pay applicable to virtually all state and local employees).

72. *See, e.g.,* Hodel v. Virginia Surface Mining & Reclamation Ass'n, 452 U.S. 264 (1981); FERC v. Mississippi, 456 U.S. 742 (1982).

73. 469 U.S. 528, 537-47 (1985). Interestingly, a staff study published in 1986 by the Advisory Commission on Intergovernmental Relations—entitled "Reflections on *Garcia* and Its Implications for Federalism"—concludes that the Court in that case correctly interpreted the Constitution. But the study goes on to argue that the interpretation exposes a "basic contradiction" in the Constitution itself. *Id.* at 51.

The study then suggests, among various ways of dealing with the claimed contradiction, consideration of a number of constitutional Amendments. These Amendments cover a broad range, from the relatively modest approach of ordering the federal courts not to leave such issues to the political process (the nub of the rationale in *Garcia*), to such radical changes as imposing explicit prohibitions on national displacement of state law or giving the states a power (on the concurrence of two-thirds of the state legislatures) to nullify any Act of Congress.

74. 112 S. Ct. 2408 (1992) (invalidating one of three federal statutory "incentives" to induce the states to work out an acceptable system for disposal of low-level radioactive waste).

75. *See* R. Cappalli, Restoring Federalism Values in the Federal Grant System, 19 Urb. Law. 493, 502 (1987).

militia,[76] and to take a variety of other actions, and the power of the Supreme Court to enforce the provisions of the Bill of Rights, other explicit restrictions on the states, and its view of the dormant Commerce Clause, the formula might well be expanded to $P = F$ (the power of the federal government (P) is as broad as the various branches of the federal government (F) wish it to be in the exercise of their lawful authority). The sole checks on each federal branch are essentially those imposed by the Bill of Rights and the principle of separation of powers—a principle addressed only to the federal government and not to the relationship between it and the states.[77]

B. The Existence of Significant State Autonomy Is Economically Counterproductive

Let us assume, then, as perhaps we must, that there is virtually no significant constitutional limit on the capacity of federal law to supersede state authority.[78] (Admittedly, the Constitution precludes the exercise of federal power for the purpose of abolishing a state without its consent, but the assumption here is that while the federal government must leave the state with its boundaries—if the state does not agree to surrender them—it may at the same time deprive the state of virtually

76. See note 23, supra, and accompanying text.

77. Samuel Beer and Vincent Ostrom have argued that the Framers essentially rejected Montesquieu's conception of a loose confederation of relatively independent small republics while at the same time relying on his theory of checks and balances as a way of avoiding excessive concentration of power within the national government itself. See S. Beer, The Idea of the Nation, in How Federal Is the Constitution? 109, 110 (R. Goldwin & W. Schambra eds., 1987) (referring to Madison's Federalist No. 10 as turning Montesquieu's argument "on its head"); S. Beer, To Make a Nation: The Rediscovery of American Federalism 285 (1993) (the authors of The Federalist relied on Montesquieu's theory of the necessity of separating legislative, executive, and judicial power as a condition of liberty); V. Ostrom, The Meaning of American Federalism 43–45 (1991) (noting differences between Montesquieu and Hamilton on the question of the virtues of a loose "confederation" and a more closely knit "compound republic"). See also H. Scheiber, note 42, supra (distinguishing between the origins of federalism, on the one hand, and the principle of separation of powers, on the other).

78. In accordance with the wise maxim, "Never say never," I acknowledge, at least for argument's sake, that Congress would have difficulty if it attempted to preempt, say, all state laws exempting charities in any degree from tort liability (see H. Friendly, In Praise of Erie—and of the New Federal Common Law, 39 N.Y.U. L. Rev. 383, 394–95 (1964); cf. S. Gardbaum, note 54, supra), or substituting for state laws on incest a uniform national law on the subject. And of course, as already noted, the Twenty-first Amendment sets limits on federal power to supersede state and local laws involving alcoholic beverages.

all authority to regulate human affairs within those boundaries.) It does not follow, however, that federal law *should* preempt all significant state laws (and indeed, no serious suggestion to do so is currently pending). To hark back for a moment to the formula $P = F$, the vital question of policy remains: how much P should F exercise in fact? Should we have a strong federal system—one in which state autonomy plays a vital role—on nonconstitutional grounds? After all, virtually no one (not even Professor Crosskey)[79] has suggested that the Constitution *precludes* the delegation of substantial authority to the states. This question of policy, or discretion, is dealt with in the remainder of this chapter, and in this section the focus is on the economic aspects of the issue. The effort here is not to argue for the value of *total* preemption of state law, but to show that the case for centralization as a matter of policy is far stronger than most federalists would be willing to admit.

1. *The Weakness of Traditional Economic Justifications for State Autonomy*

The powerful economic arguments for a strong national government are considered below.[80] But before we turn to those arguments, it is important to understand the fundamental weakness of the economic arguments for the diffusion of regulatory authority among the states.

The "traditional" economic arguments in favor of the existence of significant state policy-making authority[81] may be summarized here as resting primarily on the asserted virtues of rivalry or competition. Advocates of state autonomy start from the premise that if there is only one source of governmental power, it is far more likely that this source

79. In his extraordinary two-volume work, *Politics and the Constitution in the History of the United States* (1953), William Crosskey argued, inter alia, that the Framers intended a completely national, rather than a federal, system of government. Although the research underlying Crosskey's study was prodigious, and his arguments not without power, the core of his thesis has been generally rejected on the ground that it does not fairly reflect the nature of the Union as originally established. For critical reactions to Crosskey's work, *see, e.g.,* reviews by E. Brown and H. Hart in 67 Harv. L. Rev. 1439, 1456 (1954); I. Brant, Mr. Crosskey, and Mr. Madison, 54 Colum. L. Rev. 443 (1954); and J. Goebel, Ex Parte Clio, 54 Colum. L. Rev. 450 (1954).

In any event, even Crosskey did not deny the existence of federal authority to *delegate* many matters to the discretion of state and local governments.

80. *See* this chapter, sec. B.2.

81. These arguments are discussed in greater detail in ch. 3, sec. B.2. The use of the word "traditional" in text is perhaps inappropriate. Although some aspects of the economic arguments can be found in the ratification debates, its refinements have been developed in the present century.

will tyrannize over economic activity, disrupt the proper operation of a market economy, and make serious mistakes that either cannot be perceived or, if they are perceived, cannot readily be corrected.[82] The states, it is then argued, serve two important functions in this context. First, they establish a source of countervailing power to the federal government, and if they have significant substantive responsibilities, the burden is likely to rest on those who would take those responsibilities away—both to get the federal government to act and then to prove that federal action has in fact achieved some worthy objective. Second, the states engage in active competition with each other to attract productive investment and productive workers. This competition is enhanced by the visibility of what is happening in other states and by the mobility of industry and labor.[83] Indeed, this right of movement allows people to exercise their preferences on a wide range of issues—some of which can be considered economic only if the term is stretched well beyond its conventional meaning.

A related economic argument for the existence of significant state (and local) authority looks to the diseconomies of scale inherent in certain kinds of activities.[84] Even if it makes sense to have only one national space program (if that), it would be far less efficient for the country's schools, hospitals, roads, sanitary districts, water districts, and similar

---

82. Among the advocates of a strong federal system, a number have emphasized the value of diffused authority as a safeguard against tyranny of various sorts, both in the realm of economics and that of politics. *See, e.g.,* V. Ostrom, *The Meaning of American Federalism* (1991); V. Ostrom, Can Federalism Make a Difference?, 3 Publius 197 (1973); M. McConnell, Federalism: Evaluating the Founders' Design, 54 U. Chi. L. Rev. 1484 (1987) (review of R. Berger, *Federalism: The Founders' Design* (1987)).

83. The right of movement from one state to another (for individuals at least and, to some extent, for capital) is protected by the Constitution.

With respect to the protected constitutional right of individuals to travel from one state to another, see especially Edwards v. California, 314 U.S. 160, 178 (1941) (Douglas, J., concurring); Shapiro v. Thompson, 394 U.S. 618, 629–31 (1969). With respect to the subtler question of the ability of the states to limit movements of capital from one state to another—and the limitations on state power that may be imposed by the Commerce Clause and by provisions of the Fourteenth Amendment—see L. Tribe, *American Constitutional Law* ch. 6 (2d ed. 1988); *cf.* R. Epstein, Exit Rights under Federalism, 55 Law & Contemp. Probs. (Winter 1992), at 147, 150 (urging that "federalism provides insufficient protection for market institutions").

84. Alice Rivlin, for a number of years Director of the Congressional Budget Office, has written eloquently on this problem. *See, e.g.,* her comments in Advisory Commission on Intergovernmental Relations, *Emerging Issues in American Federalism* 73, 76 (1986) (speaking of "decision overload" at the federal level), and her longer treatment of the subject of federalism and the allocation of functions in her book, *Reviving the American Dream: The Economy, the States and the Federal Government* (1992).

activities to be directed from a single source than from a multiplicity of state (and local) sources more closely attuned to local conditions and preferences.

This summary is doubtless too brief, and the next chapter will attempt to expand on some of its more attractive aspects, but the point to be developed here is that the arguments, taken at their best, do not warrant a strong federal system in which states and localities retain significant decision-making power—at least not at the end of a century in which the world is increasingly becoming a single market for goods and capital (and even labor), and in which the existence of diffused power to make and affect policy serves primarily as a drag on this country's ability to compete effectively in the world arena.

To begin, and putting aside questions relating to any "new world (economic) order," the arguments against unrestrained national authority hinge in large part on a value judgment that is sometimes but not always made explicit—a judgment that a free and competitive market is presumptively (if not irrebuttably) preferable to government regulation.[85] Not everyone adheres to this world view, and for those who do not, the economic arguments for federalism may seem a good deal less attractive. Moreover, most of those who see the market as having virtues that exceed its defects do at the same time recognize the role of government in the many situations in which imperfections in the operation of the market require corrective government action. For these people as well, it may make more sense to undertake corrective action, whenever it is required, on a national level.

Thus, to take one of the more specific arguments for diffusion of policy-making authority, the premise of mobility (as many have noted) appears considerably overstated. Whatever constitutional rights of movement individuals may have, there are practical barriers to moving, especially for those who find themselves in the lower economic brackets in the state in which they live.[86] There are significant barriers also to

85. Clearly, this view (or a subtler variation of it) animates the suggestions of such scholars as Edmund Kitch—suggestions that he summarizes in a paper entitled Regulation, the American Common Market and Public Choice (in 6 Harv. J.L. & Pub. Pol'y 119 (1982)), and Richard Epstein, whose views are indicated in a paper entitled *The Federalist Papers: From Practical Politics to High Principle* (in 16 Harv. J.L. & Pub. Pol'y 13 (1993)) and in his article, Exit Rights under Federalism, 55 Law & Contemp. Probs. (Winter 1992), at 147.

86. *See* R. Revesz, Rehabilitating Interstate Competition: Rethinking the "Race-to-the-Bottom" Rationale for Federal Environmental Regulation, 67 N.Y.U. L. Rev. 1210, 1237, and authorities cited therein at n. 86 (1992).

the movement of capital, especially when it is tied to such fixed assets as land or substantial plant and equipment.[87] To sell in a falling market in state A in order to buy in a rising market in state B is not always an available course.

At the same time, at least with respect to capital and to an increasing extent with respect to productive and needed workers, the ability to move across international borders may be growing to the point that the importance of the right to reject the policies of a particular state by moving to another state is a diminishing one. The growing resistance in many countries to large-scale immigration is not, in the main, resistance to the creation of plant and equipment with funds coming from other countries, or to the movement across international borders of those who are unlikely to become public charges and whose talents are needed to aid in economic growth or social welfare. The point is not that international boundaries have lost their importance, or that it is just as easy to move to another country as it is to move to another state; rather, the argument is that the international mobility of goods, capital, and labor is reducing the economic significance of interstate mobility as a means of escaping the restrictive or unpopular rules of a particular state.

Second, the key economic argument for state autonomy today (although surely less critical to the thinking of the Framers or of their opponents)[88] is the value of competition among states as a way of maximizing social welfare—an argument closely tied to the right of exit already discussed. To give an example sometimes cited, if each state is free (within very broad constitutional limits, as well as reasonably broad federal statutory limits) to formulate its own policies with respect to the laws governing corporate charters and by-laws, then the states will compete with each other in order to attract corporations to incorporate there as a lucrative source of registration and related fees. Thus, the states with the most congenial laws from the viewpoint of industry—laws that will facilitate effective management *and* provide adequate protection to shareholders—will be the states that draw the most corporations.[89]

---

87. *See* R. Epstein, Exit Rights under Federalism, 55 Law & Contemp. Probs. (Winter 1992), at 147, 155–57.

88. But note Madison's reference in *The Federalist* No. 51 to the need for "opposite and rival interests" as auxiliary precautions against abuse of governmental power. Though his primary reference was plainly to the states as a countervailing force to federal power, it may well be that he was also referring to the relationships of the states to each other.

89. This view has been expressed by a number of commentators, including D. Fischel, The "Race to the Bottom" Revisited: Reflections on Recent Developments in Delaware's

(The same would be true with respect to such matters as tax structure, education, ease of intrastate movement, etc.) The overall effect, as one writer has suggested,[90] is that of a convoy: one state will occasionally pull out in front, but others will see to it that they do not fall too far behind in order to avoid the predators who are on the lookout for strays and laggards.

If one believes in the value of incremental change, this vision is a serendipitous one, but it runs aground on two shoals dreaded by all economists who espouse the virtues of unfettered competition: externalities and transaction costs. And the difficulty is that in a world in which distances are becoming less significant all the time, externalities are likely to increase, while transaction costs may well remain difficult to surmount even when communication becomes less cumbersome and expensive.

To begin with the problem of externalities, all agree that there are certain "public goods" that simply do not yield to the virtues of free market competition. Two examples often given are a lighthouse and a nuclear deterrent. Both cases present the problem of the "free rider"; if the good is furnished, people will get the benefit of it over a wide area whether they "buy" what it offers or not. Such goods—if they are to be furnished on some basis other than pure altruism—must be supplied by government and paid for through some system of taxation (although they can be purchased by governments in a competitive market, and often are).[91]

This much is surely not in dispute. The challenge is to determine which government should provide public goods—national or state. As one scholar has pointed out,[92] if all public goods were "pure" in the

---

Corporation Law, 76 Nw. U. L. Rev. 913 (1982) (also expressing the fear that in moving toward increased regulatory constraints, recent court decisions in Delaware—the leading state in this regard—may have been too responsive to "race-to-the-bottom" critiques); and R. Winter, Private Goals and Competition among State Legal Systems, 6 Harv. J.L. & Pub. Pol'y 127 (1982). See also R. Romano, The State Competition Debate in Corporate Law, 8 Cardozo L. Rev. 709, 752 (1987) (concluding that "shareholders benefit from state competition" but that "on occasion, competition may well produce laws that shareholders in some firms would not choose to adopt voluntarily").

90. J. Shannon, The Return to Fend-for-Yourself Federalism: The Reagan Mark, in Advisory Commission on Intergovernmental Relations, *Readings in Federalism: Perspectives on a Decade of Change* 119, 120 (1989).

91. For an interesting discussion of the provision of public goods in the context of a federal system, see V. Ostrom, *The Meaning of American Federalism* ch. 7 (1991).

92. *See id.*

sense that the benefit derived from them were territorially unlimited, at least within the boundaries of a country like ours, there would be no need for subnational governments to provide any of them. Since many public goods, like parks (at least small ones), are not "pure" in this sense, there may be some justification for smaller administrative units to deal with them.[93] But there is no self-evident reason why the size of those units, and the basis for raising the needed revenues to run them (including, perhaps, some form of user fees in some instances) cannot or should not be determined on a national level.

At least as important, the problem of "externalities" is also rampant with respect to government regulation of private activity. In the environmental area, for example, the residents of state A may gain enormously from the operation of a business that does little environmental damage there but wreaks havoc with the environment of adjoining (and downwind or downstream) states B, C, and D. Or, conversely, corrective environmental action in state A may cost a great deal of money, although the bulk of the benefits from the correction will be felt primarily in other states.[94]

To return for a moment to the corporate example used earlier, one problem is that the actions of a state in attracting corporations to incorporate there may prove appealing to managers and yet not be in the interest of shareholders (who reside primarily out of state), or may advance the corporation's ability to cause socially unproductive injuries to third persons. Lucian Bebchuk has persuasively countered the argument that this situation is highly unlikely to occur because (at least with respect to detriment to shareholders) the corporation would find the price of its stock falling in the event of such harm, and thus the managers would ultimately come out behind.[95] Bebchuk notes that not all appropriations by managers that are made at shareholder expense are adverse to the corporation's operational efficiency, and also points out that the argument does not even take into account those state laws that

93. See ch. 3, sec. B.2, infra.

94. For a leading discussion of the issues raised by the existence of such externalities in the environmental area, see R. Stewart, Pyramids of Sacrifice? Problems of Federalism in Mandating State Implementation of National Environmental Policy, 86 Yale L.J. 1196, 1211–19 (1977).

95. Professor Bebchuk's article, Federalism and the Corporation: The Desirable Limits on State Competition in Corporate Law, 105 Harv. L. Rev. 1435 (1992), is a response to the views advanced by such commentators as Ralph Winter, in Private Goals and Competition among State Legal Systems, 6 Harv. J.L. & Pub. Pol'y 127 (1982).

may operate to the detriment of out-of-staters who have no ownership or other equity interest in the corporation.[96]

Ronald Coase has argued that, in a world free of transaction costs, such a problem will work itself out through bargaining between the affected parties, and an efficient, socially optimal arrangement will be reached.[97] But even without transaction costs, it is undeniable that lack of sufficient resources on one side may preclude agreement, that wealth distribution will be affected by the content of the rule against which people are bargaining, and that bargaining strategies and relative bargaining abilities may profoundly affect the outcome.[98] And of course, as interesting as the theory is, bargaining is not cost free; indeed, transaction costs (tangible and intangible) are often so high in complex, multiparty, multistate situations that the very process of bargaining—at least without the direction and encouragement of some higher authority—is virtually unavailable.[99]

A major difficulty with the argument for the virtues of competition among the states, then, lies in the range of externalities that impede

96. Bebchuk has not had the last word, however, and the debate is sure to continue. Another commentator recently studied a major piece of federal legislation governing corporate affairs (the Williams Act, codified in scattered sections of 15 U.S.C., which requires certain disclosures by tender offerors) and concluded that interest groups are "as likely to skew legislation toward management interests—and away from shareholder interests—at the federal level as at the state level." Note, A Public Choice Perspective on the Debate over Federal versus State Corporate Law, 79 Va. L. Rev. 2129, 2130 (1993). Thus, the author continued, "additional resources expended lobbying federal legislators is pure social waste and should be avoided by leaving corporate regulation to the states." Id.

97. The theory is spelled out in Coase's famous essay, The Problem of Social Cost, 3 J.L. & Econ. 1 (1960).

98. Moreover, it has been argued that the outcome may well be affected by the initial allocation of the right or interest even if the overall wealth of the bargaining parties is similar. See M. Kelman, Consumption Theory, Production Theory, and Ideology in the Coase Theorem, 52 S. Cal. L. Rev. 669, 678–81 (1979). Kelman's position, which has considerable intuitive appeal, is that a person would pay less to acquire something, say a bottle of fine wine, than that same person would be willing to accept to part with it— even if we assume a given level of preference for the wine. Furthermore, the outcome of bargaining is even more likely to be affected when the overall wealth of the parties is dissimilar. See, e.g., C. Baker, Starting Points in Economic Analysis of Law, 8 Hofstra L. Rev. 939, 967 (1980).

99. For a discussion of the effect on Coasian bargaining of "positive transaction costs" (including such elements as the difficulties and expense of bringing all interested parties into the negotiations), see A. M. Polinsky, An Introduction to Law and Economics 12–14 (1983). For a discussion of the problems of transaction costs (and other obstacles to Coasian bargaining) in the context of federalism, see R. Inman & D. Rubinfeld, A Federalist Fiscal Constitution for an Imperfect World: Lessons from the United States, in Federalism: Studies in History, Law and Policy 79 (H. Scheiber ed., 1988).

full and fair competition—that preclude an environment in which those in each state bear all or substantially all of both the costs and benefits of their actions. Although even an economist trained in empirical techniques probably could not prove it, significant interstate externalities may well lurk almost everywhere, in a federal system like ours. Assuming that a country as large as the United States is big enough that the externalities resulting from national regulation of its internal affairs are reasonably limited (even if, for example, we do exploit the Colorado River to the point that what flows into Mexico is mostly salt, and even if the combined welfare of Mexico and the United States is therefore adversely affected), such a conclusion seems far less warranted on a state level. To take the area of education as an illustration, the fact of increasing mobility means that a state's commitment to quality public education may have substantial benefits beyond its borders, and that conversely, a state's own failure to provide adequate education to its residents may not harm it unduly if the state proves sufficiently attractive in other ways to draw trained and productive workers from other states. Thus, the Nation's total commitment to education, if left wholly to the states as individual polities, may well be suboptimal.

The point is not that competition in the private sector is without economic value. But when market imperfections call for some regulatory action, social welfare is more likely to be maximized when such action is taken on a national level.

A closely related argument against the value of competition among the states that is sometimes tied in with the existence of externalities involves what is frequently described as "the race to the bottom."[100] Such a race, it has been suggested, can and will occur among states—even in the absence of externalities—if two or more states are competing to attract industry. Thus, a state may rationally conclude that its overall welfare will be increased if it is able to increase investment and employment by relaxing certain regulatory standards. But if (as seems likely) other states decide to relax those same standards in order to keep (or increase) what they have, overall welfare may decline.[101] Only regulation at the

100. For a recent, impressive analysis of this issue, including a careful distinction between the "race to the bottom" question and that of externalities (as well as a thoughtful taxonomy of the forms of competition that are classified as races to the bottom), see R. Revesz, Rehabilitating Interstate Competition: Rethinking the "Race-to-the-Bottom" Rationale for Federal Environmental Regulation, 67 N.Y.U. L. Rev. 1210 (1992).

101. For a bibliography of the literature on the race to the bottom in the area of environmental regulation, see *id.* at 1210–11 n. 1.

national level can preclude such socially harmful races from occurring, and indeed, since national regulation in one area may simply move the race among the states into some other area in which the states are still free to compete, only the virtual abolition of significant state power to regulate and tax can wholly eliminate the potential harm.[102]

On the issue of economies of scale, such prominent economists as Alice Rivlin have emphasized the heavy national burden caused by over-centralization, and have urged drastic redistribution of functions—for example, leaving matters of social insurance and health care entirely to the federal government and matters of education and job training (as well as a number of other, similar areas) entirely to the states.[103]

But whatever the virtues of decentralization because large size results in diseconomies of scale—and there are frequently countervailing arguments that focus on the administrative horrors of decentralization[104]—it is hard to find in those virtues a persuasive argument for creating or maintaining the states as we know them as significant political entities possessing broad policy-making powers. As Karl Llewellyn suggested several decades ago, state lines as such seem to make little sense when it comes to a rational allocation of authority.[105] The New York metropolitan area, to take perhaps an atypical but not unique example, penetrates well into New Jersey and Connecticut, and even into more distant states like Pennsylvania. And even to the west, where states are larger and more self-contained, Denver lies only an hour's drive from large sections of Wyoming, and Chicago is easily within reach of several adjacent states.

The point can be simply summarized: even if there is a justification for some degree of decentralized administration, it does not follow that there is a justification for state governments to serve as the custodians of such decentralized authority.[106] In fact, the states may stand in the way

102. As stated by Revesz, *id.* at 1247: "In essence . . . the race-to-the-bottom argument is an argument against federalism."

103. A. Rivlin, *Reviving the American Dream: The Economy the States and the Federal Government* ch. 10 (1992).

104. *See* text at notes 111–25, *infra*.

105. *See* K. Llewellyn, The Constitution as an Institution, 34 Colum. L. Rev. 1, 38 (1934). Llewellyn went even further. While conceding that there must "always be" some guiding lines of distribution between federal and local authorities, he regarded it as far from certain that "state boundaries, or even territorial (*e.g.*, regional) lines afford" a sound basis for revising what he viewed as an "inane" pattern of distribution of functions. *Id.*

106. And even if the states are appropriate repositories of decentralized managerial authority in many instances, it does not follow that they should or must be vested with significant autonomy allowing them to make political, social, or economic decisions free

of the creation of sensible units of policy making and administration—units that may vary enormously with the nature of the problem being addressed. After all, to draw an analogy with respect to the states themselves, it is surely possible (and perhaps even more feasible as a practical matter) for a state without a guaranteed system of local home rule at the county or municipal level to delegate to geographical subunits primary responsibility for many functions, and to distinguish among functions in determining the size of the subunits to be employed.[107] Indeed, it is doubtful that any country in the world of more than minimal size, no matter how heavily centralized its government is in theory, has failed to create subunits with significant administrative responsibilities in important areas.[108]

2. *The Economic Arguments Favoring Strong National Authority*

Thus far, the economic argument has centered on an attempt to answer (in advance of a fuller presentation of the opposition) the arguments for state autonomy, but that focus has inevitably touched on the affirmative case for national power—especially the important point that both negative and positive externalities may require centralized action for their resolution.[109] This part of the argument addresses more directly the affirmative economic benefits of a strong central government in which little authority or responsibility is left to the states.

First, the argument in perhaps the most renowned of *The Federalist Papers*—No. 10, authored by Madison—is in important respects an eco-

---

from national review or control. This distinction—between managerial decentralization on the one hand and "federalism" on the other—is one of the central themes of a recent attack on the federalism "myth." E. Rubin & M. Feeley, Federalism: Some Notes on a National Neurosis, 41 UCLA L. Rev. 903, 910–14, 950–52 (1994).

107. There is a wide variation among the states on the extent and scope of local "home rule" guarantees. *See generally* J. Fordham, *Local Government Law*, and particularly ch. 2, sec. 2 (Local Units Within the State System) (2d rev. ed. 1986).

108. For example, at least since the French Revolution, France has had a strongly centralized government in which policy decisions are made at the top, and where a "Jacobin" tradition of hierarchy still prevails. *See* V. Wright, *The Government and Politics of France* 199–200 (1978). Nevertheless, much implementation of national policy is carried out by local departments. *See id.* at 201–6.

109. A negative externality arises when action in one state causes disproportionate harm in other states. A positive externality arises when significant benefits from costly action in one state accrue in other states.

A negative externality, of course, may lead a state to act (or to encourage private action) when, as a matter of overall social welfare, the action is undesirable, and a positive externality may have the opposite effect: leading a state to refrain (or to encourage private actors to refrain) when the action in question would increase overall welfare.

nomic one. The case for an extended republic with significant centralized power, he urged in this paper, was that the existence of such a republic is bound to reduce the power of factions seeking government action in order to advance their own interest rather than the broader public good. Madison recognized in his essay that the elimination of factions was incompatible with a free society, but expressed great fear (doubtless corroborated by experience under the Articles of Confederation) that individual states would yield to the power of particular factions and thus act in a manner antithetical to the public interest. A government whose power extended over a larger area and population would have two virtues that individual states would not. First, such a government would have a greater pool of candidates from which to choose representatives of experience, integrity, and wisdom. Second, and at least as significant, the range of parties and interests that would exist within the territorial jurisdiction of such a large national government would be so wide that no single faction, or small group of factions, could exercise power for selfish purposes.[110]

To be more specific, the logging, or tobacco, or rice growing, or insurance industry—or the fishermen, lawyers, birdwatchers, or dentists—may be so powerful in a particular state that the state's lawmakers, executive officials, and courts will yield to their demands when resistance might well be in the greater interest of all the present and future residents of the state itself. And the authorities will almost certainly yield when the externalities are such that the harms caused from giving in to those demands are felt primarily beyond the state's borders.

---

110. To some extent, modern public choice theory (discussed in more detail in ch. 3, sec. B.2) counters this view by arguing that cohesive, well-financed groups are likely to have a disproportionate influence—and one often inconsistent with the public interest—at the national level and that national legislators acting with an eye to reelection are likely to yield to the pressures exerted by such groups. For an excellent analysis and critique of the strengths and weaknesses of this theory, see D. Farber & P. Frickey, *Law and Public Choice* (1991).

Even adherents of public choice theory recognize, however, that private interest groups may often find it both easier and more useful to seek action at the state or local level than at the national level. Moreover, as one public choice theorist has pointed out, there are a number of situations in which "federal lawmakers will maximize public support for themselves by relegating regulatory authority to state officials." J. Macey, Federal Deference to Local Regulators and the Economic Theory of Regulation: Toward a Public-Choice Explanation of Federalism, 76 Va. L. Rev. 265, 290 (1990). Thus, Macey concludes, "deferring matters to the state legislatures" constitutes one of the strategies "by which federal politicians can offer wealth transfers to interest groups in exchange for political support." *Id.* at 291.

Second, in addition to the many problems caused by externalities, other market failures may well be correctable only on a national level. For example, disparities in economic well-being among the states or within a state may far exceed levels that are regarded as morally acceptable in modern society or that can be defended as necessary to create the incentives required to raise the general level of wealth and productivity. Yet a state may find it difficult to take any major steps to correct such disparities, even within its own borders, because of the very mobility already discussed. Heavy taxes (overt or less obvious) may well drive the state's wealthier residents to move elsewhere, while substantial benefits for the less fortunate may well attract residents of other states who are seeking to better their lot. Thus, a state trying to achieve any significant measure of redistribution may end by impoverishing itself in the attempt; surely the ability to achieve redistribution is greater at the national level even if, there too, those who seek redistribution will run into substantial internal and external constraints.[111]

Third, a federal system in which the states retain significant power has proved to be a system burdened with inefficiencies that have harmed us domestically and internationally. The examples are so many that an entire book could doubtless be written to chronicle and catalog them, but I will note here a few that are sufficiently varied to give the reader a taste of the problem.

• At the time of Hurricane Andrew in 1992, there was a desperate need for prompt emergency relief to be supplied by the national government. But such relief was evidently not made available before it had been properly requested by state officials, and for reasons still not completely clear, aid appears to have been seriously delayed by failures in the necessary communications between state and national authorities. Of course, failures in communication can take place in monolithic organizations as well. Yet how much more likely they are when two completely independent entities, each necessarily jealous of its own prerogatives, must cooperate in order to get the job done.[112]

• When we come to the raising of revenues, the problems caused by

111. For the contrary suggestion that, so far at least, federal spending has not had a dramatic effect on preexisting disparities of wealth among the states, see R. Peterson, B. Rabe, & K. Wong, *When Federalism Works* ch. 4 (1986).

112. *See* Food Gets to Florida; Distribution Snarled, Daily News of Los Angeles, Aug. 30, 1992, at N1. (Serious efforts were made, however, to avoid similar bureaucratic delays in the furnishing of federal aid following the Los Angeles earthquake in 1994. *See* Federal Agencies Rush Aid without Formal Emergency, N.Y. Times, Jan. 18, 1994, at A21, col. 1.)

our federal system are legion. As an example, states that seek to raise revenue by imposing taxes on sales of goods have run into a number of difficulties. For one, both the Due Process Clause and the dormant Commerce Clause were for many years held to preclude a state from requiring an out-of-state seller to collect and remit to the state a use tax on goods sold for use within the state, and only recently has the Supreme Court (by eliminating the due process objection) at least put it within the power of Congress to authorize a state to take such action.[113] For another, a state with a high sales tax on a product like gasoline or liquor, for example, may simply find that its residents go to nearby states with lower sales taxes (or none at all) to buy their goods, thus damaging the state's economy at least in areas near its borders. And those states that attempt to impose use taxes *directly* on their residents who buy goods elsewhere generally find such taxes to be wholly unenforceable except with respect to conspicuous goods (like automobiles) that must be registered with the state of residence.[114]

• As another aspect of the revenue-raising problem, notorious difficulties inhere in the imposition of income taxes on individuals and corporations with multistate contacts (difficulties that extend to inheritance taxes as well).[115] These difficulties may sometimes hurt the state

113. In National Bellas Hess, Inc. v. Department of Revenue of Illinois, 386 U.S. 753 (1967), the Court appeared to rely on both the Due Process and Commerce Clauses in striking down a state requirement of this kind. More recently, however, in Quill Corp. v. North Dakota, 112 S. Ct. 1904 (1992), the Court invalidated a similar state law, but exclusively on dormant Commerce Clause grounds. Congress has done nothing so far to allow the states to require out-of-state sellers to collect such taxes with respect to goods purchased for in-state use, and may well remain silent on the subject at least in part because of pressure groups (e.g., large and influential mail order businesses) that seek to maintain the status quo.

114. For a useful (though dated) discussion of the problems confronting state taxation of commodities, see J. Maxwell, *The Fiscal Impact of Federalism in the United States* ch. 14 (1946).

115. For informative discussion of the problems of multistate taxation of individual and corporate income, see *id.* ch. 13; L. Tribe, *American Constitutional Law* § 6–20 (2d ed. 1988).

On the difficulties of multistate taxation of individual income, I can testify from personal experience about the problems that arise when one is a resident of one state and earns income from property located in another that imposes a tax on that income. Those problems pale into insignificance, however, when one attempts to cope with the beartraps of multistate taxation of income in years when one has resided for a significant period in more than one state.

As to state death duties (typically, estate or inheritance taxes), case law in the Supreme Court indicates that unless total potential liability is likely to exceed the value of the decedent's estate, there may be no available remedy in an instance in which several states

that is attempting to tax its fair share of the revenue of the individual or corporation; more often, they cause nightmares for the taxpayer not simply because of the additional piles of paperwork but also because each state tries to push to the constitutional limit its authority to use as a tax base the most lucrative source of revenue available to it. Thus a company may find that in those states where its physical assets are concentrated, its taxes are based on that portion of its income that corresponds to its in-state physical assets; and in those states where its sales are concentrated, its taxes are based on that portion of its income corresponding to its in-state gross revenues.[116]

• Finally with respect to taxes, the problems of intergovernmental immunities may lead to substantial inefficiencies. Although the national government is no longer obliged to exempt from taxation the income from state and locally issued bonds,[117] it has traditionally done so, and (because of the system of progressive taxation) the result is to confer a disproportionate benefit on those in the higher tax brackets.[118] One learned commentator has described this exemption as "an evil relic" of a day when intergovernmental tax immunities received far more constitutional protection than they do today.[119]

• The powers of the states over the licensing of professionals have

---

claim jurisdiction to impose such duties. See the discussion in the various opinions in *California v. Texas*, 457 U.S. 164 (1982).

Of course, federal systems can (and do) exist in which only the central government has the power to raise revenue, but the absence of such authority at the state level would certainly diminish state autonomy.

116. Although the ability of a state to adopt an apportionment formula is not unlimited, the Supreme Court has held that uniformity in apportioning methods (and resulting absence of any overlap in the computation of taxable income) is not required by the Constitution. *See Moorman Mfg. Co. v. Bair*, 437 U.S. 267, 280 (1978); L. Tribe, *American Constitutional Law* § 6-20 (2d ed. 1988).

117. *See* South Carolina v. Baker, 485 U.S. 505, 515-27 (1988).

118. *See* J. Maxwell, *The Fiscal Impact of Federalism in the United States* ch. 16 (1946). Since the exemption has this effect, it has the character of a regressive tax. State and local borrowing authorities benefit too, of course, by being able to borrow money at lower rates of interest, but the regressive effect of the exemption could be eliminated, while retaining the benefit to state and local borrowing authorities, by a national tax on the income from state and local bonds and then a national payment of the revenue collected (after deducting administrative costs) to the borrowing authorities. Such a solution—as indicated by the parenthetical phrase in the preceding sentence—would require additional bureaucratic machinery for its implementation. Moreover, it is strongly opposed by the states because of fear of eventual federal recalcitrance, in the face of a continuing budget crunch, to turn over the revenue.

119. *Id.* at 371.

fostered anticompetitive activities by professionals, made life difficult for consumers, and hurt those professionals attempting to practice in states other than their own. Some of these barriers have been considerably weakened by the Supreme Court.[120] But it remains true, for example, that a lawyer in one state may have to retain local counsel, at significant added expense to her client, in order to litigate in the courts of that other state.[121]

• The problem runs considerably deeper than taxes, emergency relief, or professional activities. In areas not preempted by federal law, multi-state companies must have the resources to search out and comply with the laws of every state in which they do business. To paraphrase a recent comment by an attorney, it would often be far better to have one bad (i.e., unduly burdensome) federal rule on a particular topic than to have fifty less burdensome but significantly different state rules.[122]

• The problems facing multistate enterprises are especially severe in the area of potential civil liability. To take one example, almost every state has a different approach to a company's exposure to punitive damages, and many states pay little or no attention to the level of damages that may already have been levied in other states for conduct that is not only related to but is an integral part of the activity subject to litigation. So far at least, neither the federal legislature nor the federal judiciary[123]

120. *See, e.g.,* Supreme Court of New Hampshire v. Piper, 470 U.S. 274 (1985) (holding that New Hampshire violated the Privileges and Immunities Clause of Constitution by refusing to admit to the practice of law a nonresident who had taken and passed the New Hampshire bar examination; a state may discriminate against nonresidents only when its reasons are substantial).

121. In light of widely varying local procedures and customs, this need may exist as a practical matter even if (as is often not the case) the nonresident lawyer is admitted to the bar—in general or pro hac vice—in the state in which litigation is being conducted.

122. The attorney, Peter Hutt (one of the country's leading practitioners in the field of food and drug law), was so quoted in an article in the Wall Street Journal, May 10, 1993, at B4, col. 1. The article goes on to note the concern of consumer advocates that the push for uniformity "may simply mask efforts to pass federal laws that wipe out protections consumers and plaintiffs enjoy in many states." *Id.*

123. The Supreme Court's first tentative step toward limiting the ability of a state to impose punitive damages was in Honda Motor Co. v. Oberg, 114 S. Ct. 2331 (1994). In that case, the Court held that a state's limitation on judicial review of a punitive damage award was inconsistent with the requirements of due process. But the Court has yet to consider whether there are any limitations on the availability of multiple punitive damage awards in different states involving the same course of conduct. In general, efforts to establish limits on punitive damages, through the establishment of one overriding, national class action governing tort claims arising from a single incident or related series of incidents, have not been stunningly effective. Some halting steps have been taken, however,

has taken action to limit the general authority of the states in this respect.[124]

All this complexity may prove a source of income, or happiness, or both, to those who are paid to litigate the issues it generates or who study the extraordinary intricacy of our federal system. But it does little to serve the cause of efficiency, and is bound to act as a drag on an economy that needs all the help it can get if it is to retain and enhance its economic strength at a time of growing competition from other countries in every part of the globe.[125]

C. Strong National Authority Is Needed in Order to Protect the Rights and Interests of Individuals and Groups

A frequent argument for diffusion of power—and one that is explored more fully in the next chapter—is that such diffusion is necessary not only to effectuate economic competition among public bodies but to assure the preservation of individual rights and interests against the potential tyranny of a centralized government. The argument sounds splendid in theory, and indeed was emphasized in those portions of *The Federalist* that defended the role of the states in the new Union.[126] As Lord Acton put it in an oft-repeated (and usually slightly misquoted) phrase: "Power tends to corrupt, and absolute power corrupts absolutely."[127]

To a significant extent, this argument overlaps with the economic arguments relating to decentralization that have already been discussed,

---

in litigation involving such alleged mass torts as those resulting from the manufacture and use of asbestos, the production of the defoliant Agent Orange, and the manufacture and use of intrauterine devices to prevent pregnancy.

124. Several health reform proposals would limit or channel liability for medical malpractice under state law. Although criticized in some quarters for not going far enough (*see, e.g.,* N.Y. Times, Nov. 14, 1993, at sec. 4A, p. 16, col. 4), such proposals have also met with opposition from the Bar: *see, e.g.,* N.Y. Times, Sept. 24, 1993, at A26, col. 3. Broader proposals for limiting punitive damages and other exposure to awards in product liability suits have been introduced in the 104th Congress. *See, e.g.,* H.R. 10, § 103, 104th Cong., 1st Sess. (1995).

125. In his recent book, *The Endangered American Dream* (1993), Edward Luttwak argues that if the United States is to survive as a world economic power, it must develop a strong *national* strategy, emanating from Washington and involving such centralized actions as subsidies to high technology industries, and the formulation of plans to upgrade educational requirements and job training. Clearly, this approach would call for a degree of centralization inconsistent with many of the tenets of American federalists.

126. *See, e.g., The Federalist* No. 51 (Madison).

127. Letter from Lord Acton to Bishop Creighton, April 5, 1887.

and indeed, economic and political freedoms are not easily separable. Thus the right of exit, so highly prized by some as an economic incentive for each state to seek to remain attractive to investors and workers, also involves a political right—as the Supreme Court has recognized in such landmark decisions as *Shapiro v. Thompson*.[128] And Madison's thesis in *The Federalist* No. 10 is as relevant to the submergence of political rights and interests by powerful local factions as it is to the submergence of economic interests—perhaps even more so.[129] Thus, in the hope that the points made in the preceding section will be recalled, I will try not to rehearse them in addressing the arguments about political rights.

Although the importance of the states as a counterweight to the dangers of central tyranny has theoretical appeal, there is a compelling case for its weakness in both theoretical and practical terms. In the realm of theory, it is noteworthy that the Framers—intensely aware of Montesquieu's concerns about a single source of power[130]—designed a federal government with many internal checks that, in themselves, were very likely to prevent the advent of absolute power even in a government in which all authority was centralized. Among these internal checks—at least one of which has been added by subsequent Amendment—are the existence of a bicameral legislature, the President's veto power, the assurance that the ultimate control of the military will rest in civilian hands,

128. 394 U.S. 618, 629–31 (1969). Among the many authorities and sources cited as a basis for this right to travel in the *Shapiro* opinion is the opinion for the Court in United States v. Guest, 383 U.S. 745, 757–58 (1966), where Justice Stewart said: "The constitutional right to travel from one State to another . . . occupies a position fundamental to the concept of our Federal Union. It is a right that has been firmly established and repeatedly recognized." Specific constitutional sources alluded to in the *Shapiro* opinion (at 630 n. 8) include the Privileges and Immunities Clauses of Article IV, § 2 and of the Fourteenth Amendment, as well as the Commerce Clause.

129. Indeed, as noted above, Madison originally proposed (perhaps because of his fear that states would be dominated by factions) that the principal guarantees of the Bill of Rights should apply to the states. See S. Beer, *To Make a Nation: The Rediscovery of American Federalism* 291 (1993).

130. Montesquieu argued (in *The Spirit of the Laws* (1748) (Hafner Publishing ed. 1959 at 120)) that in a small republic, "the interest of the public is more obvious, better understood, and more within the reach of every citizen."

That the supporters and opponents of the new Union were aware of Montesquieu's theories is widely acknowledged. *See, e.g.,* S. Beer, *To Make a Nation: The Rediscovery of American Federalism* 219–43, 285, 295–96 (1993). While the advocates of ratification accepted Montesquieu's arguments for separation of powers on the federal level, the antifederalists went much further in support of his views on the virtues of decentralized authority. See C. Kenyon, *Men of Little Faith: The Anti-Federalists on the Nature of Representative Government* 6, 8, 23, 25, 42, in Wm. & Mary Q., 3d ser. vol. 12 (1955).

the existence of a judiciary with authority to invalidate on constitutional grounds the actions of each of the other two branches[131] (as well as its own),[132] the constitutional Amendment limiting the President to two elected terms,[133] the election of the President by means independent of the national legislature (at least in the absence of a deadlock), the power of the legislature to impeach officials of the other two branches, the necessity of the "advice and consent" of the Senate with respect to executive appointments and the making of treaties,[134] and the delegation to Congress of the authority to declare war.[135] And last but not least come the specific prohibitions against a whole range of federal actions by any of the three branches—prohibitions contained both in the Constitution itself and in the Bill of Rights.

On a more practical level, the states do not appear to have served as a bulwark of individual and group rights and interests. Writing in 1954, William Riker put the point in terms that are vivid and disturbing. If one disapproves of the values of the privileged minority, he wrote, and especially if one disapproves of racism, then "one should disapprove of federalism."[136]

131. Although the power of judicial review—to declare acts of Congress and other acts of federal and state governments unconstitutional—is not explicit in the Constitution itself, the case for the creation of this power as a fundamental aspect of the Union is a powerful one. See the discussion of historical materials in *Hart & Wechsler* 8–10.

132. The ability of the federal judiciary, and especially of the Supreme Court, to invalidate actions of the judicial branch on constitutional grounds has been of great significance in our constitutional history. Thus the Supreme Court has frequently held unconstitutional the actions of lower federal courts. (The number of such holdings in criminal proceedings is especially large.) And in such famous decisions as Erie R.R. v. Tompkins, 304 U.S. 64 (1938), the Court has acknowledged that its own course of decisions has violated the Constitution.

133. U.S. Const., Amend. XXII.

134. U.S. Const., Art. II, § 2, cl. 2.

135. U.S. Const., Art. I, § 8, cl. 11. Admittedly, the President seems to have found ways to circumvent the limitations imposed by the Constitution with respect to the making of treaties and the declaration of war, but not without controversy—most notably during the Korean and Vietnam Wars. And the existence of legislation limiting the President's power to act militarily in foreign countries without advising and consulting with the legislature (*see* War Powers Resolution, 50 U.S.C. §§ 1541–48, recently invoked by H. Con. Res. 170, directing the President to remove U.S. armed forces from Somalia by a date certain), as well as President Bush's decision to seek congressional authorization before entering the Gulf War, are powerful evidence of the continuing significance of our constitutional structure.

136. W. Riker, *Federalism: Origin, Operation, Significance* 145 (1964). (Riker's thesis as expressed in another work suggests, however, that federalism makes little or no difference in the way people are governed. *See* W. Riker, Six Books in Search of a Subject

Start with the most tragic case of all: that of slavery. To be sure, the abolitionist movement began and gathered strength in a few Northern states, and some Northern states defied federal authority by seeking to protect those who had aided in the escape of fugitive slaves.[137] But even more significantly, the proslavery movement was centered in the Southern agrarian states and may well have acquired more strength and endurance than it could otherwise have had from the states' rights arguments advanced by such theorists as Calhoun.[138] The various compromises relating to slavery that appear in the Constitution itself—especially the provision assuring that importation could continue at least until 1808[139]—might never have found their way into the document if not for the need to secure ratification from nine states (necessarily including several in the South). Indeed, the moral issues raised by slavery often became obscured by the debates over the kind of Union we had entered, and at least at the outset of the Civil War, Lincoln saw the controversy more in terms of the latter than the former.[140] Of course, one might argue that, in a sense, this proves the point of the advocates of state autonomy, since the interests of slave owners (and of others dependent on an agrarian economy that was based on the institution of slavery)

---

or Does Federalism Exist and Does It Matter?, 2 Comp. Pol. 145, 155 (1969).) On the role of the states with respect to individual rights, see also H. Scheiber, Constitutional Structure and the Protection of Rights: Federalism and the Separation of Powers, in *Power Divided: Essays in the History and Practice of Federalism* 17, 26 (H. Scheiber & M. Feeley eds., 1989) ("[T]he record of American federalism [while impressive in several respects] represents tragic failure with regard to acting as a bulwark of liberty.").

For a contrasting view, and especially for criticism of Riker's critique, see V. Ostrom, Can Federalism Make a Difference?, 3 Publius 197 (1973).

137. Thus, in Ableman v. Booth, 62 U.S. (21 How.) 506 (1859), the Wisconsin state courts had twice ordered the release (on petitions for habeas corpus) of a federal prisoner arrested, tried, and convicted of violation of the Fugitive Slave Act. The Supreme Court held in that decision, and reaffirmed in its later decision in Tarble's Case, 80 U.S. (13 Wall.) 397 (1872), that (at least under the particular circumstances presented) state courts had no power to entertain habeas corpus petitions by persons detained under federal authority.

138. For a comprehensive collection of Calhoun's views on this and related subjects, see *The Papers of John C. Calhoun* (R. Meriwether ed., 1959).

139. See U.S. Const. Art. I, § 9.

140. Explaining his focus on preserving the Union, Lincoln wrote to Horace Greeley: "My paramount object in this struggle *is* to save the Union, and is *not* either to save or to destroy slavery. If I could save the Union without freeing *any* slave, I would do it, and if I could save it by freeing *all* the slaves, I would do it; and if I could save it by freeing some and leaving others alone, I would also do that." A. Lincoln to H. Greeley, Aug. 22, 1862, reprinted in 5 *The Collected Works of Abraham Lincoln* 388 (R. Basler ed., 1953).

were defended by the Southern states against the onslaught of those whose economy and lifestyle did not depend on the institution. But this suggestion seems only to underscore Riker's point—judgments about federalism cannot be divorced from one's values, and if one is worried about protecting minorities that cannot adequately protect themselves, one should not be an advocate of state autonomy.

This view is further corroborated by the history of racism after the Civil War. No part of the country can be proud of its record on this issue, but surely the institutionalization of racial segregation reached levels in the Southern states never even imagined in the North and West.[141] And after the *Brown* decision in 1954, the year when Riker attacked the notion of federalism, the exercise of state legislative, executive, and judicial authority slowed down the process of desegregation for many years—through such devices as (1) interposition (the enactment of elaborate and intricate legislation designed primarily to impede national efforts to achieve desegregation);[142] (2) the efforts of state executives to block desegregation decrees at every turn—to the point of putting themselves in direct contempt of federal court orders;[143] and (3) the ability of state courts to create procedural barriers to the vindication of federal rights,[144] and to sustain the efforts of state law enforcement

141. Until World War 2, the District of Columbia was little more than an extension of Virginia and Maryland, and its attitudes on racial issues reflected this fact. At the same time, it is no credit to the national government—and perhaps a tribute to the structural elements of state power built into the legislative branch (especially when combined with the tradition of committee seniority)—that the national government allowed these laws and practices to persist in its own backyard and made virtually no effort to impede their operation in the South.

142. Southern state legislatures showed remarkable ingenuity after the *Brown* decision in enacting barriers to implementation—barriers that ranged from impediments to those organizations seeking to enforce black students' rights to such extreme measures as local decisions to close the public schools rather than have them desegregated. For a sampling of the Supreme Court's continuing efforts during the post-*Brown* era to confront, and usually (but not always) to strike down such actions, see Griffin v. County School Board, 377 U.S. 218 (1964); NAACP v. Button, 371 U.S. 455 (1963); Norwood v. Harrison, 413 U.S. 467 (1973). *Cf.* Palmer v. Thompson, 403 U.S. 217 (1971) (upholding decision of City Council of Jackson, Mississippi, to close public swimming pools following federal court order that the pools be desegregated).

143. See, e.g., the description of the conduct of Governor Ross Barnett and other officers of the state of Mississippi in United States v. Barnett, 330 F.2d 369 (5th Cir. 1963).

144. *See, e.g.,* NAACP v. Alabama ex rel. Patterson, 357 U.S. 449 (1958) (holding inadequate a state supreme court's procedural ground for refusal to review lower state court decision finding NAACP in contempt for failure to produce its membership lists).

officers to impede civil rights workers and even to prosecute them for what looked to many observers like trumped-up charges.[145]

Outside the area of race, the record of the states in protecting individual and group rights is no more distinguished. Although the Bill of Rights has, of course, been used to limit the exercise of national power by each of the three branches, its most significant use since the adoption of the Fourteenth Amendment has been to limit the exercise of state power against unpopular individuals or groups. The areas are so many and so well known that even a sample would seem superfluous. But surely some of the more renowned deserve mention: in the criminal field, we find such landmark decisions as *Miranda*,[146] *Mapp*,[147] *Pointer*,[148] and *Duncan*.[149] In the area of freedom of speech, most of the major decisions have involved a challenge to the exercise of state authority,[150] as have the Supreme Court's decisions on such matters as the establishment or free exercise of religion,[151] and the privacy guaranteed by the Fourth Amendment or, more broadly, by the Court's view of substantive due process.[152] And these examples are only the tip of the iceberg of the continuing need to protect individuals and groups from the exercise of state power—a need that has been recognized by Congress as well as

145. See, e.g., Henry v. Mississippi, 379 U.S. 443 (1965) (involving a criminal prosecution of civil rights leader Aaron Henry); City of Greenwood v. Peacock, 384 U.S. 808 (1966).

146. Miranda v. Arizona, 384 U.S. 436 (1966).

147. Mapp v. Ohio, 367 U.S. 643 (1961). For an interesting argument that *Mapp* and similar Supreme Court decisions have advanced professionalization, and have therefore improved the quality, of state and local law enforcement, see J. Simon & J. Skolnick, Federalism, the Exclusionary Rule, and the Police, in *Power Divided: Essays on the Theory and Practice of Federalism* 75 (H. Scheiber & M. Feeley eds., 1989).

148. Pointer v. Texas, 380 U.S. 400 (right of confrontation).

149. Duncan v. Louisiana, 391 U.S. 145 (1968) (right to jury trial).

150. There are, of course, many important decisions involving attempted restriction of speech or expression by federal authorities, but the efforts of the Supreme Court to cope with *state* activity in this area are legion. See G. Gunther, *Constitutional Law* chs. 11–13 (12th ed. 1991).

151. See *id.* at ch. 14.

152. In addition to cases arising directly under the Fourth Amendment (as incorporated in the Fourteenth), Supreme Court decisions relying in part on the right of privacy (or related notions of autonomy) as a basis for invalidating state action include Griswold v. Connecticut, 381 U.S. 479 (1965) (invalidating state restrictions relating to birth control devices); Roe v. Wade, 419 U.S. 113 (1973) (striking down state restrictions relating to abortions); Moore v. East Cleveland, 431 U.S. 494 (1977) (invalidating local housing ordinance defining a "family" so narrowly as to preclude a grandmother from living in the same house with her two grandsons). See *generally* G. Gunther, *Constitutional Law* ch. 8, sec. 3 (12th ed. 1991).

the federal courts.[153] As always, the trend has not been one directional. Recent years have seen a number of instances in which state judicial efforts to protect individuals on federal constitutional grounds have met with reversal at the hands of a more "conservative" Supreme Court,[154] as well as instances in which state courts and legislatures have used their authority under state law to extend individual rights beyond the bounds of federal protection.[155] But it is hard to quarrel with the conclusion that the historical record, viewed in its entirety, fails to support the existence of state autonomy as a critical means of protecting against abuse of governmental power. On the contrary, national power has had to be continually invoked in order to protect our freedoms against state infringement. Riker may have overstated the case, or circumstances may have moderated somewhat since he wrote, but surely Madison was not so far off the mark when he decried the dangers of the abuse of state and local power.[156]

The space devoted to the case for a strong national government has roughly approximated the space permitted for a petitioner's brief in the

153. On the legislative front, congressional actions designed to protect individuals against violations of their rights by state and local authorities cover a remarkably broad range. Illustrative of such statutes are the post–Civil War civil rights laws, especially 42 U.S.C. § 1983; Congress's extension of protection against many forms of discrimination to state employees in the 1972 amendments to Title VII of the 1964 Civil Rights Act (see Equal Employment Opportunity Act of 1972, 86 Stat. 103, 42 U.S.C. §§ 2000e(a), (b), (f), (h)); and the various voting rights laws enacted in the past several decades, e.g., 42 U.S.C. §§ 1971–1974c.

154. These instances have been especially frequent in the area of criminal procedure. See, e.g., Maryland v. Macon, 472 U.S. 463 (1985); California v. Greenwood, 486 U.S. 35 (1988); California v. Beheler, 463 U.S. 1121 (1983); Illinois v. Perkins, 496 U.S. 292 (1990).

155. In his essay, State Constitutions and the Protection of Individual Rights, 90 Harv. L. Rev. 489, 498–501 (1977), then Justice Brennan cited a number of state judicial decisions interpreting their own constitutional provisions protecting private rights more broadly than had the Supreme Court in interpreting analogous federal constitutional provisions. For a recent discussion of this trend in a number of state courts, and the suggestion that the states are unlikely ever to return to a policy of "total deference" to Supreme Court decisions interpreting constitutional rights guaranteed by both federal and state law, see G. A. Tarr, The Past and Future of the New Judicial Federalism, 24 Publius 63 (Spring 1994). In addition, a number of state statutes have banned forms of discrimination (on the basis of sexual orientation, for example) that have not been prohibited by statute at the national level. See, e.g., Haw. Rev. Stat. §§ 368, 378-2 (1993 Supp.); Mass. Ann. Laws ch. 151B, § 4 (1993); N.J. Stat. § 10:5-4 (1993).

156. See, e.g., The Federalist No. 10.

Supreme Court.[157] Though not subject to that particular constraint here, I believe the Court was right in concluding—after years of suffering through turgid "briefs"—that page limits are appropriate even for the argument of the most difficult issues. However, these concluding thoughts are a bit wordier—but only marginally so—than those customarily appearing in a Supreme Court brief.[158]

This chapter has attempted to make two main points. First, there is no legal guarantee, in the Constitution itself or anywhere else, of a decentralized system of government in which the states (and their delegates, the counties, municipalities, and towns) shall retain or receive the right to exercise significant authority over private conduct, or even to have unimpeded authority to determine their own internal governmental affairs.

Second, there are no strong policy arguments for preservation in or delegation to the states of significant power over these matters; indeed the strongest arguments cut in favor of national authority. The economic case for state autonomy, if it ever had any force, has become obsolete in a shrinking and increasingly competitive world market, and the political case founders on the shoals of history as well as on the existence of ample safeguards against tyranny at the national level.

If these points have force, the arguments for diffusion of authority among tiers of government begin to appear (to soften Riker's assault somewhat) as little more than a handy pretext—hauled out when, but only when, it is convenient to do so—for those who wish to block action at the national level that they fear will upset the status quo.

157. The Supreme Court's rules state that a brief on the merits "shall be as short as possible" (Rule 24.3) and (under Rule 33) in no event in excess of fifty pages of specified type size. Waivers of these limits are permitted in theory but seldom granted in practice.

158. The "conclusion" of a brief on the merits in the Supreme Court more often than not simply recites: "For the reasons stated, the judgment below should be [affirmed] [reversed]."

3

The Case for Federalism as a Constraint on National Authority

A. The History and Text of the Constitution, As Well As Developments during and since Its Ratification, Guarantee Both the Existence of the States and Their Right to Play a Significant Role in the Federal System

The question raised in chapter 2—whether the states preceded the creation of the Union, or vice versa—like the riddle of the chicken and the egg, may be entertaining to argue about but, in the end, not especially relevant. The important question is the nature of the federal Union that emerged when the Constitution was ratified and that has developed since that time. That Union, this chapter will show, is one in which the states play an essential role, not only in the structure of the federal government but as autonomous entities with important political powers, both actual and potential.

But on the question of our status as a society before ratification of the present Constitution, it is worth noting that the Articles of Confederation created a confederation or alliance of independent entities in the classic sense. Indeed, the closest modern analogy may well be the United Nations, although unlike the Charter of the United Nations, the Articles did cede significant powers to the central government. But the Articles not only required unanimous ratification by the legislatures of the thirteen states in order to become effective,[1] they also specifically provided that "[e]ach State retains its sovereignty, freedom and independence, and every power, jurisdiction, and right which is not by this confederation expressly delegated to the United States, in Congress assembled."[2] In the

1. Articles of Confederation and Perpetual Union, Art. 13.
2. *Id.* Art. 2.

deliberations of Congress, each state was allotted one vote,[3] and neither the power to tax nor the power to regulate commerce was delegated to Congress. Moreover, the Articles created neither an effective executive nor a continuing judicial branch with significant adjudicatory power, and Congress could not pass laws acting directly on the people nor could it seek to raise funds except by essentially unenforceable requisitions addressed to the states.[4]

It was against this background of independent state power that the Constitutional Convention was called, and it was called for the explicit purpose of amending the Articles.[5] The delegates were appointed by the governments of the states, not elected by the people, and (as in Congress under the Articles) each state had an equal vote.[6]

As to the document that emerged from that Convention, it did, as already noted, depart from the purpose for which the delegates were originally assembled, did emphasize that "the People" ordained and established the new Union, and did cede potentially broad substantive powers to the central authority. But the significance and role of the states was given too short shrift in chapter 2. In addition to the crucial structural role played by the states in the new central government,[7] the Constitution treats the states throughout as the building blocks of the new Union and, at times, is quite explicit in this respect. Thus, in Article I, which enumerates the *limited* powers of the national legislature,[8] the

3. *Id.* Art. 5.

4. *Id.* Art. 8. *See generally* M. Jensen, *The Articles of Confederation* (1940); L. Levy, The Articles of Confederation, in 1 *Encyclopedia of the American Constitution* 75 (1986).

5. For discussion of the original mandate—and in particular the insistence of Massachusetts that the purpose of the Convention was solely to revise the Articles—see J. Rakove, *The Beginnings of National Politics* ch. 15 (1979). Rakove goes on in this chapter to discuss what he describes as a critical "shift of perspective" that took place in the course of the Convention. *Id.* at 396.

6. Every state but Rhode Island sent a delegation to the Convention. For a brief but informative discussion of the background, structure, and actions of the Convention (in addition to the more extensive treatment by Rakove, cited at note 5, *supra*) see J. Roche, Constitutional Convention of 1787, in 1 *Encyclopedia of the American Constitution* 360 (1986).

7. These structural features have been alluded to in ch. 2, sec. A.1, and are discussed in some detail in ch. 4, sec. B.

8. This notion—that the powers enumerated in Article I are limited to those specified, and thus that the powers not enumerated are not delegated to the federal government—is lent additional force by a scholarly study of the Necessary and Proper Clause recently published by Gary Lawson and Patricia Granger. In their article, The "Proper" Scope of Federal Power: A Jurisdictional Interpretation of the Sweeping Clause, 43 Duke L.J. 267 (1993), the authors muster historical evidence in support of their argument that "a

Constitution equates the electorate of the lower House of Congress with the electorate of "the most numerous Branch of the State Legislature,"[9] and leaves to each state (in the absence of congressional override) the designation of the time, place, and manner of holding elections for the state's delegates to the two Houses of Congress.[10] Moreover, Article I also fortifies the states by protecting them from each other and from the federal government—specifically prohibiting any preference for the "Ports of one State over those of another," as well as the imposition by any state of duties on vessels traveling from one state to another.[11]

Article IV, already discussed in some detail,[12] continues the theme of affording national protection to the states against outside intrusion and against each other—and thus strengthening each state as a political entity—by prohibiting the alteration of the boundaries of any state without the consent of *both* Congress and the state involved, by promising to protect each state against invasion (presumably by either a foreign power or another state), and by explicitly abjuring any "prejudice" to the claims of any state to territory within the borders of the Union.[13]

Most important, it is probably a serious misreading to interpret the "Guarantee Clause" of Article IV, § 4 as simply a limitation on state power to alter its form of government to the point that it can no longer be classified as republican. The recent and thorough research of Deborah Merritt indicates that although the history of the Convention itself is slim on the point, the ratification debates contain much evidence that the clause was presented to the people (by the advocates of the new Union)

'proper' executory law must be peculiarly and distinctively within the province of the national government and therefore must respect the national government's jurisdictional boundaries. In this sense, the Sweeping [Necessary and Proper] Clause was the precursor of the Tenth Amendment's declaration." *Id.* at 273–74.

9. U.S. Const. Art. I, § 2, cl. 1.

10. U.S. Const. Art. I, § 2, cl. 1. At this writing, the Supreme Court has agreed to consider whether this clause may be construed to authorize the states to impose term limits on members of its congressional delegation. *See* U.S. Term Limits v. Thornton (No. 93–1456); Bryant v. Hill (No. 93–1828). The Court, on June 20, 1994, granted certiorari in (and consolidated) both cases for purposes of reviewing lower court decisions that invalidated state laws on the grounds that they exceeded state powers to prescribe qualifications for congressionsal delegates. 114 S. Ct. 2703 (1994).

11. U.S. Const. Art. I, § 9, cl. 6. Indeed, one significant purpose of the new Union appears to have been to *strengthen* the states by guaranteeing national defense of each state against various intrusions and incursions by outside powers, including the other states. *See* J. Zimmerman, *Contemporary American Federalism* ch. 2 (especially at 19–23) (1992).

12. *See* ch. 2, sec. A.1.

13. U.S. Const. Art. IV, § 3.

as also providing a guarantee against *federal* interference with state autonomy.[14] Thus, the clause may fairly be viewed (both textually and contextually) as protecting the essential functions of state government against national interference. And these essential functions, while fuzzy at the edges, clearly include a state's ability to determine the roles to be played by each of its branches and to control the agendas to be established by those branches.

The document as it emerged from the Convention, in short, was not the document that those with more nationalistic leanings would have preferred.[15] Important concessions had to be made along the way to those who were concerned about the survival and role of the states once the Union came into existence. And these concessions stood the supporters of the Union in good stead when the debates over ratification began.

To focus once again on *The Federalist* as one of the strongest of the briefs in support of the proposed Union, the crucial points made by Publius (in all his incarnations) about the role of the states in the new Union cannot be put down as mere selling points without substance; they were made far too often and in too many settings. And the men who wrote these documents were not simply politicians trying to sell a proposition at any cost; they were men of extraordinary depth and insight, not easily accused or convicted of hypocrisy. Thus, it is a telling argument for a truly federal Union that, for example, in *The Federalist* No. 8, Hamilton emphasized the importance of the new Union in protecting the states against each other; that in *The Federalist* No. 9, he spoke of the "sovereign power" of the states; that throughout *The Federalist* No. 39, Madison stressed the sovereign power of the states

14. *See* D. Merritt, The Guaranty Clause and State Autonomy: Federalism for a Third Century, 88 Colum. L. Rev. 1 (1988). Merritt's discussion of the ratification debates, appearing at 30–36, notes a number of comments by supporters of ratification who argued, inter alia, that this clause would operate to prevent the states from "being annihilated" by the federal government. *Id.* at 33.

15. As one prominent example, Madison (who was surely a less vigorous advocate of centralization than Hamilton and some others) had to abandon his proposal for a national veto power over state laws. *See* ch. 2, sec. A.1.

A recent and informative study of Madison's views in *The Federalist* concludes that Madison was "only a moderate nationalist, a supporter of energetic national government within a republican—and federal framework." F. Greene, Madison's Views of Federalism in *The Federalist*, 24 Publius 47, 60 (1994). As for Madison's support of a national veto power over state laws, Greene's article suggests that the veto was not seen "as an instrument for the states' complete subordination, but merely as a safeguard against state malfeasance." *Id.* at 61.

and, at one point, referred to "the assent and ratification of the States" as essential to the creation of the Union; and that in No. 45 (Madison) and No. 84 (Hamilton), the authors saw the powers delegated to the national government as so limited that (1) the states would retain a significant portion of their sovereignty (No. 45) and (2) the enactment of a Bill of Rights imposing limitations on federal authority would be superfluous (No. 84). Finally, in one of the strongest statements in support of an "extended republic," Madison conceded (in *The Federalist* No. 51) that the preservation of the states as "distinct governments" was one of the necessary "auxiliary precautions" against centralized tyranny.

As already noted, the enactment of the Bill of Rights shortly after ratification was perhaps the principal achievement of the anti-federalists in their opposition to the Union.[16] Until recently, however, the Bill was not fully understood as playing an important structural role as well as making explicit the protection of individual rights against federal invasion. In an elaborate study of the text and context of the first ten Amendments, Professor Amar has shed new light on those provisions designed to empower popular majorities (like the right to petition in the First Amendment), and to ensure popular participation in governmental affairs (as in the jury trial guarantees of the Sixth and Seventh Amendments), *and* on those provisions designed to underscore the rights and interests of state and local governments.[17] As an example of the latter, he stresses the significance of the First Amendment's Establishment Clause as both a guarantee against the establishment of religion by the national government *and* a guarantee to the states that their own decisions whether or not to establish religion (or a particular religion) within their borders would not be disturbed.[18] (As a corollary to this

16. *See* ch. 2, sec. A.1; 1 H. Storing, *The Complete Anti-Federalist* 64 (1981).

17. *See* A. Amar, The Bill of Rights as a Constitution, 100 Yale L.J. 1131 (1991). As Amar suggests in this important work, the "populist" and "localist" concerns that animated the Bill of Rights must be viewed as a part of the whole—as intimately related to the protection of individual rights in the Amendments. *See id.* at 1204.

With respect to the guarantees of jury trial (which were also provided in criminal cases in Article III itself), Amar argues that they arose from fundamentally populist and majoritarian views about the importance of curbing federal authority. *Id.* at 1182–99.

18. *See id.* at 1157–60. Established religions were not unknown at the time of the Constitutional Convention, and although some states (e.g., Virginia) were in the vanguard of efforts to prohibit state intervention and to foster individual choice in matters of religion, others (Massachusetts, for instance) assuredly were not.

For discussion of the history of disestablishment of religion in Virginia, and of the institution of freedom of religion in that state, *see* L. Lama, The Wall on a Straw Foundation: The Mythical Wall vs. The Reality of Controlled Intertwinement, 5 St. Thomas

guarantee, control over education would be left in the hands of the states.)[19] And the Second Amendment, which has proved a continuing source of irritation to the advocates of national gun control laws, appears to extend its protection against federal interference *both* to the people and to the states.[20] Thus the Tenth Amendment, which may appear tautological when considered in isolation, serves to reiterate the structural significance of the states as political entities both in the Bill of Rights and in the Constitution itself.[21]

Despite the Marshall Court's interpretation of the Constitution as authorizing the exercise of significant federal power,[22] Madison's predictions that (as a matter of public preference) the states would remain predominant[23] proved accurate at least until the Civil War.[24] The growth of national power and its exercise since then, especially in this century, have been primarily the product of the post–Civil War Amendments and their implementation, and the expansive reading that the federal courts have been willing to give to congressional authority over commerce

---

L. Rev. 581, 586 (1993); G. Leedes, Rediscovering the Link between the Establishment Clause and the Fourteenth Amendment: The Citizenship Declaration, 26 Ind. L. Rev. 469, 489–90 (1993). With respect to the establishment of religion in Massachusetts, *see, e.g.,* A. Sutherland, Establishment according to Engel, 76 Harv. L. Rev. 25, 28 (1962). ("Until 1833 Massachusetts still supported a Protestant religion by public taxation; absence from church was a Massachusetts crime until 1836.")

19. *See id.* at 1161–62.

20. *See id.* at 1162–73. As Amar recognizes, the language of the Amendment—"A well regulated Militia, being necessary to the security of a free State, the right of the people to keep and bear Arms, shall not be infringed"—is not free from ambiguity and has been the subject of a great deal of scholarly debate. For a recently published three-volume study that includes cases, articles, and other materials in the field, see *Gun Control and the Constitution* (R. Cottrol ed., 1993).

21. Amar describes the Ninth and Tenth Amendments as "The Popular Sovereignty Amendments," and argues that the Ninth Amendment—not discussed here at any length—is most significantly a declaration of the right to "alter or abolish government" rather than a statement of an unspecified set of "countermajoritarian individual rights." *See* A. Amar, The Bill of Rights as a Constitution, 100 Yale L.J. 1131, 1199, 1200 (1991).

Interestingly, Madison's original formulation of a Bill of Rights included, as its fourth proposal, an insert in Article I that was to become the core of the present Bill of Rights and that ended with the present Ninth Amendment (1 Annals of Congress 433–35) and as its eighth proposal, a new Article to be inserted in the Constitution that dealt with *both* aspects of the distribution of power: separation of powers within the national government, and the language of what is now the Tenth Amendment (*id.* at 435–36).

22. *See* ch. 2, sec. A.1.

23. *See The Federalist* No. 46 (Madison).

24. Harry Scheiber has written of the predominance of the states in establishing the prevailing legal landscape until the onset of the Civil War. *See, e.g.,* H. Scheiber, Federalism and the American Economic Order, 1789–1910, Law & Soc'y (Fall 1975), at 57, 86–100.

and over the purse, including the authority to condition grants to state and local governments.[25] But throughout this period, the Court has insisted on significant limitations on federal authority, and some of these decisions are alive and well in the 1990s.

Judicial protection of state autonomy against federal intrusion may be divided into the categories of "constitutional" and "sub-constitutional" protections, with perhaps an intermediate category where the line is at present indistinct because the Supreme Court has left it so or because the relevant doctrine appears unstable.

At the constitutional level, there are a number of important decisions, each of which marks out some aspect of state autonomy and suggests a possibly wider scope of protection in related areas. These decisions include:

• *Texas v. White*,[26] a case in which the state of Texas (as reestablished after the Civil War) was permitted to reclaim certain property that had been alienated during the War by the insurgent government of the state. For present purposes, the important aspect of the case is the Court's rationale—which stressed that Texas never ceased to be a full-fledged member of the Union (despite the efforts made to secede) because, in the words of Chief Justice Chase, the United States is "an indestructible Union, composed of indestructible States."[27] While this decision in some respects is a nationalistic one—since it considered Texas's effort to secede to have been wholly ineffective—at another, and important, level, it rested the state's claim to recover the property sought on the constitutional guarantee of the states' continued existence.

• *Coyle v. Smith*,[28] a 1911 decision by the Court holding that the Act of Congress admitting Oklahoma into the Union was invalid insofar as it sought to impose as a condition of entry a requirement that the state locate its capital in Guthrie for at least a decade. The Court said that the power to locate the state's capital—along with related powers to change locations and to appropriate funds for those purposes—were "essentially

25. *See, e.g.*, Wickard v. Filburn, 317 U.S. 111 (1942) (reach of congressional power to regulate commerce); South Dakota v. Dole, 483 U.S. 203 (1987) (power to condition expenditure of federal funds on state compliance with federal conditions).

26. 74 U.S. (7 Wall.) 700 (1868).

27. *Id.* at 725.

28. 221 U.S. 559 (1911). Interestingly, Justices Holmes and McKenna dissented without opinion. Justice Holmes was noted for writing short opinions, but this one was too short to catch his drift.

and peculiarly state powers"[29] that Congress could not have interfered with in the case of any of the thirteen original states and cannot interfere with as a condition of later admission. The Court stressed the importance of equality among the states to the harmonious operation of the Union and, relying on earlier decisions,[30] said that the Nation could not exist without the states as functioning political entities.[31]

• A series of decisions upholding an effective, though limited, inter-governmental immunity from taxation. To be sure, the earlier versions of these immunities, established in such decisions as *Collector v. Day*,[32] have fallen by the wayside.[33] But the Court's more recent decisions,

29. *Id.* at 265.

30. Especially Lane County v. Oregon, 74 U.S. (7 Wall.) 71, 76 (1868) (holding that a federal statute making U.S. notes legal tender for all debts did not preempt a state law providing that state taxes must be paid in gold and silver coin). Although the case contains a good deal of strong language about the autonomy of the states, it rests in the end on the Court's refusal to interpret the relevant act of Congress as applying to the payment of state taxes. Thus, the *Lane County* case appears to be an early example of the clear statement rules that have been applied by the Court as a kind of sub-constitutional norm and that are discussed in text, *infra*, at notes 62 and 70.

31. In South Carolina v. Katzenbach, 383 U.S. 301 (1966), the Court upheld provisions of the Voting Rights Act of 1965 as a valid exercise of congressional power under the Fifteenth Amendment even though Congress had chosen to limit certain provisions to those geographic areas where immediate action seemed necessary. "The doctrine of the equality of the States," the Court said, did not preclude this singling out because the doctrine, as expressed in *Coyle*, "applies only to the terms upon which States are admitted to the Union, and not to the remedies for local evils which have subsequently appeared." *Id.* at 328–29.

Although the holding in South Carolina v. Katzenbach, based on Congress's power to take such action under the Fifteenth Amendment, is hard to quarrel with, the Court's treatment of *Coyle* may well have been an overly restrictive one. *Coyle* fairly stands for the proposition that distinctions among states (and not merely those relating to the terms of admission) must be warranted by a clear grant of congressional authority and by an adequate basis for the distinctions drawn. In *South Carolina* itself, Congress had "learned that substantial voting discrimination presently occurs in certain areas of the country," *id.* at 328, and had chosen to deal specially with those areas.

Just as a state may select certain counties at random, in order to conduct an experiment, so the federal government may be able to select states at random for the same purpose. But random selection may also have its limits and would surely have to be justified under some test of rational selection in order to survive a *Coyle* challenge by a state that had not been the beneficiary of the experiment (or had been the target of less favorable treatment).

32. 78 U.S. (11 Wall.) 113 (1870) (precluding federal authorities from taxing the income of a state judicial officer).

33. *See* Helvering v. Gerhardt, 304 U.S. 405 (1938); Graves v. State Tax Comm'n of New York ex rel. O'Keefe, 306 U.S. 466 (1939). *See also* South Carolina v. Baker, 485 U.S. 505 (1988).

including *Massachusetts v. United States*,[34] indicate that, in order to pass muster, a federal tax imposed *directly* on state activity must not discriminate against the states (as opposed to private entities subject to the same or a comparable tax) and must not be excessive. Thus, any effort to impose a tax on an activity unique to state or local governments (a tax on prison operations or other aspects of law enforcement, for example) would be unlikely to withstand challenge.

• *Erie R.R. v. Tompkins*,[35] a decision in which the Court held that its own interpretation of the Rules of Decision Act in *Swift v. Tyson*[36] and the century that followed was unconstitutional. The *Erie* Court evidently perceived its error in *Swift* as rooted in its reliance on a grant of constitutional and statutory jurisdiction to the federal courts (diversity jurisdiction, in particular) as the basis for allowing those courts both to formulate and apply a governing common law rule in certain matters when there was no controlling state statute. Over specific objection in Justice Reed's concurring opinion, the Court indicated that the authority sought to be exercised in *Swift* and its progeny could not be conferred by Congress even if it wanted to.[37]

• *United States Steel Corp. v. Multistate Tax Comm'n*,[38] one of several cases in which the Court upheld the authority of the states to enter into an interstate agreement *without* congressional approval so long as the agreement did not increase the political power of the states (vis-à-vis the federal government). The case gave an especially broad interpretation to this authority of the states, prompting two dissenting Justices to argue

34. 435 U.S. 444 (1978). *See also* New York v. United States, 326 U.S. 572 (1946). Both cases upheld the validity of federal taxes imposed on particular state activities, but made it clear that there were limits on federal power in this area.

35. 304 U.S. 64 (1938).

36. 41 U.S. (16 Pet.) 1 (1842).

37. *See* 304 U.S. at 78–80. The Court left little doubt of its view that the Constitution itself precluded any federal authority—legislative, executive, or judicial—from preempting state substantive law (whether common law or statutory law) on the basis solely of a grant of jurisdiction in Article III to adjudicate diversity of citizenship cases. Of course, other grants of Article III jurisdiction—including judicial power in admiralty and in controversies between states—have been viewed as carrying with them the authority to formulate governing law even in the absence of statute (*see generally Hart & Wechsler* 883–85). But the grant of federal authority to adjudicate diversity of citizenship cases is different in at least one crucial respect: it is difficult to conceive of a justiciable controversy that could *not* arise in the context of a dispute between citizens of different states. Admiralty disputes and controversies between the states themselves, on the other hand, are necessarily limited in subject matter and scope. Moreover, these two categories of jurisdiction have an inherently "national" quality.

38. 434 U.S. 452 (1978).

that congressional approval (of an agreement relating to the creation of a multistate agency designed to promote uniformity of state methods of taxation) was required because of the *potential* encroachment on federal supremacy.

• *Oregon v. Mitchell*,[39] a case in which the majority invalidated an act of Congress insofar as it purported to require the states to set the age of eighteen as the minimum for eligibility to vote in state and local elections. Although a subsequent constitutional Amendment overruled the square holding on this point,[40] the rationale of the decision—that the retained power of the states to govern themselves precluded federal intrusion on so basic a matter of state governance—remains fully binding, and indeed is reinforced by the Court's most recent pronouncement in the area of protected state autonomy.

• In *New York v. United States*,[41] the Court first upheld two national legislative incentives to the establishment of sites for the disposal of low-level radioactive wastes.[42] But it then invalidated a third incentive, which required each state to take title to (and financial responsibility for) all low-level waste generated in the state if, by a certain date, the state had not taken adequate measures to provide for disposal. The Court was careful to distinguish its earlier decision in *Garcia*[43] on the ground that the challenged provision was not one simply subjecting the state to "generally applicable laws," but rather one in which Congress sought to use the states as "implements of regulation."[44] It then held that federal legislation effectively compelling a state to enact regulatory legislation was an invasion of constitutionally protected state interests even though the national government could offer financial incentives to the states for acting, could enlist state courts in the enforcement of federal law,[45] and

39. 400 U.S. 112 (1970).

40. U.S. Const. Amend. XXVI.

41. 112 S. Ct. 2408 (1992).

42. One incentive promised financial support to those states establishing sites on an independent or regional basis, and the other incentive prohibited any state from shipping low-level waste out of the state in the absence of the creation of an adequate disposal site (again on an independent or regional basis) within a given time.

43. In Garcia v. San Antonio Metropolitan Trans. Auth., 469 U.S. 528 (1985), the Court had overruled National League of Cities v. Usery (426 U.S. 833 (1976)) and held that the federal government did have authority under the commerce power to apply the provisions of the Fair Labor Standards Act to state and local employees. Protection of state interests, the Court said in *Garcia*, must be secured primarily in the national political process, not in the courts.

44. New York v. United States, 112 S. Ct. at 2420.

45. *See, e.g.,* Testa v. Katt, 330 U.S. 386 (1947).

could effectively occupy the field—leaving the states with little or no substantive power to regulate. What the national government could *not* do, the Court said, was to blur state legislative accountability to the state's residents by coercing the state's legislature to act in accordance with a federally established agenda. Significantly, the Court not only invoked the limited powers of the federal government and the emphasis on that limitation in the Tenth Amendment but also hinted at the possible applicability of the Guarantee Clause in support of its result.[46]

As noted in chapter 2, comparable efforts to protect state autonomy under the Tenth Amendment—in the *National League of Cities* case, for example—have not survived.[47] But the difficulty with the *NLC* approach—the lack of a coherent and workable rationale—may well have been avoided here. One may argue with the historical foundation of the Court's reasoning in the *New York* case,[48] as well as with its

46. See 112 S. Ct. 2432–33, where the Court stated that it need not reach the question of the applicability of the Guarantee Clause to the "take title" provision because of its reliance on other constitutional provisions. The Court then held (on the assumption that some claims under the Guarantee Clause may be justiciable) that the Act's remaining incentives did not violate the clause. Also, the Court elsewhere cited with approval the article by Merritt (88 Colum. L. Rev. 1 (1988), discussed above at note 14 and accompanying text), which relied heavily on the clause in its arguments for constitutional protection of state interests. See 112 S. Ct. at 2418.

Several lower courts have relied on the Guarantee Clause, at least in part, as a basis for their conclusions. See, e.g., Bauers v. Heisel, 361 F.2d 581, 588–89 (3d Cir. 1966) (reading 42 U.S.C. § 1983 as affording absolute immunity to state prosecutors acting in their prosecutorial capacity and stating that denial of immunity would threaten the independence of state judiciaries protected by the Guarantee Clause); Brown v. EPA, 521 F.2d 827, 837–42 (9th Cir. 1975) (holding that serious questions would be raised under the Guarantee Clause if the federal government could compel restructuring of state budgets in order to carry out federal environmental policy).

In addition, several Supreme Court decisions prior to *New York* had invoked the Guarantee Clause, including *Coyle* (text at notes 28–31, *supra*), and *Texas v. White* (text at notes 26–27, *supra*). Thus the often-cited view—based primarily on Luther v. Borden, 48 U.S. (7 How.) 1 (1849)—that claims of Guarantee Clause violation are nonjusticiable seems to have been honored in the breach in situations less politically volatile than the violent upheaval involved in the *Luther* case. In her article on the subject, Merritt argues that claims under the Guarantee Clause should be justiciable when raised by a state itself, and further argues that the notion of nonjusticiability is difficult to square with the erosion of the political question doctrine in other contexts. See Merritt, 88 Colum. L. Rev. at 70–77.

47. See ch. 2, sec. A.2.

48. See the excellent critique of the Court's historical analysis in H. J. Powell, The Oldest Question of Constitutional Law, 79 Va. L. Rev. 633, 652–81 (1993). Powell goes on to suggest, however, that the argument for the *New York* result from the standpoint of "practical wisdom" is "very powerful." *Id.* at 684. See also the less generous critique in R. Levy, *New York v. United States*: An Essay on the Uses and Misuses of Precedent,

use of precedent. But the decision has a strong intellectual and practical foundation, emphasizing as it does the aspects of the national legislation under review that focused on the states alone and that effectively coerced state legislative bodies into acting as political entities in ways that tended to distort the accountability of elected representatives in a republican system of government. The decision—limited in scope as it may be— may well survive and prosper.[49]

Several important doctrines and decisions fall into an intermediate category, where the Court has avoided the question of the constitutional limits of federal power but at the same time has strongly hinted that the question of those limits was in the mind of the majority when it reached a disposition on other grounds.

• A classic example is the Court's decision in *Murdock v. Memphis*,[50] in which the majority declined to read an amendment of the statute giving it jurisdiction over the decisions of state courts as authorizing it to resolve pure questions of state law decided by those courts. The *Murdock* case, in which the Court had to strain the interpretation of the amended statute to avoid what it clearly recognized as a difficult constitutional question, may be aptly described (along with the Court's power to review state court decisions of federal questions) as one of the "twin pillars" of our judicial federalism.

• Another important example involves a series of cases in recent years in which the Court has resisted the opportunity to hold that state (or local) legislators may be forced by a federal court to take certain kinds of legislative action in order to bring the state (or locality) into compliance with federal constitutional requirements. This constitutional issue, as in *New York v. United States*, involves the blurring of the state or local legislator's accountability to the electorate by forcing him or her to take action that neither the representative nor the electorate wishes to take. The case for the existence of national authority may well be more compelling than in *New York* because of precedent in closely analogous

---

History, and Policy in Determining the Scope of Federal Power, 41 U. Kan. L. Rev. 493 (1993). These and other critiques are discussed in further detail in ch. 4, sec. B.

49. It is significant that the Court's holding invalidating the third incentive was explicitly limited to those states that had not entered into regional compacts approved by Congress. (The Court reserved judgment with respect to this latter group.) See 112 S. Ct. at 2432. This aspect of the decision is relevant to the discussion in ch. 4, sec. C.

50. 87 U.S. (20 Wall.) 590 (1875).

areas,[51] because the obligation being enforced is one imposed directly by the Constitution, and because the enforcement is at the instance of the judiciary acting in a particular context rather than at the instance of the national legislature establishing a broadly applicable national policy. Nevertheless, the Court has resisted upholding national power in several ways: by the extraordinary holding that in a suit brought under 42 U.S.C. § 1983, state officials acting in their legislative capacity enjoy personal immunity not only from liability in damages[52] but also from the imposition of prospective relief,[53] and by several holdings reversing lower court decrees, or orders enforcing those decrees, on the ground that the lower court's failure to exhaust less drastic alternatives constituted an abuse of discretion. In one case, *Spallone v. United States*,[54] the Court reversed a decree holding individual city councilors in contempt for failing to vote in favor of an ordinance that had been agreed to by the city as part of a consent decree designed to undo the effects of constitutional violations in the field of public housing. In another case,[55] the Court held it an abuse of discretion for a federal court to require a local property tax increase in order to raise the funds needed to comply with the court's school desegregation decree. In that case, four dissenting Justices objected that the remaining aspects of the decree relating to the means of raising the required funds also implicated serious constitutional issues of invasion of state autonomy.

• While the Court has on several occasions upheld the use of the national spending power to induce states to do what the national government could not (or might not be able to) compel them to do,[56] the Court has insisted that the conditions imposed on the availability of

51. For instance, federal courts have frequently given state apportioning authorities (legislatures themselves or their delegates) the option either to reapportion legislative districts in accordance with federal requirements or to have the job done for them by the federal courts. (For an example of the Supreme Court's willingness to allow imposition of a federal court-ordered redistricting plan, *see* Connor v. Finch, 431 U.S. 407 (1977).) Although the distinctions suggested in text may be significant, or even determinative, surely state legislative action taken under this kind of threatened federal court action comes close to the sort of coercion condemned in the *New York* case.

52. *See* Tenney v. Brandhove, 341 U.S. 367 (1951).

53. *See* Supreme Court of Virginia v. Consumers Union, 446 U.S. 719 (1980).

54. 493 U.S. 265 (1990).

55. Missouri v. Jenkins, 495 U.S. 33 (1990).

56. *See, e.g.,* Steward Machine Co. v. Davis, 301 U.S. 548 (1937) (upholding, against a charge of unconstitutional coercion of the states, a federal statute providing substantial financial incentives—in the form of federal tax credits to employers—for those states enacting unemployment compensation laws); South Dakota v. Dole, 483 U.S. 203 (1987)

national funds be fairly related to the purposes of the expenditure, and that the condition not go so to the core of the state's functioning that it could be regarded as essentially coercive in nature.[57]

In what might be called the "sub-constitutional" sphere—where the federal judiciary has recognized Congress's power to preempt or to take other action intruding on state authority—the Supreme Court has been especially active in protecting state interests. The range of these cases is significant in light of the power of the judicial branch to implement federal law and policy and to bind the state courts to its decisions. A few of the most prominent examples may underscore the importance of this category.

• In a series of decisions of which *Younger v. Harris*[58] is generally regarded as the progenitor (or at least as a paradigm case), the Supreme

---

(upholding, against similar challenge, federal statute conditioning highway aid on state willingness to raise the minimum drinking age to 21).

57. Thus in South Dakota v. Dole, 483 U.S. at 206–9, the Court, while acknowledging that the spending power extended to expenditures in pursuit of the "general welfare," noted the danger to highway safety created by drunken drivers—a problem that is aggravated if minors who cannot buy a drink in their home state may travel to another state in order to do so. Admittedly, the requirement of an adequate relationship between the federal condition and a permissible federal objective may not be very robust—it was perhaps stretched close to, or even beyond, the limit in *Dole*—but the Court in *Dole* also stressed that the amount of federal money at stake (though large in absolute terms) was not a major percentage of total highway expenditures.

For a valuable discussion of the relationship between state "sovereignty" and the federal spending power—a discussion that is critical of uses of the spending power that are, as a practical matter, coercive—see L. Kaden, Politics, Money, and State Sovereignty: The Judicial Role, 79 Colum. L. Rev. 847 (1979). For a more recent critique, see Note, Federalism, Political Accountability, and the Spending Clause, 107 Harv. L. Rev. 1419 (1994) (proposing stricter federal court scrutiny of exercise of the national taxing and spending power designed to "induce" state action).

The federal Crime Bill, enacted after considerable controversy in 1994, provides for the transfer to the states of substantial funds, but also attaches a number of conditions to the transfers—especially with respect to the use of funds for penal institutions and law enforcement. Thus, one commentator noted that the bill would send "billions of federal dollars back to the states, counties and cities while at the same time giving the central Government a larger voice than it has ever had in setting policies for police and prison systems." N.Y. Times, Sept. 14, 1994, at A16, col. 1. The bill also substantially increases the number of federal crimes. *See* A Bigger Role for the Feds, 80 A.B.A. J. 14 (Oct. 1994). For a forceful assault on the notions of "germaneness" and "coercion" as limitations on federal spending power—an assault based in significant part on a close reading of Hamilton's arguments—see D. Engdahl, The Spending Power, 44 Duke L.J. 1 (1994).

58. 401 U.S. 37 (1971). For full discussion of the forerunners and offspring of the *Younger* doctrine, see *Hart & Wechsler* at 1392–1405, 1420–38.

Court has required federal courts to defer to pending state court proceedings even with respect to the determination of issues of federal law.[59] The rationale, especially applicable in state-initiated criminal (and to a lesser extent, civil) enforcement proceedings, is based largely on the state's interest in enforcing its own prohibitions and regulations in its own tribunals—subject, of course, to at least discretionary federal review of state court determination of federal questions.

• In the area of habeas corpus—and especially of efforts to use the writ to obtain federal court reveiw of the question whether a state court criminal conviction was consistent with the requirements of the Constitution—the Supreme Court has considerably cut back on the writ's availability in recent years,[60] and national legislative efforts to reverse this trend have to date been unsuccessful.

• Although the Court has recognized broad congressional power to abrogate state immunity from federal court suit under the Eleventh Amendment—at least when Congress is exercising its powers under the Fourteenth Amendment or the Commerce Clause[61]—the Court has at the same time adopted what some critics have labeled a "super clear statement rule."[62] This rule requires Congress not only to articulate but

59. Other abstention doctrines include that represented by Railroad Commission v. Pullman Co., 312 U.S. 496 (1941) (requiring federal court abstention to permit state court construction of a difficult *state* law question in cases presenting a federal constitutional issue to which the state law question is relevant). *See generally Hart & Wechsler* 1356–74.

60. *See, e.g.,* Stone v. Powell, 428 U.S. 465 (1976); Wainwright v. Sykes, 438 U.S. 72 (1977); Teague v. Lane, 489 U.S. 288 (1989); McCleskey v. Zant, 499 U.S. 467 (1991). Several historical studies suggest that this recent trend is in accord with the Supreme Court's approach to the writ in the nineteenth and early twentieth centuries, as well as with the earlier history of the writ under British law. *See, e.g.,* P. Bator, Finality in Criminal Law and Habeas Corpus for State Prisoners, 76 Harv. L. Rev. 441 (1963); D. Oaks, Legal History in the High Court—Habeas Corpus, 64 Mich. L. Rev. 451 (1966). For a very different view of the development of the writ in the United States, see G. Peller, In Defense of Federal Habeas Corpus Relitigation, 16 Harv. C.R.–C.L. L. Rev. 579 (1982).

61. *See, e.g.,* Fitzpatrick v. Bitzer, 427 U.S. 445 (1976) (Fourteenth Amendment); Pennsylvania v. Union Gas Co., 491 U.S. 1 (1989) (Commerce Clause).

62. For examples of such decisions, see, e.g., Atascadero State Hospital v. Scanlon, 473 U.S. 234 (1985); Dellmuth v. Muth, 491 U.S. 223 (1989). Both decisions were 5–4 and have been criticized as adopting a standard that serves to frustrate legislative purpose. *See, e.g.,* W. Eskridge & P. Frickey, Quasi-Constitutional Law: Clear Statement Rules as Constitutional Lawmaking, 45 Vand. L. Rev. 593, 621–23 (1992); D. Shapiro, Continuity and Change in Statutory Interpretation, 67 N.Y.U. L. Rev. 921, 956–59 (1992). In addition to being the author of the last piece just cited, I should note my participation in an amicus curiae brief submitted on what turned out to be the losing side in the *Atascadero* case. (Congress saw fit to overrule the specific holding in *Atascadero* shortly after it was rendered. See Pub. L. 99–506 § 1003, Oct. 21, 1986, 100 Stat. 1845.)

to express in explicit terms its purpose to abrogate the state's immunity if that purpose is to be judicially recognized.

• The Court's self-proclaimed authority to resort to the "dormant Commerce Clause" to strike down state legislation even in the absence of congressional preemption has been criticized from within and without the Court,[63] and, at least until recently,[64] has been sparingly exercised. Of particular significance, the Court has upheld a state's authority to use its ability as a purchaser to prefer in-state suppliers of goods and services,[65] and to use its inherent advantage as a source of material as a means of raising revenue (by the imposition of a severance tax in the case of the mining of sulphur-free coal, for example), even if the burden falls much more heavily on out-of-state purchasers than on in-state residents.[66] Thus, while a state may not overtly discriminate

63. See ch. 2, note 55. See also Justice Scalia's recent opinion concurring in part in Itel Containers Int'l Corp. v. Huddleston, 113 S. Ct. 1095, 1106–7 (1993), in which he made clear his view that the Commerce Clause "contains no 'negative' component, no self-operative prohibition upon the States' regulation of commerce," but indicated at the same time his willingness to accept (on a limited basis) the force of stare decisis in this area. That basis extended to cases in which (1) a state law "facially discriminates" against interstate commerce, or (2) is indistinguishable from a law previously held invalid by the Court.

64. In West Lynn Creamery, Inc. v. Healy, 114 S. Ct. 2205 (1994), the Court, over two dissents, struck down under the dormant Commerce Clause a state assessment payable by all milk dealers that was distributed only to in-state milk producers. Justice Scalia, concurring in the judgment, argued that the majority had written too broadly of the Court's power to protect interstate competition and contended that the result could be defended on narrower grounds.

65. See, e.g., Hughes v. Alexandria Scrap Corp., 426 U.S. 794 (1976) (upholding, over three dissents, the ability of the state of Maryland to prefer its own scrap dealers in paying a "bounty" for the destruction of automobile "hulks," and stating that nothing in the Commerce Clause prevents a state from entering a market as a buyer and in doing so, restricting trade to its own citizens).

For the strained effort of the Court in later decisions to distinguish between the state as market participant and the state as market regulator, see, e.g., South Central Timber Development, Inc. v. Wunnicke, 467 U.S. 82 (1984). For the Court's most recent allusion to the distinction between the state as regulator and the state as market participant, see Oregon Waste Systems, Inc. v. Columbia Resource Co., 114 S. Ct. 1345, 1354 n.9 (1994), a case that relied on the dormant Commerce Clause in invalidating a state's imposition of a higher fee for the disposal of solid waste when the waste was generated out of state than when it was generated within the state. (As this book went to press, it appeared that federal legislation would be enacted giving each state authority over a period of years to limit the flow into the state of waste materials from other states. See House Passes Bill to Let States Limit Trash Imports, N.Y. Times, Sept. 29, 1994, at B6, col. 1.)

66. See Commonwealth Edison Co. v. Montana, 453 U.S. 609 (1981). The decision is criticized in L. Tribe, American Constitutional Law 442 (2d ed. 1988), citing the case as an instance in which the "new realism," which Tribe views as desirable, "seems to have been tempered by an extra dose of judicial sympathy for state taxing power."

against suppliers or others from out of state in deciding what may be consumed in the state or what may travel through it (at least in the absence of a compelling justification relating to health or safety), there are available methods states can use to assist their own industries or their own residents.[67]

• In a number of areas in which competing interests may come into conflict, a state has the constitutional authority to prefer one interest over another even though both have some claim to constitutional protection. A leading example arose in the *Pruneyard* case,[68] in which the Court—after a prior decision refusing to hold that the First Amendment protected one who sought to distribute leaflets in a privately owned shopping center[69]—affirmed the authority of a state to extend protection to such activity in the face of a constitutional claim by the shopping center owner that its property rights were being infringed. The states, in other words, have substantial leeway to make policy choices in certain areas where claims of right or of substantial interest intersect, but each claim falls short of being awarded federal constitutional protection against the other.

• In a wide range of cases in recent years, the Court has demonstrated a reluctance to infer (in the absence of a clear conflict) that federal law operates to preempt state law, or to read federal preemption provisions broadly when a conflict is not inevitable and a narrower reading would save at least some state regulation.[70] One of the most recent, and visible, examples is in the area of state tort law and its relation to the preemption provisions of national legislation requiring health warnings on cigarette packages.[71]

67. Moreover, the limitations imposed on the states under the dormant Commerce Clause are in a significant respect a *guarantee* of a strong federal system. By restricting the ability of one state to discriminate against the commercial output of other states, the federal courts are protecting state interests against unfair treatment by other states. See the discussion of the *West Lynn Creamery* case, note 64, *supra*. (Compare the specific guarantees of federal protection against prejudicial treatment in Article IV, discussed in sec. A.)

68. Pruneyard Shopping Center v. Robins, 447 U.S. 74 (1980).

69. Lloyd Corp. v. Tanner, 407 U.S. 551 (1972).

70. *See* D. Shapiro, Continuity and Change in Statutory Interpretation, 67 N.Y.U. L. Rev. 921, 937 and authorities cited at n. 79 (1992). For a more extreme version of the Court's approach in the context of a challenge to preemption of state law governing the retirement of appointed state judges, see Gregory v. Ashcroft, 501 U.S. 452 (1991), criticized in Note, Clear Statement Rules, Federalism, and Congressional Regulation of States, 107 Harv. L. Rev. 1959, 1972–73 (1994).

71. In Cipollone v. Liggett Group, Inc., 112 S. Ct. 2608 (1992), the Court, dividing along several axes, held that a broadly worded preemption provision did not wholly

Admittedly, none of the decisions in this final category establishes that the states possess powers lying beyond the authority of the federal legislature to override. But they do reflect an attitude toward the role of the states in our federal system that extends well beyond the purely discretionary or policy aspects of that role. Viewed as a whole, as actions of the national judicial branch, they add up to a recognition of the relevance and importance of the states as a matter of federal *law*— federal common law, if you will. And much of this law has significant constitutional overtones.[72]

B. The Preservation of a Significant Policy-Making Role for the States Is Not Only Constitutionally Required But Also Economically, Politically, and Socially Desirable

1. *Introduction*

If the Constitution itself *must* be read to require a system in which the states retain significant rights that the national government cannot take away, then the policy issues to be faced are substantially reduced. Those who advocate the virtual elimination of the states—except perhaps as administrative or geographical entities whose powers may be effectively reduced to zero—would then be required to urge the adoption of one or more constitutional Amendments to permit such a change to occur, and the likelihood of such Amendments is not great.

---

preempt the availability of remedies under state tort law. Also, over Justice Scalia's dissent on the point, the Court squarely held that its interpretive guidelines functioned not only in dealing with congressional silence but also in construing the language of statutory preemption provisions.

72. Contrary to widespread belief, advocacy of a strong federal system is not the exclusive preserve of political or judicial conservatives. Among the Nation's most liberal Supreme Court Justices have been several who consistently favored a strong federal system in which the states played a substantial role. These Justices include Louis Brandeis—whose opinion in the *Erie* case (discussed at note 37, *supra*) was one of his favorites and who spoke enthusiastically about the states as experimental laboratories—and Hugo Black, who favored abolition of any notion of substantive due process as a restraint on the exercise of state authority (*see* Ferguson v. Skrupa, 372 U.S. 726 (1963)), who saw few if any limits to the exercise of state judicial jurisdiction over out-of-staters (*see* International Shoe Co. v. Washington, 326 U.S. 310, 322 (1945) (separate opinion of Black, J.); Mcgee v. International Life Ins. Co., 355 U.S. 220 (1957); Hanson v. Denckla, 357 U.S. 235, 256 (1958) (Black, J., dissenting)), and who spoke eloquently of "Our Federalism" in his landmark opinion in *Younger v. Harris* (discussed in text at note 70, *supra*.)

For interesting essays focusing on the views of federalism held by Justices Brandeis and Black, see M. Marcus, Louis D. Brandeis and the Laboratories of Democracy, and T. Freyer, Hugo Black and the Principles of "Our Federalism," in *Federalism and the Judicial Mind: Essays on American Constitutional Law and Politics* 75, 93 (H. Scheiber ed., 1992).

In fact, however, even staunch advocates of a decentralized system of government recognize that the Constitution can only resolve so many issues—that substantial room is inevitably left for the exercise of discretion by those vested with the power to decide.[73] Thus the question of the scope of state authority must to some significant degree turn on the economic, political, and social advantages that such a system would bring with it, and the remainder of this chapter is addressed to those issues.

2. The Virtues of State Autonomy from Economic and Related Policy Perspectives

Over the past two centuries, the American system of federalism—one in which the states have always played a significant role—has contributed to the Nation's growth and health in different ways at different times,[74] often advancing and sometimes hindering that growth and prosperity. But the overall balance is a favorable one, and on the economic front in particular, that balance continues to hold.

As indicated in chapter 2, the principal virtue claimed for a truly federal system in the present day arises from the perceived values of competition—competition between the states and the federal government for popular support and similar competition among the states themselves.[75] But in fact, the case for federalism from the perspective

73. For example, in her persuasive argument for limitations on federal power rooted in the constitutional guarantee to the states of a republican form of government, Deborah Merritt sees the Guarantee Clause as placing only "a modest restraint" on national authority. D. Merritt, The Guaranty Clause and State Autonomy: Federalism for a Third Century, 88 Colum. L. Rev. 1, 69 (1988).

74. Among historians of federalism, Harry Scheiber has been perhaps the most thoughtful chronicler of the various stages of federalism in American society. See, e.g., his articles entitled Federalism and Legal Process: Historical and Contemporary Analysis of the American System, 14 Law & Soc'y Rev. 663 (1980), and Federalism and the American Economic Order, 1789–1910, Law & Soc'y, Fall 1975, 57.

As a number of observers have pointed out, the states have played an important and often positive role: as strongholds of opposition to such unfortunate measures as the Alien and Sedition and Fugitive Slave Laws in the pre–Civil War era, as havens for escaped slaves and for the Abolitionist movement during that era, as important supporters of the transport and industrial revolutions of the mid- and late nineteenth century, as the source of much labor-protective and antidiscrimination legislation, and as supra-constitutional protectors of individual and group rights in the twentieth.

Throughout our history, of course, the scope and extent of national power has varied, but the states have never ceased to function as sources of countervailing power, as implementers of national programs, or as both.

75. See ch. 2, sec. B.1. For recent studies of the virtues of interstate competition, see, e.g., T. Dye, American Federalism: Competition among Governments (1990); G. Ottosen, Making American Government Work (1992).

of economic and related policy issues is more complex and harder to summarize. It rests on three related premises: first, that a well-conceived and smoothly operating federal system is one in which policy emerges as part of a process and from the interplay of a multiplicity of sources; second, that competition among states is bound to enhance the productivity of capital and labor in the long run; and third, that the states not only can serve, but have served, as experimental laboratories for the development of a wide range of social and economic programs.

The proposition that federalism embraces a system in which policy emerges through a continuing process of discussion and implementation by multiple governmental units is perhaps best articulated in the work of two leading advocates of contemporary federalism: Daniel Elazar and Vincent Ostrom.[76] Indeed, Elazar, in his many writings, has been at pains to stress that his view of federalism is most aptly described as a system that is "noncentralized" rather than decentralized, since the latter term carries a kind of top-down implication at odds with his view of how federalism works best.[77] Thus, Elazar argues that the least effective national programs are those in which the states are given little or no responsibility, local needs are given low priority, and local input is minimal,[78] while those that work best not only involve the states as implementing agencies but depend on the states to shape the programs in a manner that best accords with local conditions. In this view, a policy that may begin its development at the national level, will—and should— assume a different complexion and shape in every state in which it is administered. Ultimately, the experiences of the range of states will reflect back on, and redefine, the policy itself. Thus, to take a humble example, the nationally financed school lunch program assuredly benefited from the process of local implementation—a process that not only recognized the variety of local preferences but also contributed knowledge and a range of experience to the development of the program itself.[79]

76. The collected works of both authors on the subject of federalism are substantial. Among the most useful with reference to the point made in text are D. Elazar, *American Federalism: A View from the States* (3d ed. 1984), and V. Ostrom, *The Meaning of American Federalism* (1991).

77. *See, e.g.,* D. Elazar, *American Federalism: A View from the States* 3–9 (3d ed. 1984).

78. *See, e.g., id.,* at 56–58.

79. *See* R. Stoker, *Reluctant Partners* ch. 5 (1991). In this excellent study of the input of the states in developing national policies and programs, Stoker uses the school lunch program as an example involving an area of intense state and local concern. He points out that the program evolved through several phases: a constituent phase, a progressive phase, and a retrenchment phase, and that in each phase the contribution of state and local

This view is to some extent at odds with the federalistic vision of those, like Rivlin, who favor a sharper division of power between the national government and the states[80] and who worry about the overload that too much central responsibility for too many programs may entail. Perhaps the reconciliation of these somewhat different theses lies in a clearer recognition that in certain areas the national government should play little or no role (except possibly through block grants or revenue sharing).[81] But in the areas in which the national government should play a greater role, the states should ordinarily not be excluded from participation at *both* the policy development and implementation level. Indeed, these two processes are properly viewed as continuous and complementary.

The argument rooted in the value of competition among the states, especially when combined with the right of exit of capital or labor,[82] remains at the heart of the economic case for federalism. This argument in turn breaks down into several components: first, the perceived defects in Madison's theory (articulated in *The Federalist* No. 10) of the virtues of an "extended republic"; second, the weaknesses of the "race to the bottom" theory; third, the limits of the need for national action on

---

authorities was substantial. He does note, however, that the federal noose was tightened when state and local defection from the federal program became harder to achieve (because of commitments already made) (*see id.* at 149–50), and that implementing policy in the context of diffuse authority is more difficult when the issue is not one of the distribution of benefits but rather of the imposition of costs. *Id.* at ch. 6. As to that aspect—of which the problem of waste disposal is a leading example—see ch. 4, sec. C.2.

80. *See* A. Rivlin, *Reviving the American Dream: The Economy, the States and the Federal Government* (1992).

81. A good example may well lie in certain areas of criminal law enforcement involving activity essentially local in its impact.

Among the more informative studies of the history of block grants and revenue sharing in recent decades are Advisory Commission on Intergovernmental Relations, *Readings in Federalism: Perspectives on a Decade of Change* (1989) (especially at 3–12, 51–56, 109–12); D. Elazar, *American Federalism: A View from the States* ch. 4 (3d ed. 1984); R. Peterson, B. Rabe, & K. Wong, *When Federalism Works* (1986) (distinguishing between national programs that are "developmental" and those that are "redistributive"); J. Zimmerman, *Contemporary American Federalism* ch. 6 (1992). As this book goes to press in early 1995, the change in party control of the federal legislature appears to signal a revival of interest in these forms of aid to state and local governments.

82. On the significance of the right of exit, see, e.g., C. Tiebout, A Pure Theory of Local Expenditures, 64 J. Pol. Econ. 416 (1956); F. Easterbrook, Antitrust and the Economics of Federalism, 26 J.L. & Econ. 23, 32–35 (1983); C. Rose, Planning and Dealing: Piecemeal Land Control as a Problem of Local Legitimacy, 71 Cal. L. Rev. 837 (1983).

the basis of a theory of public goods; and fourth, a response to the case for virtually unlimited national power based on the inevitably of externalities in a rapidly shrinking world market.

(1) The advocates of contemporary federalism criticize—as unduly romantic and Utopian—Madison's theory that an extended republic will reduce the danger that government will yield to the blandishment of factions. The difficulty with Madison's argument, especially in the view of public choice theorists who have become quite numerous and articulate in recent years,[83] lies in his failure to appreciate the disproportionate influence that can be wielded on a national level by certain groups that may be relatively small in numbers but that are cohesive and can avoid the problem of too many free riders sharing the benefits without bearing the costs of exerting that influence.

In this view, national action is most likely when the benefits of that action are confined to a concentrated, well-organized group and the costs of the action are widely dispersed among those who are ill equipped to resist in an organized way.[84] (The least likely case for national action, of course, is the converse.)[85] Thus, the ability to achieve "redistribution of the nation's wealth"—one widely heralded advantage of national over state authority[86]—is more likely than not to take the form of redistribution from the less organized to the more concentrated, better financed, more cohesive groups. The history of national subsidies in a wide range of situations supports the validity of this view.

This rather gloomy and cynical outlook on the nature of government, to the extent that it is valid, seriously undercuts the arguments for national power based on the virtues of transcending the power of private factions and of correcting undue disparities through redistribution. If anything, redistribution is at least as likely to take the form of wealth transfers from the less organized to the more organized—transfers that may bear only the appearance of correcting disparities or of promoting the public interest in other ways. (Thus, a public housing program may end up granting far more substantial benefits to developers than to needy

83. For an analysis of the strengths and weaknesses of public choice theory, as well as a bibliography of its leading exponents, see D. Farber & P. Frickey, *Law and Public Choice* (1991).

84. For especially useful "taxonomies" of supply and demand for legislation based on cost/benefit analysis (from the viewpoint of a public choice theorist), see W. Eskridge & P. Frickey, *Cases and Materials on Legislation* 55–56 (Tables 1–1 and 1–2) (2d ed. 1995).

85. *See id.*

86. *See* ch. 2, sec. B.2.

tenants; a public health program may benefit the providers more than the receivers, etc.)

What, if anything, is the remedy for this defect of an extended republic—for the realization of what one observer called (in a slightly different context) a "nightmare for poor Madison"?[87] Some approaches avoid the issue of federalism altogether, and consider such steps as limiting the terms of elected officials and moving to a system of campaign financing that precludes significant private contributions. But both proposals have substantial flaws of their own and even raise constitutional issues.[88]

One approach not limited to measures taken at a national level looks at least in part to a healthy federalism as a helpful response. If in fact certain small, well-organized interest groups may, with relative ease, achieve their goals at a national level, the diffusion of power among a multiplicity of governments[89] may increase the difficulties such groups experience in realizing their objectives. After all, at many levels of government, those who will suffer the costs might not be so widely dispersed—they might find it far easier to organize an effective opposition than they

87. R. Stewart, Federalism and Rights, 19 Ga. L. Rev. 917, 963 (1985). Stewart here was addressing the effect of what he described as an increasing rhetoric of national rights that has helped move the battles among factions into federal courtrooms, thus circumventing many of the political safeguards of federalism that "are supposed to make national policies sensitive to state and local concerns." But his phrase seems as apt in the context of the criticisms of Madison's views from the standpoint of public choice theory.

Valuable as public choice theory has been in affording insights into the process of legislation, there is surely merit to the criticisms voiced by Farber & Frickey in their book cited at note 83, supra, and by Eskridge & Frickey, in their book cited at note 84, supra (at 57–61). For example, as the critics have observed, much legislation is difficult or impossible to explain on the basis of public choice theory, and the theory appears to pay insufficient attention to the role of the executive branch in the shaping of legislative agendas and policies. See also ch. 4, sec. C.3.

88. On the defects of term limitations, consider the loss to the effectiveness of the national legislature likely to result from adoption of a two-term limit. Surely, some of our most effective legislators have taken at least two terms to acquire the experience, influence with their peers, and other qualities needed for effective leadership.

On the constitutional issue of term limits, there are questions whether such term limits can be imposed by state or federal authorities without a constitutional Amendment. (See the reference to cases pending before the Supreme Court, note 10, supra.) On the constitutional issues raised by limitations on campaign contributions and expenditures, see, e.g., Buckley v. Valeo, 424 U.S. 1 (1976).

89. It has been reported that, taking into account not only state and federal governments but also all subdivisions of state authority (e.g., county, municipal, and township), there are over 80,000 governmental units in the United States. J. Zimmerman, Contemporary American Federalism 1 (1992).

would at a national level.[90] Under this approach, then, the very existence of dispersed authority serves as a safeguard against the wielding of excessive influence by special interests. Those interests that are strongest in particular states will find themselves vying with competing interests that have more power at a national level, and vice versa. The result is not necessarily a system of government that is both interlocked and gridlocked, but rather a greater assurance that whatever policies emerge from this olio of authority will be more likely than not to reflect the interest of a larger and more varied public.

(2) With respect to the argument for national authority based on fears of a "race to the bottom"—an argument that in its purest form asserts that such a race is likely to occur even in the absence of any externalities—a powerful response (in the context of environmental regulation) appears in a recent article by Richard Revesz.[91] Revesz begins by asking some provocative questions:

> If one believes that competition among sellers of widgets is socially desirable, why is competition among sellers of location rights socially undesirable? If federal regulation mandating a supra-competitive price for widgets is socially undesirable, why is federal regulation mandating a supra-competitive price for location rights socially desirable?[92]

90. *Cf.* J. Macey, Federal Deference to Local Regulators and the Economic Theory of Regulation: Toward a Public-Choice Theory of Federalism, 76 Va. L. Rev. 265, 290 (1990). Macey sets forth three situations in which, despite the general advantages to cohesive private interest groups in seeking nationwide legislation favoring their interests, such groups might, consistently with public choice theory, prefer to operate on a state or local level and in which national legislative officials might "maximize political support for themselves" by leaving the matter for determination on those levels.

A recent study of the operation of the Conference of Commissioners on Uniform State Laws, and particularly of the evolution of the Uniform Commercial Code, argues that the Conference—a body that has had an enormous impact on the development of state law in many fields—has tended to "produce only solutions that are the most amenable to the business special interests that dominate it." H. K. Patchel, Interest Group Politics, Federalism, and the Uniform Laws Process: Some Lessons from the Uniform Commercial Code, 78 Minn. L. Rev. 83, 162 (1993). Patchel makes a number of recommendations for improvement short of centralized lawmaking, however, including opening up the drafting process, providing the states with sufficient information to make independent decisions, and deemphasizing the need for uniform laws. But she also suggests that the Conference should not automatically rule out the possibility of recommending a nationally enacted solution rather than drafting a proposal designed for the states alone.

91. R. Revesz, Rehabilitating Interstate Competition: Rethinking the "Race-to-the-Bottom" Rationale for Federal Environmental Regulation, 67 N.Y.U. L. Rev. 1210 (1992).

92. *Id.* at 1234.

Reviewing several economic studies by other scholars,[93] Revesz then observes: "There are no formal models supporting the proposition that competition among states creates a prisoner's dilemma[94] in which states, contrary to their interests, compete for industry by offering progressively laxer standards."[95] He concludes not that a race to the bottom can never exist, but that its prevalence in theory or practice has never been established.

(3) What of the argument that "public goods" necessarily "consumed" by all—whether they pay for them or not—can and should be furnished only by a government large enough to levy the costs (through taxation) on all who receive the benefits? Part of the answer may already have been suggested in the discussion in chapter 2. "Pure" public goods, from which everyone receives equivalent benefits no matter where his location within a geographical area as broad as (or even broader than) the Nation itself, are rare. The nuclear deterrent is a classic but unusual example. Much more common, I submit, are "impure" public goods—those in which there are smaller and more definable boundaries to the available benefits. These boundaries may not reduce to a single territorial line, but at least diminish rapidly as one moves away from the center. A small public park, or a beach required by law to be open to the public, is illustrative. The more accessible the park or the beach to one's residence, the more benefit one is likely to receive from it. And public goods are also often "impure" in the sense that some sort of "user fees" are not unthinkable. Thus a highway may be a "freeway" in the true sense (as city streets must be almost by necessity), but a system of tolls can be devised—even a system that charges lower rates to the regular user on the theory that the cost of administration does not rise by the same amount with every use. Similarly, pilotage fees for the use of a port may include some element designed to pay for the cost of maintaining a lighthouse. While those fees may not be paid by all who receive benefits from the lighthouse, they do tend to concentrate the cost within the group of principal beneficiaries.

The point for federalism is that, while some public goods undoubtedly

93. See authorities cited id. at 1236–42.

94. The classic prisoner's dilemma is one in which the inability of two prisoners to communicate and to reach a binding agreement to cooperate with each other results in each prisoner rationally acting in a way that leads him to a suboptimal result. For further discussion of the nature of the dilemma, see id. at 1217–18 and authorities cited at n. 18.

95. Id. at 1242.

require a heavy dose of national authority, financing, and administration, others may benefit from some state and local participation.[96] Nobody doubts that the national government has a critical role to play in national defense, or in the administration of the larger national parks that are heavily used by people from a wide area. The question is far more debatable, however, with regard to public goods more narrowly defined geographically or more hybrid in their nature.[97]

(4) The problems raised by the existence of public goods constitute a subset of the problems raised by the existence of externalities generally— of all those instances in which the costs and benefits are not fully realized by the same group and in which significant inefficiency (too much or too little of the activity in question to maximize social welfare) is likely to result. Once again, the response to the argument that the inevitability of externalities necessitates centralized authority may lie in the range of possibilities and in a practical recognition that all decisions involve trade-offs to some degree. There are extreme examples of negative externalities in the carrying on of private activity. An enormously profitable company in a small upstream state may be polluting the water in a river that is vital to the welfare and quality of life in a large number of downstream states. One can surely imagine the state of manufacture imposing controls on itself in an effort to optimize the total balance of costs and benefits in a wide geographical area. But it seems far more likely that the upstream state, if left entirely to its own devices (and with a constitutional guarantee against at least certain forms of retribution by the downstream states), will do little or nothing, and that transaction costs may prevent the downstream states, or their residents, from organizing effectively to negotiate an efficient result. In such a case, action on a national level,

96. Admittedly, state boundaries (whose arbitrariness in many instances has already been noted) may not constitute the ideal geographic entities for the distribution of public goods. But there are two reasonable responses to this critique: (1) if the ideal unit is smaller than a state as a whole, a state may be in a far better position than the national government to delegate responsibility to that smaller unit, and (2) if the ideal unit is larger than one state, or even than several states, the machinery for interstate alliances or cooperation of various kinds may prove more appropriate than uniform national action. *See* ch. 4.

97. For an excellent discussion of the potential role of state and local governments in the purchasing and provision of public goods, and of the richly varied patterns that can exist with respect to the nature of goods generally regarded as "public," see V. Ostrom, *The Meaning of American Federalism* chs. 6, 7 (1991). *See also* J. Head, Public Goods and Multi-Level Government, in his book, *Public Goods and Public Welfare* 262–84 (1976) (suggesting, inter alia, that efficiency in the provision of public goods may *require* a significant degree of decentralization).

or at least a multistate level stimulated by national incentives, seems essential.[98]

But take a less blatant example. Following a similar illustration, assume that a manufacturer is causing significant water pollution (with its attendant social costs) primarily in the state of manufacture, but with some similar effects in downstream states. If the in-state cost is sufficiently high, and yet the state has struck the balance in favor of allowing the activity to continue (subject to some restrictions), is it so clear that the existence of some spillover effects is in itself sufficient to require action at a national level? How relevant is it that the state itself—through its elected officials—has evaluated the internal costs and benefits? That those who suffer harm outside the state are to a significant extent represented by those who suffer similar, and perhaps more drastic, harms inside the state? That in all probability at least some of the economic benefits experienced from the activity in question also spill over the state's boundaries and benefit those in other states?[99]

Perhaps this argument suggests only that if there were no other factors to weigh in the balance, leaving the states with responsibility for certain matters having external consequences is not as bad as some would have it, but that the better resolution would still be to favor decision making at a national level. But if this dialogue demonstrates little else, federalism is surely a complex subject with many facets, and if the argument derived from externalities is not overpowering (as it frequently is not), then these other factors may well tip the scales in favor either of decentralized

---

98. There has been an abundance of writing about federalism in the context of environmental law, especially on issues of interstate pollution. *See, e.g.,* W. Lowry, *The Dimensions of Federalism: State Governments and Pollution Control Policies* (1992); R. Revesz, Rehabilitating Interstate Competition: Rethinking the "Race-to-the-Bottom" Rationale for Federal Environmental Regulation, 67 N.Y.U. L. Rev. 1210 (1992); R. Stewart, Pyramids of Sacrifice? Problems of Federalism in Mandating State Implementation of National Environmental Policy, 86 Yale L.J. 1196 (1977). These works do not represent, or suggest a firm basis for developing, a consensus on the importance of state participation in policy development, and the problem is further complicated by the holding of *New York v. United States* (discussed in sec. A, *supra*), itself an environmental law case. For further discussion, see ch. 4, sec. B.

99. For sophisticated discussions of such questions as degrees of overlap and of "spillover," and of the advantages of decentralization in furthering the values of autonomy and democratic control in relation to such questions, see, e.g., J. Head, Public Goods and Multilevel Government, in his book, *Public Goods and Public Welfare* 262–84 (1974); V. Ostrom, Can Federalism Make A Difference?, 3 Publius 197 (1973).

decision making or, at least, significant state and local participation in the formulation and implementation of the relevant policies.[100]

A final economic argument for decentralization is the one articulated by Justice Brandeis[101] and often criticized as having more support in theory than in practice: the argument that the states may make a substantial contribution as "experimental laboratories" for the development of economic (and social) programs. The notion of the states as "laboratories" has two aspects: the one Brandeis evidently had principally in mind is that after thorough testing in a variety of contexts, a national solution will emerge that is suitable for implementation in every state. A related form—rooted in notions of pluralism and relativism—recognizes that given the wide variation in conditions and preferences in a country as diverse as ours, different solutions may be best for different states.

The proposition, despite its intuitive appeal, has been challenged even on the level of theory. In an article with the intriguing title *Risk Taking and Reelection: Does Federalism Promote Innovation?*,[102] Susan Rose-Ackerman argues that, in general, the answer to her question is "no" because politicians who prize reelection will be risk-averse when it comes to experiments that will succeed or fail in a short time, and indifferent to longer-term experiments unless they have discernible short-term payoffs to influential interest groups.[103] Despite the force of these points, it seems

100. For an excellent discussion in the context of pollution control, see W. Lowry, *The Dimensions of Federalism: State Governments and Pollution Control Policies* (1992) (testing a number of hypotheses, including the view that a state's ability to achieve a reasonable match between need and response depends to a significant extent on the degree of "vertical" (national) involvement in the program). Lowry concludes that both vertical involvement and horizontal competition among states are important factors in a successful pollution control program.

101. *See* New State Ice Co. v. Liebmann, 285 U.S. 262, 311 (1932) (Brandeis, J., dissenting). *See also, e.g.,* M. Marcus, Louis D. Brandeis and the Laboratories of Democracy, in *Federalism and the Judicial Mind: Essays on American Constitutional Law and Politics* 75 (H. Scheiber ed., 1992). As Marcus points out, Brandeis viewed the laboratory idea as an important path to progress because of the relatively small scale (and correspondingly low risk) of experiments undertaken in individual states.

102. Appearing in 9 J. Legal Stud. 593 (1980). For a similar, even more forcefully stated, attack on the "experimental argument for federalism," see E. Rubin & M. Feeley, Federalism: Some Notes on a National Neurosis, 41 UCLA L. Rev. 903, 923–36 (1994).

103. This brief summary undoubtedly does less than complete justice to an article that rests in large part on sophisticated techniques of analysis, but the summary does capture Rose-Ackerman's principal conclusions.

clear that over eighty thousand state and local governmental units,[104] or even fifty state units (plus some other territorial units), are more likely to engage in experiments than one national unit, especially in a country with as many regional and social differences as ours. The stark contrast in my own New England backyard among the approaches to a whole set of economic and social issues in Massachusetts, Vermont, and New Hampshire[105] lends support to this view.

Theoretical and to some extent practical support for this conclusion is furnished by the interesting work of Daniel Elazar and of those who have attempted to test his thesis. Elazar has posited three dominant "subcultures" in our Nation—the "traditionalistic," the "moralistic," and the "individualistic"—and suggests that each of these three subcultures tends to be relatively concentrated in certain areas of the country.[106] Thus, the traditionalist subculture (which emphasizes continuity and hierarchy) is concentrated in the South, the moralistic (which emphasizes the social and civic virtues) is centered in New England, and the individualistic (which is perhaps the dominant strain at this moment in our history and which, in emphasizing libertarian concepts of privatism, sees the state as playing a minimal role) is centered in certain middle states and in the West. While immigration from all over the world, as well as the movement of individuals among the states, has undoubtedly diluted these

104. The figure is taken from J. Zimmerman, *Contemporary American Federalism* 1 (1992), who reports a total of "82,237 governmental units." *Id.* The difficulty of an accurate count, particularly if all "special districts" are included, is underscored by a study entitled "Legislator's Guide to Local Governments in Illinois (Special Districts)" (Research Memorandum No. 88, 1992) (available in the author's files). This study states that with over 6,500 independent governmental entities, "Illinois has the distinction of having more local governments than any other state." *Id.* at vii.

105. It is generally believed, for example, that Vermont is less committed to hardy individualism and more committed to the environmental movement than is New Hampshire, and that these differences are reflected in the different approaches of the two states to such questions as taxation and development.

At the same time, the proximity of the two states and the high visibility to almost all Vermont and New Hampshire residents of the effects of these differences are sure to have a certain "convoy" effect on their respective policies. (For further reference to the "convoy" analogy, see ch. 2, sec. B.1.) A recent article, for example, noted that a substantial movement is building in Vermont to do more to encourage economic development in that state, even at some cost to the environment and to the values many of the state's residents place on the state's bucolic virtues. *See* S. Rimer, Vermont Debates Value of Saving a Rural Image, N.Y. Times, July 4, 1993, at sec. 1, p. 14.

106. *See, e.g.,* D. Elazar, *American Federalism: A View from the States* ch. 5 (3d ed. 1984). Elazar's theory was subjected to a variety of empirical tests in studies reported in *Political Culture, Public Policy and the American States* (J. Kincaid ed., 1982).

subcultures, and spread them more evenly throughout society, empirical studies furnish considerable evidence of their continued existence and significance.[107]

For present purposes, Elazar's thesis, as well as the empirical support for it, has at least two important ramifications. First, it underscores the likelihood of varying attitudes toward proposals for change throughout the country; and if some areas of the country are more receptive to change than others, then experiments are more likely to occur when there are many existing polities in which the experiments can be conducted. Second, the existence of the subcultures suggests a greater receptivity to particular *types* of reform, and a greater impatience with political corruption, in some areas (especially where the moralistic strain has managed to remain predominant) than in others. Thus, one might expect that certain kinds of reform movements would take root more readily in those areas.[108]

Although the actual record of the states as experimental laboratories may well be debatable, and has certainly been debated, there is no doubt that they have served that function on some important occasions. Examples include the development of workers' compensation programs,[109] experiments in public education,[110] welfare reform,[111] health care,[112]

107. *See id.*

108. *See, e.g.,* L. Ritt, Political Cultures and Political Reform," in *id.* 143. Admittedly, the force of this point is somewhat undercut by the many factors that have weakened the predominance of these strains in virtually every part of the country. Thus, political corruption on a fairly grand scale is far from unfamiliar to residents of New England.

109. Wisconsin was one of the leaders in developing a successful system of industrial and unemployment insurance. *See* Steward Mach. Co. v. Davis, 301 U.S. 548, 587 (1931). On the general issue of state leadership in this area, as well as in a number of other areas discussed in text, see, e.g., A. E. D. Howard, The Values of Federalism, 1 New Europe L. Rev. 142, 145–56 (1993); L. Kaden, Politics, Money, and State Sovereignty: The Judicial Role, 79 Colum. L. Rev. 847, 853–57 (1979). For further discussion of the role of the states in contributing to the development of national policies, see R. Stoker, *Reluctant Partners* (1991).

110. The extraordinary work of Horace Mann and others in developing universally available public education at the elementary and secondary levels in Massachusetts is well known (*see, e.g.,* R. Downs, *Horace Mann: Champion of Public Schools* 149–54 (1974)), as is the growth of institutions of higher public education in California and other Western states (*see Education in the States: Historical Development and Outlook* 119–26 (J. Pearson & E. Fuller eds., 1969)), where private universities had not had an opportunity to flourish in the eighteenth and nineteenth centuries.

More recently, a referendum in California put to the voters the question whether to adopt a "voucher" system that would dramatically change the relationship between public and private education. *See* Newsweek, Oct. 11, 1993, at 64–65; New Republic, Nov.

taxation systems,[113] penology,[114] environmental protection,[115] and a number of other subjects.[116] Sometimes, observers have expressed gratitude that these experiments are localized and that those who feel aggrieved by them can go elsewhere.[117] Sometimes, an idea born and bred in a particular state serves as a basis for developments in other states or throughout the Nation.[118]

Advocates of state autonomy who base their arguments essentially on

15, 1993, at 4. The article in the New Republic urged California voters to support the referendum on the ground that the proposal was "a perfect opportunity to apply Brandeis' famous dictum that the states are laboratories of democracy. Let one or two of them try it. See if it works." *Id.* Ultimately, however, the referendum was soundly defeated. *See* In Wake of Defeat, Voucher Backers Vow a Stiffer Fight, Los Angeles Times, Nov. 4, 1993, at A1.

111. New Jersey was one of the early jurisdictions to experiment with various programs of welfare reform. *See, e.g.,* Trenton Welfare Change Being Felt, N.Y. Times, Dec. 5, 1993, at 49, col. 2.

On November 1, 1993, the Wall Street Journal (at A24, col. 1) reported that the national administration had approved "a Wisconsin welfare reform experiment, the toughest proposed by any state, that would cut off cash benefits for recipients after two years." *Id.* The plan would not guarantee the recipient a job, but would provide job training, child care, health care, and job placement assistance to those whose benefits expire. Later, Wisconsin went even further and enacted a law under which it would leave the federal welfare system entirely within five years. *See* N.Y. Times, Dec. 11, 1993, at 1, col. 3. (Also, other states, including Virginia and Illinois, have recently received federal approval to conduct welfare reform experiments, and in the case of Virginia, the experiment was to occur in individual counties. *See* Boston Globe, Nov. 24, 1993, at 10, col. 1.)

A number of states have recently come up with further proposals for change, even while change at the national level is under consideration. *See, e.g.,* Oklahoma Gets Approval to Link Welfare and School Attendance, N.Y. Times, Jan. 26, 1994, at A19, col. 1; U.S. Approves Colorado Welfare Shift, Boston Globe, Jan. 13, 1994, at 5, col. 4; J. DeParle, States' Eagerness to Experiment on Welfare Jars Administration, N.Y. Times, Apr. 14, 1994, at A1, col. 5.

Such state experimentation in this field is often subject to challenge on grounds of federal preemption, as shown by a case pending in the Supreme Court at the time this book went to press. *See* Edwards v. Healy, 12 F.3d 154 (9th Cir. 1993), cert. granted *sub nom.* Anderson v. Edwards, 115 S. Ct. 41 (1994) (granting review of lower court holding that a state rule broadly defining an "assistance unit" for purposes of a federal aid program was invalid).

112. Hawaii has been a leader in the development of a program of universally available health care. *See* State Health Insurance Program Act, Haw. Rev. Stat. Ann ch. 431n (Micchie 1994) (establishing program "to ensure that all residents, regardless of age, income, employment status, or any other factor, have access to health insurance coverage which will provide basic medical services necessary to sustain a healthy life"). Recent, intensive discussion of proposed health care reforms have recognized the contribution that individual states can and should be allowed to make; *see, e.g.,* J. Mashaw & T. Marmor, The States as Health Care Labs, N.Y. Times, Aug. 18, 1993, at A15. And at this writing, several proposals for reform give states considerable discretion to develop their own

economic grounds have been heard to suggest that the ideal role of the central government is to ensure that the right of movement from state to state is not impeded for people or for capital—to ensure an interstate common market through enforcement of specific constitutional prohibitions and of the dormant Commerce Clause.[119] But there is provocative scholarship suggesting that, from the viewpoint of a proponent of free interstate trade, even this minimal role for the national government may be unnecessary and counterproductive. A paper by Edmund Kitch, which

programs (including single-payer systems) or to enter arrangements with other states. *See, e.g.,* the report in the Wall Street Journal, White House Makes It Easier for States to Set up Single-Payer Health Systems, Oct. 25, 1993, at A22.

For a persuasive presentation of the view that Congress has impeded state efforts to experiment in this area (even in Hawaii, which did receive a limited congressional exemption from national preemption under ERISA), and that the Supreme Court must actively intervene if the states are to fulfill their important experimental function, see Note, Federalism Myth: States as Laboratories of Health Care Reform, 82 Geo. L.J. 159 (1993).

113. The variation in state approaches to taxation is documented (as of the end of World War 2) in J. Maxwell, *The Fiscal Impact of Federalism in the United States* chs. 13–15 (1946). For more up-to-date information, see Hellerstein & Hellerstein's *Cases and Materials on State and Local Taxation* (5th ed. 1988).

As a New Englander, I can attest to the remarkable disparity between, say, Massachusetts—which depends on property taxes, sales taxes, business and personal income taxes, and a state lottery, as well as the usual assortment of user fees—and New Hampshire, which does not tax individuals on earned income but relies far more heavily on the property tax, has no sales tax on most consumer items (except those especially likely to hit tourists), and derives a good deal of revenue from state-owned liquor stores and from business taxes. These different approaches appear to have widely varying costs and benefits as economic conditions change—and to some extent, the "convoy" effect (see ch. 2, sec. B.1) has its impact, as in the case of the hard-fought decision by Connecticut, after many years, to follow the pattern of most nearby states and adopt a state income tax.

Of course, the availability of federal tax deductions for state and local individual income and property taxes (but not for sales taxes) constitutes a form of federal subsidy or "tax expenditure" that is bound to affect state choices.

114. Once again, Massachusetts has been recognized as taking the lead (for good or ill) in the development of new methods of treatment of youthful offenders. *See* M. Miller, Lawmaker Attitudes toward Court Reform in Massachusetts, 77 Jud. 34 (1993); J. Miller, *Last One over the Wall: The Massachusetts Experiment in Closing Reform Schools* (1991). And some jurisdictions are beginning to experiment with the subcontracting of the operation of penal institutions. *See, e.g.,* 650-Bed Private Prison Planned for Greenwood, Commercial Appeal (Memphis, Tenn.), June 3, 1992, at A14 (discussing existing or proposed subcontracting in a number of jurisdictions). The influence of federal law in this area, however, should not be slighted. For discussion of the impact of recently developed constitutional standards on the operation of state and local prisons and jails, see M. Feeley & E. Rubin, Federal-State Relations and Prison Administration, in *Power Divided: Essays on the Theory and Practice of Federalism* 63 (H. Scheiber & M. Feeley eds., 1989).

Penology, of course, extends to matters of sentencing as well, and although major sentencing reforms have developed (and been widely criticized) at the national level, many changes have occurred or are being considered at the state level. Thus, the drive

served as the subject of a symposium over a decade ago, argued that during the period of the Articles of Confederation, the predominant economic relationship among the states was one of free trade, and that this relationship was achieved as a matter of mutual self-interest rather than national enforcement.[120]

Kitch takes the argument one step further. Open and unfettered competition among the states, he suggests, has been thwarted primarily by

in California and other states to increase substantially the penalties for repeat offenders (*see, e.g.*, N.Y. Times, Dec. 26, 1993, at sec. 1, p. 1, col. 4), contributed to change on the national level. *See* 18 U.S.C. § 3559, as amended by the Violent Crime Control and Law Enforcement Act of 1994, Pub. L. No. 103–322, at § 70001, 108 Stat. 1796, 1982–84.

115. For discussion of state participation in the development of environmental policy (including the protection of natural resources), see, e.g., W. Lowry, *The Dimensions of Federalism: State Governments and Pollution Control Policies* (1993); R. Stoker, *Reluctant Partners* chs. 4, 6 (1991).

116. In the area of tort law, no-fault reform has spread in varying forms throughout the states, and now, in addition to a wide range of experiments in the area of medical malpractice, several states (including New York and Utah) are considering instituting systems of no-fault compensation for victims of medical injuries. *See* K. Post, Fault-Free Malpractice, 80 A.B.A. J. 46 (Jan. 1994).

117. In a symposium on federalism appearing in 6 Harv. J.L. & Pub. Pol'y (1982), Lino Graglia argued that one of the advantages of "localism" is that people who are unhappy with social experiments can go elsewhere, and he used a recent development in Santa Monica, California (a development he described as "setting the price of housing by government decree"), as an example of a community program that caused only a ripple at a local level but that would have led to chaos had it attracted national support. *Id.* at 25. Whether or not one agrees with Graglia's assessment of the Santa Monica experiment, it is hard to deny his point that local experimentation permits a substantial reduction in the risks of experiments going awry.

118. Surely, Wisconsin's development of industrial compensation and insurance programs is a leading example. Hawaii's experiment in seeking to provide universal health care may prove to be another. We may well discover, however, that what works reasonably well in an island economy with a fairly stable population and other advantages may fail when tried in an entirely different context. Indeed, this very possibility supports the room afforded for state discretion in a number of the health care proposals now under consideration.

119. This view is the clear purport of R. Epstein, Exit Rights under Federalism, 55 Law & Contemp. Probs. (Winter 1992) at 147; *cf.* R. Collins, Economic Union as a Constitutional Value, 63 N.Y.U. L. Rev. 43 (1988) (arguing that dormant Commerce Clause doctrine is designed to detect and prohibit protectionist actions by states that are hostile to economic interests in other states).

120. Kitch's paper is presented and commented on extensively in *Regulation, Federalism, and Interstate Commerce* (A. D. Tarlock ed., 1981). There is no doubt of the correctness of part of Kitch's thesis; at that time, the central government was in no position to enforce an interstate common market. As to the other part of his thesis—the actual existence of free trade among the states—the evidence seems shakier, resting (as Kitch admits) on several studies of available records by one scholar. *See id.* at 17–19, 98.

congressional overreaction to the Supreme Court's decisions under the "negative" Commerce Clause.[121] Thus, to cite an intriguing example given by one of the commentators on Kitch's paper, Oklahoma may have had a good reason for preventing or limiting the export of minnows in order to protect a dwindling supply, but the Supreme Court nevertheless chose to strike down the limitation as an unwarranted interference with commerce among the states.[122] The next step could have been (though it was not in this case) a legislative decision to regulate trade in minnows at the national level, and perhaps even to establish a National Commission authorized to issue (or withhold) permits to those who wish to transport the little fellows across state lines. The end result, of course, would be to stifle a free market even more drastically than did the original state limitation.[123]

3. Liberty and the Social Virtues of State Autonomy

The virtues of decentralization transcend the more traditional economic arguments discussed in the preceding section, though they are not un-related and, in some instances, arise out of the same structural and theoretical premises.

(1) For example, one of the stronger arguments for a decentralized political structure is that, to the extent the electorate is small, and elected representatives are thus more immediately accountable to individuals

121. See, e.g., id. at 46, 123.

122. In Hughes v. Oklahoma, 441 U.S. 322 (1979), the Court struck down, as discriminating against commerce in violation of the dormant Commerce Clause, a state statute that proscribed the transport outside the state (for sale) of natural minnows seined or procured from waters within the state. In answer to the argument that the prohibition was a legitimate conservation measure, the Court responded that the means chosen unnecessarily discriminated against out-of-state purchasers. An earlier decision allowing comparable restrictions on the ground of state ownership of "wild animals" was overruled.

Justice Rehnquist, joined by Chief Justice Burger, dissented. He argued that the state law was a legitimate conservation measure and that it did not adversely affect interstate commerce in minnows (since it allowed the export of hatchery minnows).

With characteristic verve and, some would say, overkill, Lino Graglia described this decision as an "unauthorized, presumptuous, officious interference with what should be the right of the people of the states to practice self-government." Regulation, Federalism, and Interstate Commerce 71 (A. D. Tarlock ed., 1981).

123. The growth of free trade areas, and of common markets, beyond national boundaries may actually serve to revitalize, or in some instances to vitalize, regionalization on a subnational level. As national boundaries tend to lose their significance, local areas find themselves with more discretion and flexibility to exploit their natural advantages (and less ability to lean on their own governments to protect themselves from international competition).

and their concerns, government is brought closer to the people, and democratic ideals are more fully realized.[124] Indeed, the ultimate form of democracy, or something very close to it, may be achieved in the New England Town Meeting, in which the entire "electorate" is eligible to consider, debate, and vote on substantive matters of general importance, and the elected representatives have essentially managerial responsibility. Such an argument, which does not resonate in classic economic terms, surely has its economic implications. Economists recognize that each individual has personal preferences about how public funds should be raised and allocated, and the greater the role an individual can play in making those decisions, the more that individual's preferences are likely to be influential—thus maximizing the general welfare. Indeed, if the electorate is relatively small, it is more likely to be homogeneous in a number of respects, and thus the group as a whole is more likely to reflect widely shared sets of preferences.[125] Elazar's provocative theory of cultural subsets and their geographic concentration in particular areas[126] supports this view.

Perhaps this theory does not in itself warrant decentralized authority along the lines drawn by state boundaries. Thus, to paraphrase Llewellyn's point[127] (but to a slightly different purpose), state lines may be arbitrary in two different but important ways. First, some interests may be regional in nature and thus involve groups of states. Second,

124. Support for a small polity, not always for democratic reasons but for reasons that included internal stability and homogeneity, trace back not just to Montesquieu, who influenced all those who fought for and against ratification, but also to Plato and Aristotle (who emphasized not democracy but community) and Machiavelli (in the *Discourses*). Machiavelli and Montesquieu, of course, were aware that smallness could operate as an obstacle to effective self-defense, but alliances, confederations, or other leagues for mutual defense could be formed in an effort to deal with that problem. For a discussion of the views of these and other theorists (especially David Hume and James Harrington), and their impact on the thought of the Framers and their opponents, see S. Beer, *To Make a Nation: The Rediscovery of American Federalism* (1993).

125. For a discussion of the value of federalism to an "optimistic" pluralist, who believes in the virtues of majority rule in embodying and summarizing private preferences, see T. Merrill, Chief Justice Rehnquist, Pluralist Theory, and the Interpretation of Statutes, 25 Rutgers L.J. 621, 631, 655–57 (1994).

The argument also finds support in recent communitarian scholarship. *See, e.g.,* A. Rapaczynski, From Sovereignty to Process: The Jurisprudence of Federalism after *Garcia,* 1985 Sup. Ct. Rev. 341, and the wide range of authorities (from Stanley Fish and Richard Rorty to Cass Sunstein and Frank Michelman) cited in E. Rubin & M. Feeley, Federalism: Notes on a National Neurosis, 41 UCLA L. Rev. 903, 906–7 (1994).

126. *See* text at notes 106–7, *supra.*

127. *See* ch. 2, sec. B.1, note 105 and accompanying text.

the goal of realizing democratic values to the maximum extent feasible may not be significantly enhanced by reducing the relevant polity from one of some 280,000,000 (the United States) to one of, say, 30,000,000 (the state of California). In either case, the size of the electorate and its heterogeneity tend to dwarf participation by the individual and to frustrate the recognition of small group preferences.

There are several responses available to a defender of a strong federal system—a system based on the states as presently constituted as at least an appropriate starting point for a diffusion of governmental authority that increases democratic participation and that recognizes individual and small group preferences. First, California is, of course, the most populous and thus a highly atypical state. At the other end of the scale, such states as Wyoming and New Hampshire are sufficiently small that electors are likely to know their representative personally—at least their representative in the larger chamber of the state legislature—and are likely to have met and discussed issues with that representative on a number of occasions.[128] Even if one were to discount the five largest and smallest states and to concentrate on the middle range, the analogy to Wyoming and New Hampshire retains much of its force.[129] Thus, in a middle-range state like Massachusetts, it is not difficult to get to know (and to discuss issues with) one's representative in the local community's governing body and even one's representative in the lower chamber of the state legislature, if not the upper chamber as well.

Second, to the extent that the democratic ideal is more fully realized on a municipal or town level,[130] the states are in a far better position

---

128. This is especially true in a state like New Hampshire—even though its population is larger than Wyoming's—because its lower house is the largest in the Nation (including the national House of Representatives) and because the state covers a relatively small territory. Indeed, Concord (New Hampshire's capital city) is a remarkably small community within easy driving distance of any part of the state.

As one who has had a part-time residence in New Hampshire for many years, I have known the state representative from my district through several transitions. The person who, until recently, served in the lower house of the state legislature ran a local market and real estate agency, and we often discussed local political issues at the checkout counter.

129. As noted in the text paragraph that follows, every state is divided in turn into local governmental units with significant policy-making responsibilities, and in which the average voter who is willing to make even a minimal effort is likely to know his or her representative.

130. *See* G. Frug, The City as a Legal Concept, 93 Harv. L. Rev. 1057 (1980). In this provocative article, Frug argues that realization of what he calls "public freedom"—the enhancement of citizen participation in basic decisions—can best be achieved by conferring significant power on municipalities, power analogous to that currently enjoyed by private

to respond to local pressures for home rule than is a more remote and centralized government. And indeed, de facto or de jure home rule has strong roots in our state traditions and is a central aspect of political life in the vast majority of states.[131]

Third, to the extent that regional interests transcend state lines, the states are often able to negotiate regional compacts (sometimes without any requirement of federal approval), or enact reciprocal laws that effectively reflect those regional interests. These formal or informal regional alliances, more fully discussed in the next chapter,[132] are doubtless facilitated by the existence of individual polities within the region that can make the decisions to enter into such alliances as circumstances warrant. It would be far harder to determine and impose the appropriate scope of such alliances from above if state polities did not exist (although the central government may contribute substantially as a facilitator of interstate cooperation).

(2) The story told in chapter 2—stressing the neglect or overriding of individual rights by state institutions and the necessity of national

---

corporations in the management of their affairs. In a more recent article, Decentering Decentralization, 60 U. Chi. L. Rev. 253 (1993), Frug develops and refines his proposals in an elaborate critique of the view that decentralization would attribute to cities "the subjectivity of the centered self." Id. at 257. Rather, he offers an alternative vision in which municipal power is modeled neither on a notion of the autonomous individual nor on a notion of a "nation state," but instead on what he calls a "decentered self." Id. at 284–87.

My purpose here is not to parse or to criticize this thesis, but simply to suggest that advocates of decentralization may well view the states as simply a starting point for the full realization of the potential of the citizenry.

131. See generally J. Fordham, Local Government Law, and particularly ch. 2, sec. 2 (Local Units within the State System) (2d revised ed. 1986). Frug, whose work is referred to at note 130, supra, would of course opt for greater devolution of power to local government units.

132. See ch. 4, sec. C.2. Outstanding examples of formal alliances include regional authorities governing the use of water resources. Instances of less direct and formal cooperation include state laws allowing the banks of one state (or other institutions or licensed professionals) to operate in other states affording reciprocal privileges. See, e.g., Conn. Gen Stat. § 36–553 (1993) (allowing such reciprocity with respect to banks in other New England states); Mass. Gen. L. ch. 167 A, § 2 (1993) (same). (The issue has been substantially mooted by the recent passage of a federal law—P.L. 103–328, 108 Stat. 2338—allowing banks to set up nationwide branch networks.)

For an important Supreme Court decision holding that a particular interstate agreement relating to the rationalization of state taxation systems did not require congressional approval in order to become effective, see United States Steel Corp. v. Multistate Tax Comm'n, 434 U.S. 452 (1978).

(legislative, judicial, or executive) intervention to protect those rights—is grossly oversimplified. That the national government has played such a role on significant occasions—has even gone to war with those states that, in retaining slavery, persisted in abridging basic human rights—is undeniable. But another side to the story cannot be ignored—a side that acknowledges the role of the states in protecting individual and group rights and interests.

This other side begins with the crucial right of exit already discussed in a number of contexts. Just as religious persecution led the Puritans to leave England, so comparable persecution led Roger Williams to Rhode Island, and after formation of the Union, led the Mormons to Utah. The significance of the right of exit persists to this day, allowing, for example, those who fall out of sympathy with the orthodoxy that may predominate in one state to seek refuge in another. Thus, the excommunicated Mormon may choose to cross the Utah border into Colorado (or even to go further east if necessary to escape unwanted associations); the environmentalist frustrated by New Hampshire's prevailing libertarianism and receptiveness to development may find happiness in the more ecologically conscious hills of Vermont; one who objects to the homophobia or antipornography stance of a state may escape the prevailing attitude (an attitude that may well be reflected not only in social mores but in city ordinances and state laws) by a small journey across a state line—a point that led Justice Harlan to argue that state restrictions on publication should be viewed more tolerantly than restrictions running nationwide.[133] The existence of separate polities, in sum, when

133. In his separate opinion in Roth v. United States, 354 U.S. 476, 496 (1957) (Harlan, J., concurring in part and dissenting in part), Justice Harlan argued (in a case involving governmental power to proscribe or punish the distribution of obscene material) that "the domain of sexual morality is pre-eminently a matter of state concern," id. at 502. Even more to the point, he suggested that "[t]he danger is perhaps not great if the people of one State, through their legislature, decide that 'Lady Chatterley's Lover' goes so far beyond the acceptable standards of candor that it will be deemed offensive and non-sellable, for the State next door is still free to make its own choice. At least we do not have one uniform standard." Id. at 506.

Justice Harlan's approach gains support from the language of the First Amendment, which, despite Justice Black's repeated emphasis on the Amendment's words "no law" as an argument for an absolute right to speak, also limits its proscription to "Congress." Nevertheless, one who believes that the Fourteenth Amendment does restrict the states from interfering with fundamental liberties (perhaps through the Privileges or Immunities Clause rather than the Due Process Clause) would surely find it hard to accept the view that a resident, say, of Montana might have to travel hundreds, or even thousands, of

coupled with a reasonable degree of mobility, may significantly enhance individual freedom whenever a state acts against personal preferences in a manner that is difficult or impossible to challenge as a matter of federal law.

To carry this point one step further, competition among states may increase individual liberty just as it has been argued to increase economic welfare. As an example, consider the advent of no-fault divorce. Once the Supreme Court held that a divorce granted in one state is entitled to full faith and credit in every other (so long as the plaintiff spouse has established the jurisdictional prerequisites for obtaining the divorce),[134] the willingness of states like Nevada to allow ex parte divorces on easy terms was a significant factor leading other states to follow suit—and to go even further in relaxing the prerequisites for dissolution. First, those responsible for the policy in states with restrictive divorce laws realized that it made little sense to afford another state a source of revenue that not only transferred wealth to that other state but at the same time rendered their own, less tolerant laws essentially ineffective for those who could afford the journey. Second, it became morally difficult for a state to operate with a set of divorce laws that (whether the state liked it or not) effectively permitted consent divorce, or even divorce on demand over a spouse's objection, for those who could spend the money to travel elsewhere but denied the same privilege to those too poor to make the trip. Thus, after a slow beginning, the notion of no-fault divorce became

---

miles beyond the borders of his own state in order to buy a book that is protected against federal censorship by the First Amendment, and that the Montana resident might also be prohibited by Montana law from bringing the book back home with him.

134. *See* Williams v. North Carolina, 317 U.S. 287 (1942); Williams v. North Carolina, 325 U.S. 226 (1945). The jurisdictional prerequisite, the Court said, was the domicile of the spouse seeking the divorce. *Id.* at 229.

Although under the second *Williams* decision, the existence of jurisdiction to grant a divorce could be challenged by another state or by an absent spouse, the determination of the state granting the divorce is entitled to respect, and indeed was later held to lie beyond jurisdictional challenge by a spouse who had entered an appearance in the original proceeding (Sherrer v. Sherrer, 334 U.S. 343 (1948)), or by a child whose parent had not contested the divorce (Johnson v. Muelberger, 340 U.S. 581 (1951)). Following these decisions, efforts by absent spouses, or other states, to challenge out-of-state ex parte divorces shrank almost to the vanishing point, especially with the advent of no-fault divorce laws, discussed below. *See generally* J. Areen, *Family Law* 392–410 (3d ed. 1992).

This discussion applies to divorce itself, but not to such issues as custody, property division, or support obligations.

virtually universal in this country, even though the states still differ in a number of significant details.[135]

The no-fault divorce story is a complicated one, of course, because the evolution of state law—which is reminiscent of the "convoy" metaphor discussed earlier[136]—has not occurred without dissension and even backlash. Undoubtedly, the greater ability of a discontented spouse to obtain a divorce without the consent of the other spouse—or of two consenting spouses to obtain a divorce with no grounds other than a desire to do so—constitutes *both* an increase in the scope of individual liberty and a source of distress to many. First, it pains those who, for religious or moral reasons, do not favor easy terms of divorce.[137] Second, recent studies have indicated that the spread of no-fault divorce has not proved as beneficial to women as it has to men.[138] Thus, like many important social changes, this one has been seen to have adverse effects both on the preferences of some individuals and groups and on the practical interests of others. Indeed, for one who favors regulation in the sphere of moral conduct, this story may constitute a kind of "race to the bottom" analogous to the race criticized by some exponents of national regulation in the economic field.

Nevertheless, the story remains one of significant contribution to the growth of individual choice resulting from the exercise of state power to enact legislation in the field of family law and relationships. That no-fault divorce would have developed so rapidly (or at all) on a national scale in a country as large and heterogeneous as ours seems highly unlikely had our polity been one that vested all legislative power in one centralized body.

A final set of examples in this category consists of those instances in which the states have consciously gone further—either by statute or in interpreting their own constitutions—than has the federal government

135. *See generally* J. Areen, *Family Law* 340–55 (3d ed. 1992). As Areen points out, *id.* at 340 n. 1, the concept of "no-fault divorce" first appeared in the nineteenth century, but the movement to adopt this approach did not gather great momentum until the 1960s, and by 1985 "every state . . . had adopted, at least in part, a 'no-fault' approach to divorce." *Id.* at 340.

136. *See* ch. 2, sec. B.1.

137. Indeed, as Areen notes, in *Family Law* 355–58 (3d ed. 1992), religious principles and civil laws occasionally come into fierce conflict in the area of divorce.

138. For references to the academic literature, see *id.* at 343. For an especially critical analysis of the impact of no-fault divorce laws, see M. Fineman, *The Illusion of Equality: The Rhetoric and Reality of Divorce Reform* (1991).

in protecting minority or individual rights. Although these instances may, in total, fall short in both quantity and quality when compared with the converse cases in which national power has been used to sustain individual rights against the assertion of state power, the affirmative contribution of the states is far from negligible. Beginning with state resistance to the Alien and Sedition Acts,[139] and continuing through the era when state officials refused to cooperate in the enforcement of state and federal laws dealing with fugitive slaves and requiring the extradition of those who assisted in their escape to free territory,[140] the story extends to the present day. Thus New Jersey—as a prominent example—stands out as a jurisdiction that has interpreted its own

139. The Virginia and Kentucky legislatures declared the Alien and Sedition Acts of 1798 unconstitutional. *See* Virginia Resolutions of 1798, in 4 *The Debates in the Several State Conventions on the Federal Constitution* 528 (J. Elliott ed., 2d ed. 1901); Kentucky Resolutions of 1798 and 1799, *id.* at 540. Kentucky's resolutions were drafted by Jefferson and Virginia's by Madison (who had plainly become more partial to the rights and interests of the states than he had been in his role as Constitution-maker). *See* H. J. Powell, The Original Understanding of Original Intent, 98 Harv. L. Rev. 885, 926 (1985); 17 *The Papers of James Madison* 190, 341–46 (D. Mattern et al. eds., 1991). (While the resolutions were not adopted by other states, they undoubtedly had an impact on national reaction to the laws, which were ultimately repealed.)

For a recent, very different effort at state nullification (which plainly reflected a strong measure of popular discontent), see N.Y. Times, Jan. 19, 1994, at A10, col. 1, reporting an announcement by Governor Casey of Pennsylvania that he would defy a federal directive requiring state Medicaid programs to pay for abortions in case of rape or incest even when the state law requirement of prompt reporting of the rape or incest had not been met. The number of states following Pennsylvania's lead by May of that year had grown to eleven. *See* Boston Globe, May 7, 1994, at 3, col. 1. By August, at least five states had been ordered by federal district courts to follow the federal directive. *See* St. Louis Post–Dispatch, Aug. 17, 1994, at 6A.

140. In Kentucky v. Dennison, 65 U.S. (24 How) 66 (1861), the governor of Ohio had refused to comply with Kentucky's request for extradition of one who had aided in the escape of a slave. The Supreme Court, after holding that the Ohio governor had violated his duty under the Constitution, refused to enforce Kentucky's request on the ground that the governor's duty was only a "moral" one and not enforceable in a federal court suit. (The holding was later overruled, and the duty to extradite held legally enforceable, in Puerto Rico v. Branstad, 483 U.S. 219 (1987), partly on the ground that *Dennison* was "the product of another time [in which federal power rested on a far less firm foundation]" and that the concept of federal-state relations represented by the *Dennison* decision "is fundamentally incompatible with more than a century of constitutional development." Puerto Rico v. Branstad, 483 U.S. at 230.)

For a related decision during the same era as *Dennison*, in which a Wisconsin court granted habeas corpus to one held in federal custody for aiding in the escape of a fugitive slave, see Ableman v. Booth, 62 U.S. (21 How.) 506 (1859). The Supreme Court in that case held that Wisconsin lacked power to grant a writ of habeas corpus under the circumstances presented.

constitution to afford greater protection against search and seizure and a more generous measure of equal protection than is afforded under federal law.[141] And other states and localities have enacted statutory protection of individual and minority rights—especially against both public and private discrimination—that exceed the protections afforded by federal law.[142] Thus in a well-known paper, then Justice Brennan—clearly discouraged by what he saw as the failure of the Supreme Court to preserve and extend individual rights—encouraged the states to use their own legal resources to build on the progress that had been made at the national level.[143]

(3) The story told in chapter 2—of national protection of the individual against the oppression of the states—is oversimplified in another respect, a respect similar to the complexities inherent in the development of no-fault divorce. The story assumes (and here I plead guilty to having made such assumptions in some of my own earlier work)[144] that the individual is pitted against the state, and that the national government, like the cavalry, rides to the rescue of the individual. Sometimes, this simple way of looking at a case is fairly accurate—cases like those involving the validity of a state or local law requiring an unwilling student to salute the flag and pledge allegiance in a public school,[145]

141. *See* State v. Johnson, 346 A.2d 66 (N.J. 1975) (imposing a heavier burden on the state than did the federal Constitution in order to establish the validity of a search); Southern Burlington County NAACP v. Township of Mt. Laurel, 336 A.2d 713 (N.J.) (invalidating exclusive zoning ordinance), *appeal dismissed and cert. denied*, 423 U.S. 808 (1975).

142. An interesting example, as interpreted by the state's supreme court, is California's antidiscrimination statute (known popularly as the Unruh Civil Rights Act), West's Ann. Cal. Civil Code § 51 et seq. The Act has been interpreted to preclude business enterprises from excluding *any* class from access to their services on the basis of a generalized prediction that the class "as a whole" is more likely to misbehave than some other classes. Marina Point, Ltd. v. Wolfson, 640 P.2d 114 (1982) (Cal. 1982).

143. W. Brennan, State Constitutions and the Protection of Individual Rights, 90 Harv. L. Rev. 489 (1977). For those sharing this outlook, federalism serves essentially as a "one-way ratchet"—increasing the scope of civil or other rights above a federal floor that may or not be seen as adequate to the task at any given time. For some observers, however, the potential costs of such "independent state review," which can include wasteful duplication, uncertainty, and the loss of local legislative responsibility, may well exceed the benefits. *See, e.g.,* E. Maltz, The Dark Side of State Court Activism, 63 Tex. L. Rev. 995 (1985). A good discussion of this trend and its likely continuation in the future may be found in G. A. Tarr, The Past and Future of the New Judicial Federalism, 24 Publius 63 (Spring 1994).

144. *See, e.g.,* D. Shapiro, Mr. Justice Rehnquist: A Preliminary View, 90 Harv. L. Rev. 293, 294 (1976).

145. West Virginia State Board of Educ. v. Barnette, 319 U.S. 624 (1943) (holding such a requirement invalid). Notably, however, the *Barnette* decision overruled a then-recent

of a state rule barring a criminal defendant from testifying under oath at his trial,[146] or of a system of justice in which a state judge's salary goes up in proportion to the fines he imposes.[147] And, surely, the story is unassailable when the national government (first through executive decree and then through constitutional Amendment) decided to outlaw the existence of slavery in any state or territory.[148]

But often—and perhaps even in some of the examples just given—the story is more properly viewed not as simply pitting the individual against the state but as a conflict of individual or group interests; when looked at in this way, the state may be seen as the defender of one set of private interests against another. Several examples may help to make the point clearer.

First, in a criminal prosecution for child abuse, the question may arise whether hearsay accusations by the child should be admissible in evidence, or whether (if admissible) they should be sufficient in themselves to sustain a conviction.[149] If the state courts admit the evidence, the issue could be phrased in terms of the interest of the "state" in obtaining a conviction, on the one hand, and that of the defendant asserting the violation of his Sixth Amendment confrontation rights, on the other. But it may be closer to the mark to view the issue as one of striking the proper balance between the rights of the accused and the interests of the victim in obtaining vindication (and even a measure of revenge), and of deterring similar crimes against this or similar victims in the future. Perhaps the latter interests do not rise to the level of constitutional protection, so that the balance is not in this instance one of competing constitutional claims, but the conflict is nevertheless real and personal. It

---

Supreme Court precedent and evoked a vigorous dissent from Justice Frankfurter in defense of the state's prerogative to require such a display of support for the Nation.

146. For a summary of the case law in the Supreme Court, see C. Whitebread & C. Slobogin, Criminal Procedure § 28.06(a) (3d ed. 1993).

147. *See* Tumey v. Ohio, 273 U.S. 510 (1927).

148. The Emancipation Proclamation, declaring that all persons held in slavery in certain designated states and territories were and should remain free, was an executive proclamation issued by President Lincoln on January 1, 1863, in the midst of the Civil War. The Thirteenth Amendment, which went into effect in 1865, prohibits slavery or involuntary servitude (except as punishment for crime) throughout the United States or any place subject to its jurisdiction.

149. The Supreme Court, by a 5–4 vote, recently held that admission of the hearsay statements of the alleged child victim in such a case violated the Sixth Amendment because the statements lacked sufficient guarantees of trustworthiness. Idaho v. Wright, 497 U.S. 805 (1990).

is not merely a clash between the individual defendant on the one hand and the state as a faceless institution on the other. To the extent that we choose to describe the conflict as one involving "state interests," we may (or may not) give those interests greater constitutional weight, but we should not let the label obscure the fact that the state's side of the balance often serves as a proxy for the individual or group interests that the state is seeking to protect.

This example could be repeated throughout many aspects of the criminal process in which the state has rejected an individual's constitutional challenge to a criminal conviction. The individual or group interest that underlies the state's position may be especially weak in some instances—as when the defendant is barred from testifying under oath solely because of an ancient tradition that has long since ceased to apply in analogous contexts.[150] But in other instances—such as the question whether to admit evidence unlawfully seized in a trial for a crime against the person—the interest is plainly substantial. Judge Cardozo refused, in 1926 (while he was serving as a state judge), to apply as a matter of New York state law a rule adopted in the federal courts under which, in Cardozo's famous aphorism, "[t]he criminal is to go free because the constable has blundered."[151] Such a refusal may no longer be (entirely) an option open to the state courts. But Cardozo's point retains its intrinsic force as a stark reminder that the balance is a difficult one to strike.

As a second example, the point about the nature of "state interests" is especially vivid in cases involving claims under the Establishment or Free Exercise Clauses of the First Amendment. Thus, in a challenge to the use of public property for displays or ceremonies having religious significance, the state serves as representative for those who wish to have such displays or take part in such ceremonies, and who see the challenge as one to their own associational and religious freedom.[152] It is true that nonpublic spaces may be available to these people, but it is also true that such spaces may be more costly and less accessible, and that those who object to a particular display in a public facility (that carries with it no abusive message) are not severely harmed by that display.

150. *See* note 146, *supra*, and accompanying text.

151. People v. Defore, 150 N.E. 585, 587 (N.Y. 1926).

152. For a recent decision highlighting the difficulty of accommodation in this area, see County of Allegheny v. ACLU, Greater Pittsburgh Chapter, 492 U.S. 573 (1989) (holding unconstitutional a display of a nativity scene on the main staircase of a county courthouse, but rejecting a constitutional challenge to the county's display of a Jewish Chanukah menorah placed next to a Christmas tree and a sign saluting liberty).

The case thus involves a closer and more difficult balance between conflicting individual and group interests than does the case of *requiring* an unwilling student to recite the pledge of allegiance. Any injury to others from invalidating this latter requirement seems to arise solely from the psychological impact of knowing that not everyone joins in one's particular views—an injury one should be prepared to suffer in a free society.[153] The injury from being unable to use particularly accessible public facilities for a display or activity one wants to enjoy is more direct and more troublesome, and when the state defends its "interest" before the courts, it is serving as parens patriae for the individuals who claim such an injury.

Third, when the state defends its compulsory education laws against, say, the efforts of Amish parents to take their children out of school before the parents were permitted to do so under state law,[154] the clash may be seen as one between the interests of the individual parents and those of "society" in imposing its educational views and values.[155] But is it less accurate to view the state also, and even more significantly, as representing the interests of the *children* in at least being exposed to a larger society than that of their own family—an interest that they may be unable to present on their own and that will enhance their personal choice about how they will spend their lives?[156] To the extent that the law now recognizes a growing sphere of the rights of children (and not

153. I assume that the ceremony—the pledge of allegiance, for example—is not *prohibited* but rather is conducted in a manner that allows objectors not to participate.

154. *See* Wisconsin v. Yoder, 406 U.S. 205 (1972) (holding that a state would violate the Free Exercise Clause by punishing a member of the Old Order Amish for his refusal to send his children to school after they had completed the eighth grade but before they had reached the age of sixteen).

155. Indeed, Chief Justice Burger, speaking for the Court in the *Yoder* case, recognized the argument that a child taken out of school at a relatively early age might be ill equipped to deal with the demands of an open society, but ultimately concluded that the state had failed to show with sufficient particularity how its admittedly strong interest in compulsory education would be adversely affected by granting a limited exemption to the Amish.

156. The Court in *Yoder* declined to consider the possible claims of the children that they might wish to continue their schooling; the children, the Court said, "were not parties to this litigation." *Id.* at 231. But those claims did play a prominent role in Justice Douglas's separate opinion, which stated: "As the child has no other effective forum, it is in this litigation that his rights should be considered. And, if an Amish child desires to attend high school, and is mature enough to have that desire respected, the State may well be able to override the parents' religiously motivated objections." *Id.* at 242 (Douglas, J., dissenting in part). *See also* M. Minow, Putting Up and Putting Down: Tolerance Reconsidered, in *Comparative Constitutional Federalism* 77, 96–98 (M. Tushnet ed., 1990).

merely of the state as guardian or ward) to object to certain kinds of parental treatment,[157] this way of looking at the case seems far less strained, even if the children themselves remain silent throughout the litigation. After all, even antipaternalists acknowledge the appropriateness of a certain degree of governmental paternalism toward those who are still minors.[158]

As a final example, although many others could be cited, challenges to zoning laws frequently pit the interests of one individual or group against another. Thus, zoning laws that prohibit the location of "adult" theaters in certain neighborhoods are not simply institutional decisions that certain "state interests" outweigh individual liberty interests.[159] The laws often represent a solid consensus of local opinion that certain activities ought not to be carried on in neighborhoods where families live and play. Once again, the state, in defending these laws, is serving as representative of the individuals or groups who support them on intensely personal grounds.

Of course, even if the states did not exist, these views would doubtless be persuasively presented, the conflicts would be acknowledged, and some accommodation would be reached at the national level. But the existence of the states as polities ready and willing to advocate such views surely lends them considerable weight and political force.

If this analysis is valid, the existence of the states as separate political entities having significant legislative powers is essential to a continuing dialogue about the proper resolution of the clash of interests between individuals and groups.[160] And every time a claim of constitutional right against the state is sustained, it does not follow that the role of the states

157. The range of situations in which children may file legal claims based on treatment by their parents (claims ranging from actions in tort to actions for termination of the parental relationship) and may participate through counsel in proceedings affecting their custody is canvassed in J. Areen, *Family Law* (3d ed. 1992), especially at chs. 8 and 10.

158. At least if the definition of what constitutes a "minor" is not too far-reaching. *See* D. Shapiro, Courts, Legislatures, and Paternalism, 74 Va. L. Rev. 519, 547 (1988) (referring to "infan[cy]" as an appropriate basis for paternalistic action). One old enough to vote (under the terms of a constitutional Amendment) and to serve in the military is hard to classify as a minor in this sense, even if state laws forbid that person to buy a drink with any alcoholic content.

159. In City of Renton v. Playtime Theatres, Inc., 475 U.S. 41 (1986), a divided Supreme Court upheld an ordinance providing that "adult motion picture theaters" may not be located within one thousand feet of any residential zone, single- or multiple-family dwelling, church, park, or school.

160. This suggestion builds on the views put forth by Cover and Aleinikoff in a valuable article on the dialectical virtues of federal habeas corpus as a means of fostering

as defenders of private interests has gone down a notch. Often, the result simply means that, rightly or wrongly, a close and difficult balance has been struck in favor of the challenger and against those individuals or groups who are on the losing end of the challenge.

(4) There is another respect in which the state can serve as an important safeguard of liberty, and that is as a guardian of *federal* rights. Two of the leading scholars in the field of federal jurisdiction have stressed this function in closely related contexts. First, in his famous dialogue, Henry Hart insisted that however complete the power of Congress may be to strip the federal courts of their jurisdiction to determine the scope of federal rights (even federal constitutional rights), the state judicial systems remain available (and ultimately unassailable by Congress) as safe harbors for the vindication of those rights.[161] Second, Akhil Amar has urged the states to consider adopting what he describes as "converse-1983" provisions—that would create a "statutory" *Bivens*[162] action for those whose federal rights have been violated by federal officials.[163] Moreover, Amar argues (in a controversial part of his paper) that the state would be free in defining this cause of action either to reject or limit certain defenses accorded to the defendant under "federal common law" in administering the *Bivens* doctrine.[164] Whether or not Amar's

---

debate between state and federal judicial systems. The article, suitably enough, is entitled Dialectical Federalism: Habeas Corpus and the Court, 86 Yale L.J. 1035 (1977).

161. *See* H. M. Hart, The Power of Congress to Limit the Jurisdiction of Federal Courts: An Exercise in Dialectic, 66 Harv. L. Rev. 1362, 1401–2 (1953). At the end of this essay, when "Q" asks for an answer to the argument that Congress may indeed be able to strip the federal courts of jurisdiction to pass on issues of constitutional import, "A" responds that ever since 1787 the state courts in these circumstances "are the primary guarantors of constitutional rights, and in many cases they may be the ultimate ones." *Id.* at 1401.

Under this approach, a decision like Tarble's Case, 80 U.S. (13 Wall.) 397 (1872), would have no proper place, at least if broadly interpreted to preclude state courts from entertaining federal habeas corpus petitions by federal prisoners no matter what restrictions were placed on the availability of habeas relief for those prisoners in the federal courts.

162. In Bivens v. Six Unknown Agents of the Federal Bureau of Narcotics, 403 U.S. 388 (1971), the Supreme Court allowed (in the absence of any relevant statute) a private damages action against a federal officer by one who had been injured by that officer's violation of the claimant's constitutional rights. For the story of the evolution of this doctrine, see *Hart & Wechsler* at 926–35, *Hart & Wechsler* 1993 Supp. 121–23.

163. A. Amar, Of Sovereignty and Federalism, 96 Yale L.J. 1425, 1512–17 (1987). Amar speaks of "converse-1983" because a federal statute, 42 U.S.C. § 1983 (dating from 1871), affords a private remedy to those persons injured by violations of federal law committed by persons acting under color of *state* law.

164. *See id.* at 1515–17. Amar supports not only the possibility of individual "strict liability" under such statutes, but of direct federal government liability as well. Some questions raised by this argument are summarized in text.

thesis is sound in this latter respect—and it may raise difficulties under the Supremacy Clause to the extent that federal common law in this area strikes a balance that the Supreme Court has found appropriate and that Congress has not rejected—Amar's underlying point has significance and force. The states have often served, and should serve, as protectors of federal rights to whatever extent federal law permits, either as a supplement to federal protection or as institutions capable of filling the gaps left open by lack of effective federal enforcement. If the states did not exist as strong political entities, they would be in no position to afford such protection.

(5) Finally, even the story of state resistance to such decisions as *Brown v. Board of Education*[165] has its affirmative side. The point has been suggested by Daniel Elazar,[166] who acknowledges that the existence of state power facilitated the prolonged opposition to implementation of *Brown*;[167] after all, the notion of "interposition" had its roots in the existence of state and local authority. But he then points out that the ultimate collapse of state-imposed segregation in the South and the emergence of black citizens as a social and political force that has surely transformed that region of the country "was not simply a consequence of superior federal strength in a contest with a number of recalcitrant states." Rather, it "marked a major change in the attitudes of the dominant groups in those states," and an upsetting of established customs that would have been far harder to accomplish simply by the issuance of decrees from a centralized source.[168] The existence of diffused power, in other words, may have prolonged the struggle, but it has also contributed to the durability of the ultimate outcome—a durability that can only be further strengthened as black Americans begin to play a major role (as they surely have) in state and local institutions. Federalism, in other words, has served both to impede and ultimately to promote the progress on this front.[169]

---

165. 347 U.S. 483 (1954). Some examples of state resistance to this decision and its aftermath are given in ch. 2, sec. C.

166. *See* D. Elazar, *American Federalism: A View from the States* (3d ed. 1984).

167. *Id.* at 11–14.

168. *Id.* at 13–14.

169. And as Elazar concludes in his discussion of this issue, "it is the nature of American federalism that once a new consensus is achieved, these matters are again entrusted to the states and their local populations." *Id.* at 14.

It is perhaps ironic, but at the same time supportive of the argument in text, that in one of its most controversial recent decisions, Shaw v. Reno, 113 S. Ct. 2816 (1993), the Supreme Court cast grave doubt on the validity under the federal Constitution of North

The case for a vigorous federal system in which the states play a significant policy-making role—is a complex and forceful one. It rests first on a firm constitutional foundation, one that takes into account the assumptions of the Framers and the arguments for ratification as well as the text itself. But it also rests on a strong pragmatic base—a base that finds its justification both in the economic virtues of interstate competition and in the role that the states inevitably play in protecting liberty and in reconciling conflicting individual and group interests.

Carolina's effort to draw a particular congressional district in a manner that was likely to increase the number of black congressional representatives from that state.

4

Striking the Balance: Federalism and Dialogue

A. Introduction

Anyone who has come this far will, I hope, agree with me on at least one central point: federalism matters. To be sure, many who believe fervently in the virtues of a "democratic republic" have shown less than wholehearted agreement with this point. They have found the rhetoric of decentralization—of a "healthy" federalism—useful when they are opposed to a particular national policy, and have rejected it with little hesitation when it stands in the way of a policy they favor. For them, federalism may be little more than a pretext—a useful port when the winds of change are blowing against them on a national level, but a valueless concept when they find themselves advocating national action.[1]

Yet in an ironic sense, even the views of these skeptics contribute to the force of my conclusion. Federalism becomes part of the debate because it does matter to many, and because it should. Just as the deceiver may profit from the fact that truth-telling is generally regarded as a virtue,[2] so the argument appealing to principles of federalism helps the

1. See the remarks of Lino Graglia, cited in ch. 1, note 26; see also A. Anderson, The Meaning of Federalism: Interpreting the Securities Exchange Act of 1934, 70 Va. L. Rev. 813 (1984), discussed in ch. 1, note 25; L. Kalman, Abe Fortas and Strategic Federalism in Law and Politics, in *Federalism and the Judicial Mind: Essays on American Constitutional Law and Politics* 109, 110, 112 (H. Scheiber ed., 1992) (noting Fortas's "strategic federalism" when, as a lawyer, he sought to keep the federal courts from interfering with the election of his client, Lyndon Johnson, to the Senate, and also quoting the comments of Fortas's law partner, Thurman Arnold, that federalism was a species of "procedural theology").

For a pervasive critique of the federalism "myth" that alludes to the frequent use of federalism arguments as mere pretexts for advancing other, substantive agendas, see E. Rubin & M. Feeley, Federalism: Some Notes on a National Neurosis, 41 UCLA L. Rev. 903, 948 (1994).

2. François, Duc de la Rochefoucauld, may have said it best some three hundred years ago: "Hypocrisy is an homage vice pays to virtue." *Maximes* (Maxim 218) (3d ed.

disbeliever because it is perceived as important to many, and because it is an essential aspect of our polity. Just as the advocates of greater state autonomy do not seriously suggest reducing the federal government to pure "night watchman" status (recognizing, as they must, that many problems other than national defense and foreign policy require national initiatives and even national regulation), so the advocates of greater exercise of national power recognize the existence of the states not simply as geographical entities but also as significant centers of the regulation of human affairs.[3]

The importance of federalism, in my view, derives from several sources: its firm basis in our constitutional structure, its pragmatic justifications in economic, political, and social terms, and the contributions it has made and can continue to make in a constructive dialogue. Indeed, the value of this essay may lie not only in the presentation of a dialogue *about* federalism but also in its effort to underscore the strength of federalism as *itself* a dialogue about government. In this sense, neither argument—the case for unrestrained national authority or the case against it—is rhetorically or normatively complete without the other.[4]

B. The Constitutional and Structural Bases of Our Federal System

The debate over the extent to which the Constitution itself protects the integrity and autonomy of the states in our federal system can perhaps never be fully resolved because there were so many conflicting forces at

rev. and augm. 1983). *See also* D. Shapiro, In Defense of Judicial Candor, 100 Harv. L. Rev. 731, 737 (1987) ("Indeed, even arguments for occasional deception depend for their effectiveness on a background of truthfulness, for the deception loses its point if it is not believed.").

3. Examples, many of which have already been mentioned, extend to so wide a range of human activity that merely to attempt a catalog may be misleading. The fact is that we all take for granted the enormous role of state and local governments—perhaps in large part for reasons of history and tradition, but also, as I try to suggest below and have hinted throughout, because of the strong pragmatic and democratic considerations favoring such an arrangement.

4. As indicated in the Introduction, I do not propose, in this final chapter, to tie up every loose end that may be left unresolved by the briefs in the preceding chapters, any more than a judge deciding a controversy is obligated to resolve every point of disagreement between the parties. Indeed, an effort to do so would be at odds with one aspect of my thesis: that a principal virtue of the dialogue is that it stresses the need for continuing accommodation of competing, and in many instances, equally compelling, considerations.

work at the time of the founding and because so much has happened politically and technologically since the adoption of the Constitution.[5] Nevertheless, I think it fair to draw some conclusions, both about the design of the Framers, as reflected in the text of the document and the context in which it was adopted, and about the impact of subsequent developments.

As to the document that emerged from the Constitutional Convention, and that was ratified ultimately by all thirteen of the original states, this document did not represent the undiluted nationalistic yearnings of some of its strongest advocates.[6] Indeed, the necessity of compromise within the Convention, the strength of the anti-federalist opposition,[7]

5. Among the valuable studies relating to the background and context of the Constitutional Convention and of the ratification debates—a number of which have already been cited—are M. Jensen, *The New Nation: A History of the United States during the Confederation, 1781–1789* (1950); J. Rakove, *The Beginnings of National Politics* (1979); S. Beer, *To Make a Nation: The Rediscovery of American Federalism* (1993); G. Wood, *The Making of the Constitution* (1987); G. Wills, *Explaining America: The Federalist* (1981); H. Storing, *The Complete Anti-Federalist* (1981) (especially vol. 1), and two works that take almost diametrically opposite views of the nature of the federal union: R. Berger, *Federalism: The Founders' Design* (1987), and W. Crosskey, *Politics and the Constitution in the History of the United States* (1953). A writer whose work is most helpful both for its own insights and for the criticism of the work of others is H. Jefferson Powell, in such articles as The Modern Misunderstanding of Original Intent, 54 U. Chi. L. Rev. 1513 (1987), and The Oldest Question of Constitutional Law, 79 Va. L. Rev. 633 (1993).

Among those who have written about the transformation of American federalism since the Constitution was ratified, one of the most informative is Harry Scheiber. *See, e.g.,* Federalism and the Economic Order, 1789–1910, 10 Law & Soc'y Rev. 57 (1975); Federalism and Legal Process: Historical and Contemporary Analysis of the American System, 14 Law & Soc'y Rev. 663 (1980). Scheiber is also the editor of several valuable collections of essays on the legal and political history of American federalism including *Federalism and the Judicial Mind: Essays on American Law and Politics* (1992), and *Federalism: Studies in History, Law, and Policy* (1988).

A new, extensive study of the history of American federalism, with special emphasis on the significance of such extra-constitutional entities as political parties and the administrative bureaucracy, is currently being undertaken by Professor Larry Kramer, who views such a study as essential to an understanding of modern federalism and, especially, of the appropriate role of the federal courts. Letter and draft manuscript from Professor Kramer to the author, April 28, 1994. (Just as this book was going to press, Professor Kramer's manuscript appeared in published form in a Symposium on Federalism's Future in the Vanderbilt Law Review. *See* L. Kramer, Understanding Federalism, 47 Vand. L. Rev. 1485 (1994).)

6. As indicated in a recent article and in other studies, Madison himself, though a strong supporter of greater central authority than afforded in the Articles of Confederation, was also a believer in the importance of divided power when he made his contributions to *The Federalist Papers (see, e.g.,* F. Greene, Madison's Views of Federalism in *The*

the defense by the proratification forces that stressed the continuing importance of the states,[8] all buttress this conclusion. Without rehearsing the points already made about the context in which the Constitution was adopted,[9] I believe that three aspects of the text itself are worthy of repetition.

First, the powers granted in Article I constituted a list of enumerated, albeit broad, grants of regulatory authority, and recent scholarship suggests that even the Necessary and Proper Clause had its deliberate, jurisdictional limits.[10]

Second, a number of key provisions of the Constitution are designed to guarantee to the states national protection against each other—protection that they may have been given (in whole or in part) in the text of the Articles of Confederation but that were essentially unenforceable under those Articles.[11] Indeed, in addition to other safeguards, the states

Federalist, 24 Publius 47 (1994) (discussed in ch. 3, note 15))—a belief that became even stronger in his later years. *See* ch. 3, sec. A.

7. The story of the opposition to ratification is told in a number of places, but perhaps nowhere more effectively than in the multivolume work by Herbert Storing, *The Complete Anti-Federalist*. In volume 1, published in 1981, Storing summarizes the primary materials contained in the succeeding volumes, pays tribute to the anti-federalists for their contributions (including their unrelenting and, in the event, successful pressure for a Bill of Rights), and sympathizes with their admiration for small-scale republics and their passion for community. But in the conclusion to his first volume, Storing concedes that ultimately, the anti-federalists lost the debate "because they had the weaker argument." *Id.* at 71.

8. *See* the discussion in ch. 3, sec. A.

9. A further word may be in order about *The Federalist Papers*. A recent and thoughtful note argues that this work, in the end, does not provide a clear consensus as to the constitutional system of federalism, and that it should not be regarded as a means of determining the original intention of the Framers. J. Ducayet, Publius and Federalism: On the Uses and Abuses of the Federalist Papers in Constitutional Interpretation, 68 N.Y.U. L. Rev. 821 (1994). The author concludes, however, that the work does provide a useful source as a "sophisticated theory of political psychology," *id.* at 825, and that with respect to our system of government, Publius (Hamilton, Madison, and Jay) viewed it as a "compound" of national and local elements giving rise to "fluid and dynamic arrangements" enforced less by rigid legal divisions than by the ordinary political process. *Id.* at 865.

10. *See* G. Lawson & P. Granger, The "Proper" Scope of Federal Power: A Jurisdictional Interpretation of the Sweeping Clause, 43 Duke L.J. 267 (1993) (discussed in ch. 3, note 8).

11. The Articles of Confederation did contain several important guarantees, e.g., "free inhabitants" of a state (excluding "paupers, vagabonds, and fugitives") were assured the "privileges and immunities of free citizens in the several states," as well as "free ingress and regress to and from any other State," the same privileges of trade and commerce in another state as the state's own citizens, and "[f]ull faith and credit" in each state to every other state's records, acts, and judicial proceedings (Article 4). The Articles

are assured national protection against aggressive action by their sister states (as well as foreign powers) and afforded further protection (on appropriate request) against insurrection from within.[12]

Third—and here I find most persuasive the thoughtful and informative work of Deborah Merritt[13]—the Constitution explicitly gives the states more than territorial integrity guaranteeing their borders against change without their consent; they are also afforded a guarantee of a republican form of government—a guarantee that is most naturally and plausibly read as a promise of protection *both* against upheaval from within *and* intrusion from without. In other words, the Constitution did not simply ensure the survival of the states as territorial units that might or might not possess political integrity; it contemplated, and even assured, their continued survival as political entities. The Supreme Court was thus transcending rhetoric when it spoke so eloquently in *Texas v. White* of an "indestructible Union, composed of indestructible States."[14]

If the states were guaranteed continued existence as politically functioning entities, then the most recent effort to articulate and give greater substance to this notion in *New York v. United States*[15] is a worthy one. Indeed, the decision may be the most coherent and effective effort to address the constitutional underpinnings of federalism to have emerged from the Supreme Court's continuing struggle with the issue over two centuries. The political integrity of a republican form of government does center on the accountability of elected representatives to their electorate, and although it may be wholly appropriate to confront one's representatives with hard choices (e.g., do you want to accept these outside funds under these conditions?), it crosses the line to *coerce* them to take legislative action for which they then become accountable to the people who chose them.[16] Such coercion not only undermines their

---

also contained a number of important prohibitions, e.g., no interstate treaties without congressional consent, no imposts or duties that would interfere with any treaties entered by the United States, and (in the absence of actual invasion or other limited circumstances) no engagement in war without the consent of Congress (Article 6). But since authority for effective national judicial and executive branches was notably absent from the Articles, these guarantees and prohibitions were essentially precatory.

12. U.S. Const. Art. IV, § 4.

13. D. Merritt, The Guaranty Clause and State Autonomy: Federalism for a Third Century, 88 Colum. L. Rev. 1 (1988), discussed in ch. 3, sec. A.

14. 74 U.S. (7 Wall.) 700, 725 (1868).

15. 112 S. Ct. 2408 (1992), discussed in ch. 3, sec. A.

16. Two recent lower federal court decisions—involving provisions of the "Brady" handgun law that require local officials to conduct background checks on prospective

responsibility and accountability; it masks the ultimate accountability of the federal authorities that forced them to act as they did.[17] It is perhaps a partial answer that elected representatives at the state level can always say they were dragooned into action and that the real fault lies at the federal level; but this retort smacks of a kind of buck passing by responsible officials that has never proved especially appealing in a democratic society.[18]

---

handgun buyers—have reached opposite conclusions on the application of the *New York* rationale to the federal imposition of duties on state law executive (law enforcement) personnel. Compare Koog v. United States, 852 F. Supp. 1376 (W.D. Tex. 1994) (upholding imposition), with Printz v. United States, 854 F. Supp. 1503 (D. Mont. 1994) (invalidating imposition).

17. To be sure, the line between inducement and coercion is thin and may not even have been drawn at the right place in the *New York* case, but all lines drawn in the law cause difficulties at the margin; that does not necessarily destroy their significance. The evanescence of the distinction between inducement and coercion has been recognized by the Supreme Court itself; *see, e.g.,* South Dakota v. Dole, 483 U.S. 203, 211 (1987). And a number of commentators have noted the powerful force that financial inducements can exert. *See, e.g.,* L. Kaden, Politics, Money, and State Sovereignty: The Judicial Role, 79 Colum. L. Rev. 1 (1979); R. Stewart, Federalism and Rights, 19 Ga. L. Rev. 917, 957–59 (1985); J. Zimmerman, Contemporary American Federalism 112–23 (1992); Note, Federalism, Political Accountability, and the Spending Clause, 107 Harv. L. Rev. 1419 (1994).

In a recent symposium on health care reform, Professor Candice Howe explores in depth the constitutional implications of a wide range of proposals for utilizing state administration and state revenues as part of a national health care program. C. Howe, Constitutional Impediments to National Health Care Reform, 21 Hastings Const. L.Q. 489 (1994). Her discussion of the applicability of the *New York* rationale to seven pending bills provides a fascinating case study of the implications of that decision and its relation to congressional power under the Spending and Commerce Clauses. *But see* D. Engdahl, ch. 3, n. 57, *supra,* for a critique of the inducement/coercion distinction in spending power cases.

18. The *New York* decision is not above criticism, of course, and it has had its share. *See, e.g.,* J. Choper, Federalism and Judicial Review, 21 Hastings Const. L.Q. 577 (1994) (arguing that claims of federalism arising under the Tenth Amendment should be nonjusticiable); M. Redish, Doing It with Mirrors: *New York v. United States* and Constitutional Limitations on Federal Power to Require State Legislation, 21 Hastings Const. L.Q. 539 (1994) (arguing that the Court wrongly equated an unwarranted "enclave" (or state sovereignty) approach and an "enumerated powers" approach that recognizes broad but not unlimited national regulatory authority); H. J. Powell, The Oldest Question of Constitutional Law, 79 Va. L. Rev. 633, 652–81 (1993), discussed in ch. 3 at note 48; R. Levy, *New York v. United States*: An Essay on the Uses and Misuses of Precedent, History, and Policy in Determining the Scope of Federal Power, 41 Kan. L. Rev. 493 (1993).

As Professor Levy's title suggests, he argues at length that Justice O'Connor is guilty of "misleading case citations and a slanted reading of an ambiguous historical record." *Id.* at 533. He also questions much of the reasoning—challenging, for example, the distinction between financial inducements and the threat of preemption on the one hand, and the

What of the argument that, whatever the design of the original document, we have been through several traumatic events since then, especially the Civil War and the New Deal, that have dramatically altered the state-federal balance?[19] The significance of those events should surely not be slighted; and the scope of federal power today is in many respects far broader than even the most nationalistic of the Founders might have hoped. Moreover, the present extent of federal power is the result not only of social and political but of technological changes that have turned the Nation into a far more unified whole as well as a unitary player in global political and economic struggles.

Yet despite these dramatic changes, several crucial aspects of our federal system remain largely unaffected. The principal changes, I believe, are the expansion of federal power through the various pronationalistic Amendments adopted since the Civil War,[20] the changing attitude of the Supreme Court toward the breadth of power available to federal authority under such rubrics as the Commerce Clause—changes that even most present-day federalists admit are essentially irreversible[21]—

"take title" provisions on the other. Yet at the same time, he acknowledges that the result of the case may be correct and that "principles of federalism provide plausible arguments in [its] favor." *Id.* at 533.

Admittedly, the argument of a state legislator that he or she was forced to yield to irresistible federal pressure may find a sympathetic audience and absolve the legislator of accountability to the electorate. (But should it?) Moreover, the effort of the Court in *New York* to distinguish the well-accepted authority of the federal government to impose obligations on state judicial systems (*see, e.g.,* Testa v. Katt, 330 U.S. 386 (1947)) is not wholly convincing, and the Court's determination that Congress may not readjust property rights and obligations within a state as a form of "inducement" may be a bit too casual and weakly reasoned. Indeed, the Court might have been wiser to have acknowledged more clearly that it was breaking new ground, and to have relied squarely on the Guarantee Clause rather than an amalgam of general notions of state sovereignty, limited national powers, and the Tenth Amendment. But withal, the case strikes me as a strong effort to articulate a meaningful floor for the constitutional limits of national power in our federal system. Perhaps it is only a beginning; I doubt that it will prove a dead end.

19. In his recent book, *We the People* (1991), Bruce Ackerman argues that two of the most significant events in our history as a republic have been the post–Civil War Reconstruction Era and the New Deal. The first of these, in his view, effectuated the transfer of power from the states to the federal government, while the second further submerged what was left of state authority in a new era of economic centralization and executive authority.

20. These Amendments are described in ch. 2, sec. A.2.

21. Certainly, nothing in Justice O'Connor's strongly pro-state-autonomy approach in cases like FERC v. Mississippi, 456 U.S. 742, 775 (1982) (O'Connor, J., concurring in part and dissenting in part) and New York v. United States, 112 S. Ct. 2408 (1992), suggests a reappraisal of the scope of congressional power to regulate *private* activity

and the changes in technology that have increased the significance and impact of externalities and have made state regulation less likely to achieve truly efficient results.

Stacked against these changes, however, are some noteworthy features of our social structure that remain remarkably close to the original design. While state political autonomy, and the subjects states may regulate free from any hazard of national control, have been narrowed in theory and in practice, it remains true that a remarkable proportion of the regulations that affect our daily lives—on such matters as the uses of property, education, local transportation, family relations, the definition of liability-creating civil and criminal conduct, and many others—continue as primarily the subject of state and local control. Admittedly, some of these matters—perhaps many of them—could be shifted in greater part to national control, but is it simply inertia, or the influence of disproportionately powerful pressure groups, that has kept this from happening to a larger extent than it has? I don't believe so. I believe rather that the profound observation of Hart and Wechsler over forty years ago that federal law in this country is "generally interstitial in its nature,"[22] while less pervasively accurate than when it was first written, still holds for reasons best explained in institutional terms that leave the cynicism of the hard-line realists well behind.[23]

The enduring significance of state and local authority derives at least in part from certain constitutional understandings about the federal system. Those understandings, while not acting as absolute restraints on

---

under the Commerce Clause. (One recent article does make a forceful case for restricting exercise of national power over interstate commerce to instances of clear externalities militating against efficient state action, but the thesis of the article is unlikely to influence the course of constitutional development. See J. Leboeuf, The Economics of Federalism and the Proper Scope of the Federal Commerce Power, 31 San Diego L. Rev. 555 (1994). (Indeed, whatever the merits of the thesis, there may be far too much water under the bridge to permit such a step.)

22. H. Hart & H. Wechsler, *The Federal Courts and the Federal System* 435 (1953). The authors conceded in their brief note on this subject that the federal legislative product had expanded considerably since the inception of the Republic, but maintained that "[f]ederal legislation, on the whole, has been conceived and drafted on an ad hoc basis to accomplish limited objectives. It builds upon legal relationships established by the states, altering or supplanting them only so far as necessary for the special purpose." *Id.*

23. The editors of the second and third editions of *Hart & Wechsler* (of whom I am one) have barely altered the text of this brief note as it appeared in the first edition. The reason for this continuity, I maintain, is not inertia—much of the text and organization of the entire book has been substantially changed—but rather the editors' continuing acceptance of the accuracy and utility of the observation. See *Hart & Wechsler* 533–34.

dramatic exercises and extensions of federal power, nevertheless assure the continued existence of the states as countervailing forces, and their ongoing ability to resist national control. Perhaps this element has been better captured by Justice O'Connor, in her partial dissent in *FERC v. Mississippi*[24] and her opinion for the Court in the *New York* case, than ever before. It is an element that assures that the states can never be reduced to mere administrative units of a centralized system—that whatever regulatory power they may have over a particular subject at a given time (and in theory at least, it may be very little), they will always have the political capacity to function as alternative sources of authority and to resist incursion from without (and especially from above). This aspect of our federal system has served different purposes at different eras in our history—and surely, not all state contributions have been humane, progressive, or in furtherance of democratic ideals. But the states, as noted in chapter 3, have proved themselves as sources of organized resistance to slavery and even to questionable foreign adventures, as well as of important social, educational, and political reform.[25] Today, they serve as sources of healthy competitive rivalry and experiment both in the economic and the political aspects of our lives, as well as havens and even refueling stations for the political party that finds itself temporarily out of power at the national level. Tomorrow, they may help to fulfill a different purpose—but they will, and should, continue to be there.

Yet federal authority to preempt state regulation is, as a constitutional matter, undoubtedly very broad. Why is it then that, given the dramatic expansion of federal power recognized by the courts over the last century, the states have retained such a central role not simply as

24. 456 U.S. 742, 775 (1982) (O'Connor, J., concurring in part and dissenting in part). In this opinion, Justice O'Connor focused on the fundamental importance, in assessing the autonomy of any political entity, of "the power to choose subjects for legislation" (*id.* at 785), and concentrated her fire on what she alleged to be the federal government's interference with the setting of that agenda. This opinion, I believe, laid the groundwork for the Court's decision in *New York v. United States*, a decade later, and indeed the *New York* decision casts doubt on the continuing validity of the *FERC* rationale.

25. See generally ch. 3, sec. B.2.

With respect to the reference in text to "foreign adventures," note the resistance of several governors to Presidential decisions to call up the National Guard for "training" missions abroad—resistance discussed in Perpich v. Department of Defense, 496 U.S. 334 (1990). Although the Court in *Perpich* held that a governor's consent is not constitutionally required under these circumstances, the case was made difficult by the wording of the "Militia Clauses" of Article I (clauses 15 and 16 of § 8). And the resistance of the popularly elected governors in each instance served as an important expression of popular concern over the actions taken by the national government.

administrators of federal programs, but as independent sources of law and policy? Is it merely the consequence of inertial forces, backed by well-organized, private interests that, in at least some instances, stand to lose from a transfer of power to the national level?[26] I think there are also significant structural reasons for the retention of state authority in so many areas of general importance.[27] These structural factors have been noted in the work of several scholars, including Herbert Wechsler[28] and Martin Diamond,[29] and their work underscores what Diamond called the "compound" nature of American federalism[30]—the built-in role of the states in the administration of the central government. The structural features begin with the makeup of the bicameral national legislature—a lower house in which each state is assured of at least one representative (and in which state delegations frequently seek to share common interests crossing party lines) and an upper house in which every state is guaranteed two and only two Senators.[31] The structural elements built into the Constitution also include the election of the Presi-

26. *See generally* J. Macey, Federal Deference to Local Regulators and the Economic Theory of Regulation: Toward a Public-Choice Explanation of Federalism, 76 Va. L. Rev. 265 (1990).

27. However, a number of scholars dissent vigorously from the view (endorsed by the Court in *Garcia* and by the writings discussed in text) that the various structural features of the federal government serve in any meaningful way to protect state interests. *See, e.g.,* W. Van Alstyne, The Second Death of Federalism, 83 Mich. L. Rev. 1709, 1724 (1985), L. Kramer, note 5, *supra.*

28. H. Wechsler, The Political Safeguards of Federalism: The Role of the States in the Composition and Selection of the National Government, 54 Colum. L. Rev. 543 (1943).

29. *See, e.g.,* M. Diamond, The Federalist on Federalism: Neither a National nor a Federal Constitution but a Composition of Both, 86 Yale L.J. 1273 (1977). *See also* B. LaPierre, The Political Safeguards of Federalism Redux: Intergovernmental Immunity and the States as Agents of the Nation, 60 Wash. U. L.Q. 779 (1982); J. Choper, *Judicial Review and the National Process* (1980).

30. *See* M. Diamond, note 29, *supra,* at 1273.

31. The makeup of the House of Representatives is specified in U.S. Const. Art. I, § 2, that of the Senate in *id.* § 3. And in a remarkable provision appearing in Article V on the amending process, the Constitution explicitly prohibits any state (without its consent) from being deprived of "its equal Suffrage in the Senate."

I have always wondered whether this guarantee of "equal Suffrage" could be modified by *two* Amendments—the first deleting this sentence of Article V and the second modifying equal suffrage. But the question is likely never to materialize, regardless of its academic interest, because of the moral force of the prohibition. Clearly, the "Connecticut Compromise," providing for equal suffrage in the Senate, was regarded as essential not only to the formation of the new Union but also to its continuation. (It is true, however, that the force of the Compromise has been diluted by the provision in the Seventeenth Amendment for the direct popular election of Senators from each state—rather than their designation by the state legislatures.)

dent through an Electoral College system that, whatever its peculiarities, tends to focus Presidential campaigns on appeals to the electorate on a state-by-state basis.[32] And the constitutional theme continues through a number of other structural provisions—notably the requirement of a weighted majority of state legislatures for approval of any constitutional Amendment.[33]

Such features, combined with a variety of other factors,[34] help to ensure that significant state interests will be accorded recognition at the national level. Thus, when the Supreme Court held in *Garcia* that state employees were, after all, subject to federal minimum wage requirements, Congress was quick to respond with at least some relief—including permission to the states to afford compensatory time off instead of paying costly overtime rates that would otherwise be required by federal law.[35] And the complaints voiced by many states that they are being forced to pay too large a share of the cost of many present and contemplated federal programs are clearly being heard in the halls of Congress.[36]

32. The provisions governing the Electoral College, originally provided for in Article II, have been significantly modified in the Twelfth Amendment. And while I am convinced that they do enhance the significance of state interests in the conduct of Presidential campaigns, their operation has evolved in ways that were doubtless unintended by the Framers. *Cf.* Ray v. Blair, 343 U.S. 214 (1952) (discussed in ch. 1, note 26).

33. The requirement that three-fourths of state legislatures must approve an Amendment before it becomes effective appears in Article V. (Article V also permits, as an alternative, approval "by Conventions" in three-fourths of the states if that method is proposed by Congress.) And Akhil Amar has recently argued that Article V is not the exclusive means of amending the Constitution. See A. Amar, The Consent of the Governed: Constitutional Amendment outside Article V, 94 Colum. L. Rev. 457 (1994) (discussed in ch. 2, note 29).

34. Additional, nonstructural checks on federal power are suggested by B. LaPierre, The Political Safeguards of Federalism Redux: Intergovernmental Immunity and the States as Agents of the Nation, 60 Wash. U. L.Q. 779 (1982). And Professor Kramer's study in process (see note 5, *supra*) seeks to explore the role of informal, unplanned institutions (especially our unique political party system and our complex federal-state administrative bureaucracy) in protecting state interests.

35. For the story of this and other congressional responses to the *Garcia* decision, see Z. Baird, State Empowerment after *Garcia*, 18 Urb. Law. 491, 512–13 (1986). Baird argues—rather unconvincingly in my view—that even though Congress did act quickly in this instance, its action indicates only that the states can "win a single battle in a crisis atmosphere." *Id.* at 513. For me, it is a powerful example of the Diamond-Wechsler thesis discussed above.

36. *See* J. Cushman, Congress Limits Federal Orders Costly to States, N.Y. Times, Feb. 2, 1995, at A1. This article describes passage, in the second month of the 104th Congress, of legislation (reportedly endorsed by the White House) that would require assessment of

These aspects of our governmental (and social) system are in an important respect buttressed by the Supreme Court's reluctance to read national legislation as imposing burdens on the states, or as preempting state laws, in the absence of a clear legislative statement. Although criticism has been leveled (and in my view quite properly so), at the more extreme versions of this approach,[37] the milder version, best described as a rebuttable presumption of noninterference with or nonimposition on the states, fits well with the structural and related elements just discussed. As a result of the Court's approach, the national authorities must squarely address state concerns if they wish to override those concerns in establishing a uniform, national policy that effectively supersedes existing variations among the states.

C. The Exercise of Discretion

The analysis in section B attempts to establish a meaningful constitutional floor for our federal system—one that fixes in that system a role for the states that cannot be diminished. At the same time, it recognizes a "sub-constitutional" area of considerable breadth where strong forces work toward the continued recognition of state authority but do not compel it. It is that area to which this section is addressed: what should be the starting point of analysis when national authorities have discretion to replace state regulation and establish uniform policy? And

---

the costs to the states of any proposed national mandates and would also require a specific provision whenever such a mandate was imposed without reimbursement of those costs. Efforts to limit the reach of the legislation (for example, by excluding environmental protection laws) were uniformily rejected.

As an example of congressional responsiveness in another field, the recently enacted federal crime bill bars federal judges from setting caps on prison populations that would force release of prisoners to prevent overcrowding. See 18 U.S.C. § 3626 (b) (i), as amended by the Violent Crime Control and Law Enforcement Act of 1994,. Pub. L. No. 103–322 at § 20409, 108 Stat. 1796, 1827. (I pass over with only this brief reference the question of the power of Congress to limit available constitutional remedies. See Hart & Wechsler 372–73, 379–80, 395–98.)

As a final example, it appeared as this book was going to press that Congress was about to enact a law responding to pressure from a number of states for authorization to limit imports of trash from out of state. See ch. 3, note 65.

37. See W. Eskridge & P. Frickey, Quasi-Constitutional Law: Clear Statement Rules as Constitutional Lawmaking, 45 Vand. L. Rev. 593 (1992); D. Shapiro, Continuity and Change in Statutory Interpretation, 67 N.Y.U. L. Rev. 921, 956–59 (1992). The difficulty with these more extreme versions of the canons of statutory interpretation is that they go beyond the approach of forcing the legislature to confront difficult issues of federalism and frustrate even relatively clear legislative efforts to address and to deal with those issues.

what are the principal functions to be served by national authority in a system like ours? Unfortunately, clear answers, even if ascertainable in light of present conditions, are not immutable but rather are necessarily contingent on time and place. What may seem most appropriate today may seem foolishly out of tune with tomorrow's needs. And if that is true, it is the continued flexibility and room for productive debate that may constitute the true genius of the system.

Nevertheless, I believe the enduring validity of several considerations deserve emphasis—considerations involving, first, the appropriate placement of the burden of persuasion when questions of the national role are being debated; second, the significant contributions the states can make as political entities in any allocation of governmental authority (including their potential as participants in what I describe as "intermediate federalism"); and finally, the essential role of the national government in a strong federal system.

1. *Allocating the Burden*

Given the virtues of a federal system in which the starting point for the exercise of authority is at the state level (or lower), I think it appropriate that the burden rest—as I believe it traditionally has—with those who advocate the exercise of national power.[38] Thus, to invoke an example much debated in the press and the law reviews, if there is to be a single national law of product liability, we must ask its proponents to shoulder the burden of explaining why each state cannot express its preferences on this score with respect to the balance it wishes to strike between the interests of consumers and manufacturers. Perhaps it can be shown that decentralized decision making in this area is "structurally skewed toward inefficiently plaintiff-favoring laws."[39] Or that the "convoy" effect—encouraged by the movement toward relative uniformity that has resulted from the efforts of such organizations as the American Law

38. For expression of a similar view, see A. Wildavsky, A Bias toward Federalism: Confronting the Conventional Wisdom on the Delivery of Government Services, 6 Publius 95 (1976). Wildavsky points to increasing evidence that the quality of service declines with size. (In California, for example, studies indicate that size of school district is negatively correlated to student performance.) *Id.* at 119. Wildavsky also argues that in addition to the goal of efficiency, society should keep an eye fixed on the goal of creativity—a goal more likely to be achieved in a pluralistic context.

39. The quote is from B. Hay, Conflicts of Law and State Competition in the Product Liability System, 80 Geo. L.J. 617, 652 (1992), who argues that the issue is one on which "the jury is still out," especially since, as Hay concludes, the choice of law process in such cases "prevents states from exporting the major costs of their laws." *Id.*

Institute and the Commissioners on Uniform State laws—has proved inadequate to the task of affording sufficient protection to the conflicting interests involved. Or that the hazards of punitive damage exposure in multiple jurisdictions are so great that the movement of goods in commerce, or the health of industry, is unduly threatened by overexposure to liability. Perhaps an appropriate showing in any of these respects may justify partial federal intervention in what until now has been essentially left to the states.[40] But interestingly enough, we find ourselves still at a point where the relevant product liability rules are predominantly state rules, and where most participants in the debate—while perhaps disagreeing on the precise nature of the burden—seem to accept the placing of that burden on those who would establish the need for federal intervention.[41]

That the burden in many areas properly rests on the advocates of centralization is supported by more than tradition. When a state takes a regulatory step—either towards or away from governmental intervention and control—the step is one that is far more easily compared with the success or failure of different approaches in other states and far easier to modify or reverse than a uniform change on a national level.[42] Moreover,

40. Recent Congresses have seen a number of efforts to limit product liability. *See, e.g.,* H.R. 1854, 103d Cong., 1st Sess. (1993); H.R. 1910, 103d Cong., 1st Sess. (1993); S. 711, 100th Cong. 1st Sess. (1987); H.R. 2729, 98th Cong., 1st Sess. (1983); S. 44, 98th Cong., 1st Sess. (1983); H.R. 5214, 97th Cong., 1st Sess. (1981). Such efforts have been generally unsuccessful despite a significant measure of administrative support for "tort reform" during the 1980s. For an example of an effort that is now pending, see H.R. 10, § 103, 104th Cong., 1st Sess. (1995).

41. There are notable exceptions, of course, to the predominance of state rules, including limited preemption in the area of product liability for the marketing of cigarettes (see the various federal provisions governing cigarette labeling and warnings and the related preemption provisions, interpreted in Cipollone v. Liggett Group, Inc. 112 S. Ct. 2608 (1992)), and limited immunity from liability for defamation as a result of a series of Supreme Court actions under the First Amendment. (And at present, there are strong moves to place various caps or other limits on medical malpractice and commercial product liability.) But such nationally ordained exceptions remain islands in a sea of state law.

42. In a memorandum written to me during the delivery of the Rosenthal Lectures, Professor Marshall Shapo of Northwestern Law School noted, among other points relating to the issue of tort reform, that (1) there appears to have been no "race to the bottom" among the states in this field, (2) tort reform at the state level "provides many venues for creativity" while at the same time serving to "limit the damage" that might result from a misconceived experiment on a broader level, and (3) any nationally imposed change would inevitably be variously interpreted by different state and federal courts (and such differences might take a generation to iron out at the Supreme Court level). See also Professor Shapo's testimony in opposition to a bill to provide a national uniform product

the step is considerably more likely to take account of local needs and preferences than is a nationwide revision dictated from the top.[43]

2. The Contributions of the States

At a number of points in this dialogue, questions have been raised about the relevance of state boundaries, or even about the relevance of the states themselves, to many of the arguments for decentralized authority. Since state boundaries are in significant part the product of historical events (including some purely haphazard ones) and seem to lack present utility, it might be argued that they make as little sense today in terms of a rational system of government as the colonial boundaries imposed on ethnic and tribal groups in Africa and Europe—boundaries that have served more as the cause of friction and even civil war than of harmony.[44]

A few examples may help to illustrate the point. First, to think of the states as on any kind of a par in terms of their constitutional role seems bizarre when we compare a state as small as Rhode Island (smaller than some of our national parks) with a state as large as California—large both in territory and population. Surely, some of the states are far too small to be able to take any major regulatory actions that do not have significant external costs or benefits, or both, and are also far too small to constitute efficient administrative units for any kind of national program. (Moreover, these small states are especially likely to be vulnerable to the factionalism Madison so clearly saw as a danger to the public interest.) Other states are so large that they too cease to be useful as administrative units, and their inevitable heterogeneity leads to the loss of one of the asserted virtues of federalism: polities sufficiently small and homogeneous that the citizens are likely to have similar preferences as to how resources should be allocated and liberty restricted or unrestrained.

Continuing with the argument, one who sees little value in existing state boundaries might urge that many of the virtues of decentralization

---

liability law. Hearings on S. 1400 before the Senate Comm. on the Judiciary, 101st Cong., 2d Sess. 31–38 (1990).

43. A recent example of the general tendency to resist efforts to achieve national uniformity arose when it appeared that national standards were being devised for higher education. See A. Dembner, Colleges Fear Loss of Control under New Law, Boston Globe, Nov. 20, 1993, at sec. National/Foreign, p. 1.

44. Compare the reference to Karl Llewellyn's challenge to the present-day relevance of state boundaries in ch. 2, sec. B.1.

could be achieved without them—by setting up administrative units that recognize present-day realities with respect to metropolitan areas, ethnic groupings, and the like.[45] Moreover, to the extent that Brandeis's experimental laboratory thesis is valid, such experiments can well be attempted by the national government; indeed, examples at the judicial level involve the use of certain federal districts to attempt innovative methods of dispute resolution, as well as recent legislation asking each federal judicial district to come up with its own plan to reduce the costs and delays of litigation.[46]

These arguments surely have merit, and were we writing on a completely clean slate, we might well shrink from establishing state boundaries along what now seem (at least in parts of the country) to be quite irrational lines. As the ALI Study of Federal Jurisdiction said some years ago, "[r]ivers that used to divide now serve to unify,"[47] and state lines that once made sense now serve only to change the speed limit or the quality of the road surface for frustrated drivers commuting to work.

Yet there are, I believe, several powerful reasons why existing state boundaries should be respected and should continue to be utilized as the starting point for analyzing the virtues (and limits) of contemporary federalism. Indeed, in my view some of these reasons not only justify this approach but make a case for its superiority over any method that we might look to as an alternative.

(1) To begin, there is the simple fact that the states already exist (and most have long existed), not simply as administrative units but as political entities, and that any effort to restructure the nation along "more rational" lines would run into a sea of practical (not to mention constitutional) difficulties. Perhaps this is just a variation of a long-standing concern of mine—that arguments that start from a "clean slate" neglect the fact that the slate is not blank and that the existing state of affairs—even if not the best of all possible worlds—does represent the accumulated efforts and wisdom of generations of our predecessors.

---

45. As noted in ch. 2, note 105, Llewellyn himself went further and, in an aside, seemed to question virtually any territorial basis for allocating authority.

46. See Title I of the Judicial Improvements Act of 1990, 104 Stat. 5089–98 (codified in part, as amended, in 28 U.S.C. §§ 471–82).

47. American Law Institute, *Study of the Division of Jurisdiction between State and Federal Courts* 131 (1968). The statement was made in connection with a proposal to deny an individual access to a federal court on grounds of diversity of citizenship in any district in which that individual had his principal place of business or employment (even if he was a citizen of another state).

If this makes me a Burkean conservative at best (and an unthinking defender of the status quo at worst), then so be it.[48]

(2) A related point is a more positive one. Existing state institutions are more than administrative units that could perhaps be set up along more rational administrative lines. They are active polities, with their own governmental structures equipped to serve as the source of their own law and policy and as critics, or sometimes outright opponents, of federal proposals. Even when reduced to participation in some federally devised scheme, the states have the capacity to contribute their own ideas and objections to the implementation and thus to the development of that scheme. Indeed, it is this element of reciprocity—the notion that the states and their subdivisions do not simply implement but help to mold and create national programs—that constitutes one of the principal strengths of federalism in the eyes of some of its most eloquent advocates.[49]

(3) Another related point is also a more positive one. We may count ourselves fortunate, I think, not only that the states vary widely in size and population but that few if any states constitute truly homogeneous groupings of individuals along ethnic, racial, or religious lines.[50] Although there are many who see federalism as the best alternative to civil war among conflicting groups who loathe each other for nationalistic, tribal, religious, or racial reasons—and indeed, some form of federation may be the last, best hope for survival in many parts of the world—others have argued forcefully that the stronger the forces of ethnicity (or other similar factors) within each unit in a federal system, the less chance the federation itself has of surviving and prospering as a political entity: the centrifugal forces are simply too great.[51]

The case of Cyprus is a particularly tragic but still far from unique

48. My Burkean leanings are revealed in several earlier pieces, especially D. Shapiro, Continuity and Change in Statutory Interpretation, 67 N.Y.U. L. Rev. 921, 943–50 (1992); Reflections on the Allocation of Jurisdiction between State and Federal Courts, 78 Va. L. Rev. 1839, 1840–41 (1992).

49. See, e.g., D. Elazar, American Federalism: A View from the States, especially chs. 1, 5 (3d ed. 1984); V. Ostrom, The Meaning of Federalism, especially chs. 8, 9 (1991); R. Stoker, Reluctant Partners (1991).

50. To the extent the states have adopted home rule provisions de facto or de jure, the further devolution of political self-rule may well lead to greater homogeneity at these lower political levels, but always subject to a significant extent of state review and control.

51. See D. Elazar, International and Comparative Federalism, in a symposium on federalism appearing in 26 Pol. Sci. & Politics, No. 2 (1993), at 190–95.

example.[52] In light of the extreme tension between the Greek majority and the Turkish minority on the island, an effort was made to resolve the crisis through a form of federalism. A sophisticated constitutional structure was devised that provided a detailed formula for power sharing between the two groups—groups that were geographically concentrated in different parts of the island and thus could realize a significant degree of self-government. The plan foundered, however, because the Greek majority did not want to share power and so sought to convert the island into a "fairly unitary" state essentially dominated by Greek interests.[53] The result was armed conflict between the two groups (with Greece and Turkey themselves involved in the conflict), and the eventual de facto dissolution of the federation with the substitution of virtual partition of the island. When some desire later developed on the part of the Greeks to return to the original federation, the Turkish population, with the backing of Turkey itself, evinced no interest in change. A similar, but more peaceful story, may be told about the dissolution of Czechoslovakia, with some current talk about economic cooperation, or even more, between the two now independent states (of Slovakia and the Czech Republic), but little talk of political reunion.

In light of such examples, and the conviction of observers of the subject that strong ethnic or similar divisions among federal units does not bode well for the survival of a healthy federal union, we should, I think, be gratified that so many of our states lack the ethnic or racial cohesiveness that seems sure to exacerbate tensions within a federal system.

In a sense, the states—as additional sources of conflict resolution— serve the function some unions serve in dealing with employers. Each local (or each union in a multiemployer bargaining unit) must adopt a bargaining stance that reflects the resolution of conflicting interests within its membership—including clashes among junior and senior employees, skilled and unskilled employees, male and female, black and white. Similarly, the states frequently must adopt legislative positions (or lobbying positions at the national level) that reflect the diversity within them. This diversity may be considerably less than that existing at the national level, and thus it is no surprise, for example, that states heavily

52. The summary in text is derived from B. Akzin, Where Do We Stand, in *Constitutional Design and Power-Sharing in the Post-Modern Epoch* 239, 248 (D. Elazar ed., 1991).
53. *Id.*

dependent on tobacco growing will adopt proindustry legislation, oppose burdening the industry with "sin taxes," and lobby at the national level for protection against foreign competition.[54] But surely the pattern within the states is such that we are unlikely ever again to see an issue so divisive as the debate over slavery. Even a state as heavily dependent on automobile manufacture as Michigan doubtless contains its share of free trade advocates willing to argue the virtues of open competition with manufacturers of cars in other countries. And on an issue such as health care reform, while views may differ from state to state and from region to region, virtually every viewpoint is sure to claim some support in virtually every state.

In sum, the states in our federal system serve not only as a countervailing force to federal power, but as an additional moderator of their own internal conflicts. Efforts to establish units with more internal homogeneity might well backfire, by contributing to the increase of conflict and divisiveness at the national level.

(4) To the extent that efforts should be made to maximize democratic self-government (epitomized by the New England Town Meeting), the states are surely in a better position than the central government to move significantly in that direction. It is certainly a less daunting task for advocates of home rule on the municipal level to make themselves heard in the corridors of state capitals than in Washington.[55]

54. The influence of the "tobacco lobby," and of the Senators and Representatives from the tobacco-growing and -processing states, is a matter so widely known as to be an appropriate candidate for judicial notice. As an interesting recent example, a provision was inserted in the final stages of the 1993 budget bill that affords special protection to domestic tobacco growers. *See* M. Janofsky, A Curb on Imported Tobacco Aids Farms and Philip Morris, N.Y. Times, Sept. 29, 1993, at A1, col. 1. The provision, of course, had no relation whatever to the primary subject matter of the bill and was probably passed without even the knowledge of the overwhelming majority of members of Congress.

55. This point has its limits, however, and some observers have noted that during the period of relatively lavish federal spending on state and local projects, cities frequently attempted (with some success) to bypass state governments and establish direct relations with the dispensing powers in Washington. Indeed, the cities have resisted the tendency, through such means as federal revenue sharing and block grants, to increase the powers of the states to determine how federal funds should be spent. For an argument that there is no necessary link between state authority and local self-rule, see E. Rubin & M. Feeley, Federalism: Some Notes on a National Neurosis, 41 UCLA L. Rev., 903, 940–41 (1994).

For further discussion of these issues, see D. Elazar, *American Federalism: A View from the States* ch. 4 (3d ed. 1984); D. Elazar, Fiscal Questions and Political Answers in Intergovernmental Finance, in *Federalism and Intergovernmental Relations* 158 (D. Wright & H. White eds., 1984); B. Harman, The Bloc [sic] Grant: Readings from a First Experiment, in *id.* at 187.

(5) Even in the many instances when the states prove too small for the efficient provision of public goods, or for the internalization of both the costs and benefits of the decisions about resource allocation, the states can and should serve as valuable intermediaries in arriving at the best available accommodation of conflicting interests. Such an accommodation is not likely to be reached by making a decision at the top whose implementation is mandated on a regional or other subnational basis. From the standpoint of the range of popular preferences and of cost efficiency, the best resolution may be to facilitate regional cooperation—a kind of "intermediate federalism"—among states with roughly parallel (or even conflicting) interests. That the states already exist, with all the machinery necessary to regional administration, and that the Constitution adds to potential state power by authorizing interstate compacts (some of which require congressional approval) may well be one of the outstanding (and most underutilized) strong points of American federalism.[56]

A radical version of this thesis was suggested a few years ago in an essay by Robert Golembiewski.[57] In this essay, he recognized the dangers of centralized power, especially when no effective checks to the exercise of that power existed, and he also recognized the values of competition and experimentation at a subnational level. Acknowledging that the growth of externalities often made the states inappropriate vehicles for decision making, he proposed a system of "areal governments" presided over by the President—a system in which minimum standards would be set at the national level but in which wide discretion would be given to each area both in implementing those standards and in deciding whether or not, and in what respects, to exceed them. An area would often encompass a number of states, and would be sufficiently large

56. The possibility of interstate cooperation of various kinds is further discussed below. In *Regulation, Federalism, and Interstate Commerce* (A. D. Tarlock ed., 1981)—noted in ch. 3, sec. B.2.—there was considerable, but inconclusive, discussion of interstate cooperation (through compacts or other alliances) among a group that, in general, was oriented in favor of decentralized government. *See, e.g., id.* at 126–28, 136–40.

For an early discussion of the history and potential uses of interstate agreements, see F. Frankfurter & J. Landis, The Compact Clause of the Constitution—A Study in Interstate Adjustments, 34 Yale L.J. 685 (1925. In their conclusion, the authors state: "We must not deny ourselves new or unfamiliar modes in realizing national ideals. Our regions are realities. Political thinking must respond to these realities." *Id.* at 729.

57. *See* R. Golembiewski, Organizing Public Work, Round Three: Toward a New Balance between Political Agendas and Management Perspectives, in *The Costs of Federalism* 237 (R. Golembiewski & A. Wildavsky eds., 1984).

to reduce the likelihood of significant externalities. Competition among areas would be encouraged, but always subject to national oversight. The role played by the individual states in this new federacy was left somewhat fuzzy—indeed the proposal as a whole was acknowledged to be tentative—but Golembiewski suggested that substantial enabling legislation and interstate agreements would be required for the areal concept to be realized.

As I have suggested at several points along the way,[58] the idea of activity on a regional, multistate level is an attractive one in several respects—one that maintains many of the advantages of a strong federal system but at the same time diminishes some of the weaknesses adhering to the present arbitrariness of many state boundaries. Golembiewski's idea may be a good deal more compatible with our existing constitutional structure, and a good deal more feasible in the near future, than he realized. The very existence of states constitutionally capable of acting on their own and of combining with others in formal and informal ways may well improve the chances that such regional arrangements will succeed.

Many examples, both actual and imaginary, could be cited, but three illustrations drawn from different areas may help put some flesh on the idea. The first derives from existing law—the Low-Level Radioactive Waste Policy Amendments Act of 1985[59] that was the subject of the Supreme Court's landmark decision in *New York v. United States*.[60] New York, the petitioner in the case, was objecting to the coercive effect of the law on a state that had to that point decided to go it alone—that had not taken advantage of the opportunity offered by federal law to (1) enter into a multistate arrangement for waste disposal that, if approved by Congress, would (2) allow the multistate group after a certain date to exclude waste shipped to it from states not part of the agreement. Part (2) of this authorization gave the states entering such agreements more extensive exclusionary powers than they would have when acting alone.[61] As a result, the vast majority of the states—

58. *See, e.g.,* ch. 1; ch. 2, sec. B.1; ch. 3, sec. B.2.

59. 42 U.S.C. §§ 2021b et seq.

60. 112 S. Ct. 2408 (1992).

61. In Philadelphia v. New Jersey, 437 U.S. 617 (1978), the Court held invalid (under the dormant Commerce Clause) a New Jersey statute prohibiting the importation of most solid or liquid waste from other states. *See also, e.g.,* Fort Gratiot Sanitary Landfill, Inc. v. Michigan Department of Natural Resources, 112 S. Ct. 2019 (1992).

some forty-four in all—had in fact entered such multistate agreements at the time of the litigation, and the agreements had been approved by Congress.[62] Obviously impressed by this achievement, the Court was careful to note in its opinion that its theory of federalism did not necessarily permit states that had entered such arrangements to raise objections like those raised by New York and accepted by the Court.[63]

Does this mean that New York did better by refraining from multistate cooperation than did those states that were "induced" to enter such agreements? Not at all, since New York emerged from the case with the same daunting problems of waste disposal with which it began. And the ability of the agreeing states to exclude waste coming from New York could only intensify those problems.

In many ways, then, this Act and its outcome (to date) reflect some of the strongest features of American federalism. States that might be unable to surmount the transaction costs of multistate bargaining, but that did have the political potential to act effectively in conjunction with others, were encouraged by federal law to combine to seek regional solutions to one of our most pressing current problems.[64] These solu-

---

62. The history of these developments is described both in Justice White's dissent in the *New York* case, 112 S. Ct. at 2435–38 (White, J., joined by Blackmun and Stevens, JJ., dissenting), and in a comprehensive (pre-*New York*) article by D. Berkovitz, Waste Wars: Did Congress "Nuke" State Sovereignty in the Low-Level Radioactive Waste Policy Amendments Act of 1985?, 11 Harv. Envtl. L. Rev. 437 (1987).

63. "While New York has received the benefit of the Act in the form of a few more years of access to disposal sites in other States, New York has never entered a regional radioactive waste compact. Any estoppel implications that might flow from membership in a compact, see West Virginia ex rel. Dyer v. Sims, 341 U.S. 22, 35–36 (Jackson, J., concurring) thus do not concern us here." New York v. United States, 112 S. Ct. at 2432.

64. *See* Berkovitz, note 62, *supra*, at 487–90. In his book, *Reluctant Partners* ch. 6 (1991), Robert Stoker compares the relative success of the low-level radioactive waste disposal program (which was worked out with the consultation and cooperation of the substantial majority of states) with the disappointing progress of national efforts to develop a disposal program for high-level radioactive waste. Of course, the latter problem may simply be more intractable than the former, but Stoker points out that while the level of consultation and cooperation on the problems of high-level waste disposal was intended to be substantial, Congress in fact allowed forty-seven states to get behind a "screw Nevada" bill (*id.* at 169), which evoked a veto by Nevada that Congress could but probably would not override.

See also R. Ofierski, Nuclear Waste Policy Act, 22 Envtl. L. Rev. 1145, 1160–61 (1992). Although the Department of Energy has indicated that a Nevada repository will be ready for business by the year 2010, many believe it will never open. (For further discussion of Nevada's position, see J. Davenport, The Federal Structure: Can Congress Commandeer Nevada to Participate in Its High Level Waste Disposal Program?, 12 Va. Envtl. L. Rev. 539 (1993).)

tions necessarily left room for the flexibility appropriate to the different activities and needs of different regions. That the approach was far from ideal, however, is surely underscored by the failure of a state as important as New York to find its way into a regional alliance that would probably have mooted its challenge to the incentive system established by Congress.

Take another example from a completely different realm. Pro– and anti–gun control forces have vigorously debated the meaning of the Second Amendment's guarantee of the right to bear arms, but irrespective of the merits of that debate, two points seem fairly clear. First, whatever limits the Amendment imposes on the federal government, the Amendment is not a provision of the Bill of Rights that will, or should, be applied to restrict the power of the states. Indeed, a forceful argument can be made that the structure of the Amendment was designed in significant part to *protect* the existence of state militias as an aspect of popular democracy and "the right of the people to bear arms." [65] To read the Privileges and Immunities Clause, the Due Process Clause, the Equal Protection Clause, or any other provision of the Fourteenth Amendment as somehow extending this restriction to the states would be so ironic that even one who shared Justice Black's version of incorporation theory would be likely to balk.[66]

Yet if the Second Amendment—whatever restrictions it places on Congress—does not limit the ability of the states to restrict the sale and use of firearms, it remains true as a practical matter that states can do little without multistate cooperation and federal support. State

---

65. *See* A. Amar, The Bill of Rights as a Constitution, 100 Yale L.J. 1131, 1162 (1991) (suggesting that the Second Amendment's "core concerns are populism and federalism"). Amar concedes that the words "the people" in the Second Amendment can be read broadly to protect "arms-bearing outside of military service," *id.* at 1164 n. 153, and cites for this broad view S. Halbrook, What the Framers Intended: A Linguistic Analysis of the Right to "Bear Arms," in a symposium on gun control in 49 Law & Contemp. Probs. (Winter 1986), at 151. *See also* S. Levinson, The Embarrassing Second Amendment, 99 Yale L.J. 637 (1989).

For discussion of Supreme Court authority upholding national power to regulate individual use of firearms, see L. Tribe, *American Constitutional Law* 299 n. 6 (2d ed. 1988). For a recent three-volume study that includes cases, articles, and other materials on the constitutional status of gun control, see *Gun Control and the Constitution* (R. Cottrol ed. 1993). For an exploration of the history and origins of the Second Amendment, see J. Malcolm, *To Keep and Bear Arms: The Origins of an Anglo-American Right* (1994).

66. Lawrence Tribe, in his treatise on *American Constitutional Law* (2d ed. 1988), states that invocation of the amendment as a restriction on state or local gun control measures would be "extremely problematic." *Id.* at 299 n. 6.

boundaries are simply too porous, and many states simply too small, for any realistic hope that gun control legislation on the state level will have much impact.

What, then, are the options open to an advocate of more stringent gun control laws? Under a narrow interpretation of the Second Amendment, the answer is national legislation backed up by national power.[67] But even under a more expansive interpretation of that Amendment, the anti–gun control forces do not necessarily emerge victorious. The dormant Commerce Clause may block any individual state from acting on its own to restrict interstate transportation, and practical considerations may frustrate such attempts in any event. But do not the possibilities for effective regulation increase substantially if states can form broad regional alliances involving mutual cooperation and, to the extent necessary, obtain congressional approval of any interference with commerce that might otherwise result? Would even a broad reading of the Second Amendment preclude Congress from giving its blessing to state cooperation in this area, or even from offering substantial inducements to the states to cooperate in this way and substantial support if they do? Surely not, if the Supreme Court decided *South Dakota v. Dole*[68] correctly.

To select just one more example from among many,[69] bargaining costs and related factors may preclude effective agreements among upstream and downstream states (or upwind and downwind states) with respect to the optimal level of allowable pollution produced and consumed by each of the concerned states. The answer may well lie, then, in top-down legislation simply imposing a federal solution. But may there not be

---

67. Recent efforts to curb use of firearms, in addition to nationally prescribed waiting periods and prohibitions on sales of assault weapons or any sales of firearms to minors, include proposals for proscription of the manufacture or importation of certain types of ammunition. *See, e.g.,* H.R. 3355, 103d Cong., 1st Sess. §§ 311, 313, 416, 622, 623, 2907 (1993). *See also* Senator Moynihan's proposal, in Guns Don't Kill People. Bullets Do, N.Y. Times, Dec. 12, 1993, at sec. 4, p. 15, col. 2 (advocating a 10,000 percent tax increase on certain especially lethal bullets); Real Cost of Handgun Ammunition Act, S. 1616, 103d Cong., 1st Sess. (1993).

68. 483 U.S. 203 (1987). The Court in this case upheld the use of the federal spending power to "induce" the states to take action (raising the minimum drinking age to twenty-one) that—the Court assumed for purposes of the case—Congress could not have mandated directly in light of the Twenty-first Amendment.

69. For an interesting proposal for an interstate compact in an entirely different area (that of complex, multistate litigation), see American Law Institute, *Complex Litigation: Statutory Recommendations and Analysis* 165–66, 457–59 (1994); *see also* L. Feldman, The Interstate Compact: A Cooperative Solution to Complex Litigation in the State Courts, 12 Rev. Litiga. 137 (1992).

signal advantages—in terms both of democratic values and recognition of regional differences—in providing the opportunity and incentive both for the origination of policies by individual states and for multistate bargaining on these issues, subject to a significant measure of federal review and, if necessary, control?[70]

3. The Role of the National Government

Lest the concluding thoughts in this dialogue sound more like a panegyric to decentralized authority and state autonomy than they are intended to be, I should stress at the outset of this section that I do not intend the listing of matters appropriate for national action to be exhaustive. Thus, as an obvious example, matters of international relations and national defense are plainly appropriate subjects for national determination, and the establishment of a national currency is clearly and quite properly delegated to national authority. These (and other matters) are not further discussed here because I believe they lie well beyond the areas of useful debate.

But within the area of controversy, I believe there are at least five ways in which national action can serve a valuable purpose in ensuring the existence of a healthy federal system. These deserve emphasis both because they help illuminate the significance of central power *and* because in some instances they suggest some alternatives to the present, more preemptive exercises of that power.

First, the exercise of national power is appropriate in areas where there is a perceived need for public goods that simply will not be supplied unless national authority (both revenue raising and policy making) is brought to bear. Although national defense may be the strongest example, it is surely not the only one. The Coast Guard performs many

70. Among the many studies of environmental regulation in the context of American federalism (several of which are cited in ch. 3, note 98), one of the most recent, and provocative, is W. Lowry, *The Dimensions of Federalism: State Governments and Pollution Control Policies* (1992). Lowry focuses on regulation in selected states, but at the same time looks at developments throughout the country in terms of the extent of national involvement, the form and extent of state action, and the degree to which state responses to particular problems match the perceived need. Among his important conclusions are that state initiatives have contributed substantially to effective control, and that the matching of need and response is significantly correlated with what he describes as the degree of "vertical" (i.e., national) involvement in the particular program. *See id.,* at ch. 6.

Note that the encouragement of interstate cooperation, as in the matter of low-level radioactive waste disposal, combines important elements of national involvement and state participation in both the development and implementation of policy.

functions that have little or nothing to do with national defense, and that cannot be wholly financed on a fee-for-service basis. So do national parks designed for use by a broad spectrum of the national population and not simply by those from a particular area or region.

At least a subdivision of this category, and one that may be more deserving of a category of its own, consists of those areas in which the externalities of conduct within a state (and especially the negative externalities) are so great, and the costs of bargaining so high, that only national action can deal effectively with the problem.[71] This subject has already been discussed in some detail,[72] but it should be noted here that national uniformity may not always be the preferred solution in such a case—that the facilitation of regional cooperation (frequently with the stipulation of a nationally established regulatory floor) may have many advantages.

Second, there are bound to be areas of administration where economies of scale can be achieved only on a national level—although before any such conclusion is reached, serious consideration should be given to administration on a multistate or regional basis. Without purporting to be definitive, I would imagine that questions of minimum requirements for safe air traffic, for example, if not left to the open market,[73] can be more efficiently managed on a national than on a state-by-state or regional basis. Moreover, there seems relatively little to be gained by leaving the subject of air safety to interstate or interregional competition, especially when the federal government is constantly in a

71. *See, e.g.,* R. Stewart, Pyramids of Sacrifice? Problems of Federalism in Mandating State Implementation of National Environmental Policy, 86 Yale L.J. 1196, 1215–16 (1977). This important article, written during the regime of National League of Cities v. Usery, 426 U.S. 833 (1976) (discussed in ch. 2, sec. A.2), rejects Harold Laski's well-known attack on the utility of American federalism in the twentieth century (*see id.* at 1266), defends the value of decentralized decision making in a number of areas relating to the environment, but stresses the need for national action when overall welfare is impaired because of the presence of significant spillover effects, or when national intervention is warranted in order to pursue certain "national moral goals." *Id.* at 1265. In general, Stewart maintains, "[s]ubstantial reliance on state and local action and judgment is inevitable." *Id.* at 1266.

72. *See* ch. 2, sec. B.1; ch. 3, sec. B.2.

73. A committed advocate of the free market might urge that safety regulation is not needed because airlines with poor safety records will simply not attract passengers and will thus fall victim to safer competitors. But a good many people may die in the process of working out the free play of market forces. Similar responses may be apt in other fields of safety regulation—especially those involving food and drugs.

position to compare its own criteria with those of other countries whose safety records and judgment we respect. Similarly, when some degree of market failure may be due to lack of information available to those residing throughout the country, a single source of regulation requiring adequate disclosure (such as the Securities and Exchange Commission) seems plainly preferable to a plethora of competing and inconsistent sources.[74]

Third, the exercise of national power (not just judicial but legislative and executive as well) is a critical part of the ongoing dialogue on the appropriate scope of private rights. The effort in chapter 3 to highlight the role of the states in representing individual and group interests that might not otherwise be heard took as given the significance of effective enforcement of the Bill of Rights by the federal courts and the faithful articulation and implementation of rights against discrimination by both the courts and other national bodies. Surely, the civil rights revolution wrought by the legislation in the 1960s—so artfully guided through Congress by Lyndon Johnson[75]—is one of the great accomplishments of national authority in recent decades. That not every aspect has proved successful, and that we are still a long way from the goals of the movement for mutual respect and for equality of opportunity to work and live where one chooses, cannot, I believe, be attributed to defective national legislation. Our shortfall is, rather, the result of the inability of laws alone to alter attitudes and social conditions.

Fourth, when some redistribution of the nation's wealth is warranted and supported by the electorate—and especially redistribution from wealthier to poorer states—the federal government must play a role. Here, the public choice theorists leave one skeptical that redistribution at the national level can do more than redistribute from those with less clout to those with more, and the amount of clout possessed by a particular group is not necessarily correlated to its worthiness or

---

74. A related point is that administration at the national level may eliminate wasteful overlap and inefficiency—a point supported by the illustrations in ch. 2, sec. B.2. The difficulty with carrying this argument too far, however, is that some degree of inefficiency may well be a necessary price to pay for the advantages of decentralization, just as some degree of inequality among the resources of particular states may be a fair price to pay for the benefits to be obtained from interstate competition.

75. Especially the comprehensive Civil Rights Act of 1964, 78 Stat. 241, as amended, principally 42 U.S.C. §§ 1971, 2000a et seq., and also in scattered sections of 5, 28, and 29 U.S.C.; and the Voting Rights Act of 1965, as amended, 42 U.S.C. §§ 1973 et seq.

its contribution to the public welfare. But for reasons well stated by thoughtful critics of the theory,[76] I am not so pessimistic on this score. Moreover, whatever the chances of successful redistribution through national efforts, they strike me as greater than if such matters are left entirely to the states. Indeed, it is hard to see how bargaining among the states (at least without some federal inducements or even coercive measures) will effect any kind of meaningful transfer from the wealthier states to the poorer ones. Moreover, even with respect to a state that is willing to implement some redistribution within its borders—shifting assets from the wealthier residents and entities to the poorer—I suspect that the more ambitious such a program, the more likely it is (given the right of exit) to drive both affluent residents and investment capital to other states.[77] I recognize that altruism is not unknown, and that its significance is often underrated, but it cannot be depended on to do the whole job. The use of federal funds or other techniques to provide aid and encouragement for redistribution may make all the difference.

Of course, redistribution is a risky business at best—always creating the danger that it will reduce individual incentives and thus overall productivity, that it will lead to overdependence, and that the programs devised will transfer more wealth to the bureaucracy and the intermediaries than to the intended beneficiaries. But a healthy federal system may play a useful role in tempering the urge to achieve equality of result regardless of the costs.

Fifth, the national judiciary can play (and has played) a significant "sub-constitutional" role in ensuring that the legislature has squarely faced up to its political responsibilities before a national statute will be

76. See, e.g., D. Farber & P. Frickey, Law and Public Choice (1991); W. Eskridge & P. Frickey, Cases and Materials on Legislation 57–61 (2d ed. 1995), and authorities cited therein. Among the critiques are empirical studies indicating that in many instances, lobbying groups have countered each other so effectively that legislators were left with considerable leeway; studies demonstrating the extraordinary range and diversity of present-day lobbying groups; studies indicating that the desire for reelection is just one of a number of factors motivating legislators to act; and arguments that public choice theory fails to account for a great deal of legislation, as well as for the significance of the role played by the executive branch (and even, on some occasions, the judicial) in the development and active pursuit of legislative goals.

77. Massachusetts has recently taken action to reduce substantially the burden of state inheritance taxes, which were thought to be a significant factor (along with the intolerable climate) in driving older residents to spend their declining years in other states. See Mass. Gen. L. Ch. 65C, §§ 2, 3, 3A (1993) (amended July 1, 1992); P. Howe, Plan to Cut State Tax Gathers Bipartisan Steam, Boston Globe, June 24, 1992, at Metro/Region, 28.

interpreted to preempt state regulatory law. The judicially developed rule that preemption must be clearly expressed or implied—a rule that has not always been forcefully applied in this area,[78] and that is susceptible to abuse if applied too stringently—doubtless invigorates the structural protections afforded to the states in our national government.[79]

Finally, and perhaps most relevant to the ideas I have tried to develop here, the national government can serve as facilitator of effective multistate bargaining—of the growth of "intermediate federalism." If many problems are best dealt with on an "areal" or regional basis, and if transaction costs of various kinds are effective stumbling blocks to multistate cooperation, then the federal role as facilitator *and* as the wielder of both carrots and sticks cannot be underestimated.

Take, for example, an instance in which there is a need to develop an effective tristate mass transportation system for use by commuters to a metropolitan center (or centers) from all three states. Bargaining among the three states, with little or no federal encouragement or prodding, *may* lead to the development of the most efficient system from the standpoint of cost and effectiveness. But there may be many barriers to effective bargaining among the states involved. The three states may vary widely in their available resources: one may have much less incentive than the others to play a role in the development (because its costs will outweigh the benefits to its residents, although total benefits in the tristate area will plainly exceed total costs); another may have more to gain from a particular approach than do the others. (Thus, the state with the largest metropolitan center may fear—and the others may hope—that in the absence of an effective mass transport system, the state that now has most of the business will lose large chunks of it to the other states, even though the most efficient result may be to retain or even enhance the degree of concentration.) Finally, the establishment of a multistate authority with sufficient power to run the mass transit system effectively

78. In the field of labor law, the Supreme Court was surprisingly willing to find that the 1947 amendments to the National Labor Relations Act effected a broad replacement of state law, even though the evidence of congressional purpose was sparse, to say the least. *See Hart & Wechsler* 897 and n. 3.

79. Moreover, as discussed in earlier chapters, the federal judiciary has afforded significant protection to state interests in a number of other "sub-constitutional" doctrines. *See* ch. 1; ch. 3, sec. A. And most of these doctrines, even if subject to criticism in particular applications, are, I believe, sound in their basic premises. *See* D. Shapiro, Continuity and Change in Statutory Interpretation, 67 N.Y.U. L. Rev. 921, 937, 947 (1992); D. Shapiro, Jurisdiction and Discretion, 60 N.Y.U. L. Rev. 543, 580–85 (1985).

may be unattainable (under Supreme Court decisions)[80] unless Congress gives its blessing to any multistate agreement that is reached.

A considerable number of contributions might be made at the national level in such a case. First, some federal financial support may be offered, not simply as an incentive to reach an accord but as a way of equalizing the resources among the participating states. Second, an independent federal study may make it clear to all the states involved that a particular result is the most beneficial from the standpoint of the total welfare of all three states, and the national government might then be able to establish incentives (or disincentives) designed to encourage realization of that result. Third, the national government might wish to establish certain minimum standards that any such system has to meet (in terms of safety and financial soundness), leaving the states involved to bargain over any aspects of the system that they conclude should exceed those standards. Finally, Congress may—for constitutional reasons— have to give its approval to all or part of the agreement because of the enhancement of state political power that is inherent in the implementation of the accord. In doing so, Congress can make sure that the agreement does not contain elements of cartelization that will adversely affect nonparticipating states, or confer undue benefits on "free riders," or conflict with other national or regional arrangements. If such elements are found, their alleviation or even elimination can be made a condition of national approval.[81]

This last point is offered not only as a complement to the earlier discussion of the advantages of regional cooperation among states, but as an alternative to the tendency to nationalize any problem that transcends state boundaries and to search for a uniform result that effectively

---

80. For general discussion of Supreme Court doctrine in this area, see L. Tribe, *American Constitutional Law* § 6-33 (2d ed. 1988).

81. In an interesting discussion of the potential of interstate agreements for dealing effectively with problems transcending a single state's boundaries, one commentator voiced concern that interstate agreements might become too ready a vehicle for the formation of anticompetitive, socially undesirable cartels. See *Regulation, Federalism, and Interstate Commerce* 131–32, 138–39 (A. D. Tarlock ed., 1981). Surely, the ability of representatives from other states to object to congressional approval of anticompetitive agreements that would cause harm to residents of those other states would serve as an important safeguard against such a development. (That such a safeguard might not be foolproof, however, is suggested by the discussion of an interstate oil compact, supported by the federal government, which was adopted in the 1930s and which, according to one commentator, allowed Texas and Louisiana "to act just the way Saudi Arabia and Iran did under OPEC." *Id.* at 138.)

preempts state laws. As the Supreme Court itself has come to recognize in some important recent decisions, the fact that a problem cannot be resolved simply on the basis of state law operating of its own force does not mean that the alternative is almost certainly a uniform national rule. That may have been the view of earlier twentieth-century cases dealing with the nature and scope of federal common law,[82] but more recent decisions have recognized that even federal common law can effectively accommodate state and local interests when the need for uniformity is not sufficiently compelling.[83]

The picture that is limned here is surely more complex than one that operates essentially from the top down, and the complexity may not always be worth it. But as I have tried to suggest, complexity does not always mean gridlock: it can result in leeway for the exercise of discretion and creativity, and for recognition of the unique qualities of almost every problem.

D. Some Concluding Thoughts: Federalism as a Dialogue

Perhaps an effort to sum up the arguments for and against centralization cannot succeed because, as even this survey suggests, the debate is too rich and complex to be captured in a brief conclusion. Yet at the risk of oversimplifying, I will hazard a few concluding remarks.

There are, I believe, at least three strong centripetal forces in a society like ours. First, Madison's insight[84] retains its intuitive appeal, and surely its force can in some critical instances be empirically demonstrated. If factions are an inevitable (and not wholly undesirable) aspect of a society that is not run on despotic principles, then the power of any individual faction—especially one that speaks for a narrowly defined interest—is likely to be less of a threat to the public interest in an extended republic. There will, for example, be so many lobbies competing for public favor that the executive and (to a lesser extent) the legislature will have a freer hand to take action in the public interest.

Second, there is an inevitable impatience with the waste and overlap inherent in dealing with governments on several levels instead of just

---

82. *E.g.*, Clearfield Trust Co. v. United States, 318 U.S. 363 (1943), criticized on this point in H. Friendly, In Praise of *Erie*—and of the New Federal Common Law, 39 N.Y.U. L. Rev. 383, 410 (1964).

83. *See, e.g.*, United States v. Kimbell Foods, Inc., 440 U.S. 715 (1979).

84. In *The Federalist* No. 10.

one. It is hard enough, for example, to obtain approval from a local government to build a small extension on one's house if the owner has to get the approval of both the zoning board and the historical commission. How much harder, and more costly, must it be for a multistate operation to get the necessary approvals for, say, the marketing of a new product if the approval of three federal agencies and at least one agency in every state is required? Even the private citizen who does little but hold down a job must worry about paying taxes at two or three levels of government, and is frequently chagrined to discover that what is tax-free at one level of government (or at least subject to a lower rate of tax) is taxed at the highest rate at another level.[85]

Third, the moral and practical forces favoring equality look toward the virtues of uniformity not only as a cost-saver but as something approaching a natural right. Why should the quality of public education be so much better in state A than across the river in state B? (The question, of course, arises within states as well, but a state's political and judicial machinery is at least capable of addressing that problem.) Why should the level of local taxation be so much higher in state B than state A? The drive for uniformity, in other words, is not simply born of the desire to achieve efficiency and avoid waste; it is part of an understandable lack of sympathy for what may seem pointless disparity of result in a country that places great value on considerations of fairness and equality. Such considerations provide a powerful incentive for redistribution, or at least for the establishment of national minimum standards supported by the expenditure of national funds.

At the same time, there are at least three strong centrifugal forces at work. (That the number is the same as that of the centripetal forces is surely irrelevant to the appropriate balance. It probably has more to do with the mystical qualities of the number three.) First, a lack of certainty as to what is "right"—a skepticism that is in many ways the hallmark of modern thought—leads one not only to be tolerant of variation but to desire it for its own sake. A process of continuous comparison can help lead to surer choices among competing alternatives, and when the choice is essentially a matter of subjective preference, the right of exit stands as a guarantee, at least to those capable of moving, that their

---

85. Thus some income taxable at high rates in Massachusetts is tax exempt under federal law while other income—interest paid on federal government bonds, for example—is taxed at ordinary progressive income rates by the federal government but is not taxed at all by the state of Massachusetts.

subjective preferences will be honored. Even for those less mobile, the "convoy" effect is bound to have an impact as one state loses capital and labor to another.

Second, and closely related (perhaps the three factors are closer to two), a system of decentralized polities has value for those who believe in the virtues of competition at every level of human endeavor. The existence of healthy, functioning governmental systems below the national level increases the likelihood that national minimum standards of behavior will be accepted in some quarters but found insufficient in others, and (in a different vein) helps assure that the states will effectively compete with each other, as well as with the national government, to create an environment conducive to productivity. One need not be an undeviating follower of Adam Smith, or Milton Friedman, to appreciate the force of this argument and to recognize that some degree of countervailing power is one of the best structural means of ensuring against the dangers of abuse inherent in the existence of political power. Related to this argument is the point, already discussed in some detail, that state courts and other state institutions may serve as effective participants in a dialogue about the best and most effective means of protecting *federal* rights.[86]

Finally, the existence of state political power, and its national corollary of local power within the political subdivisions of a state—serve the important function of bringing democracy closer to the people. There is no doubt that the desire to achieve this goal constituted an important strain in the political theory of the nineteenth century, that it moved the anti-federalists profoundly and gave rise to some of their most effective arguments against ratification, and that those who urged ratification tried their best to reassure those who feared the erosion of state and local institutions. That these institutions thrived with so little federal interference for so many years lends support to the understandings on which ratification was based.

Perhaps I have labored the point too hard already, or have at least implicitly indicated my own view of the strength of the federal system as originally established and as it now appears to exist. First, I am persuaded that it would require repeal of the Constitution itself to

---

86. See the analogous discussion of the role of federal and state courts in the handling of post-conviction petitions by state prisoners in R. Cover & T. A. Aleinikoff, Dialectical Federalism: Habeas Corpus and the Court, 86 Yale L.J. 1035 (1977).

abolish it. Even the power of Congress, especially with the cooperation of the other national branches, to displace virtually all state substantive regulation of private conduct does not undermine the validity of this point. Such action will not occur because there are too many contrary premises built into our constitutional and social structure, because the states retain a significant role in shaping national policy, and because the people themselves would not stand for it. But even if the vigor of the federal system were to be sapped to a much greater degree than it already has been, the continued existence of the states as viable political entities, and thus as competing sources of power and opposition, would remain a basic part of the constitutional fabric.

The second, and equally fundamental, strength of our federal system is that it affords the flexibility to assert national power when the need is manifest, and to retreat from that assertion when circumstances change. Thus the true genius of American federalism lies in the continuing, and constitutionally assured, basis for dialogue—for moral, political, economic, and social debate over the merits of the allocation of power (both in general and in particular instances) among the various branches of government. What began in these lectures, then, as an effort to bring an advocate's experience to bear on the problems of federalism ends, for me, as a lesson in the value of a system that depends on dialogue and on vigorous advocacy for its health and its growth.

Postscript on the Decision in United States v. Lopez

On April 26, 1995, well after this book was in page proof, the Supreme Court, in a sharply divided 5-4 decision, held unconstitutional an Act of Congress making the possession of a gun within 1000 feet of a school a federal crime. The Act, the majority held, could not be sustained (as the government had argued) under the commerce power vested in Congress in Article I.

The decision, United States v. Lopez, 115 S. Ct. _____(1995), is referred to as pending, and as raising important issues, in footnote 63, at page 31 of the text. As indicated in the text at page 30, no previous Act of Congress regulating private activity has been invalidated on this ground for some sixty years, ever since the famous "switch in time" in 1937.

The breadth of the various opinions for the five member majority suggests that the opinion may herald a significant change in the scope of congressional discretion, in exercising the commerce power, to preempt state regulation. But, like New York v. United States, discussed at length in text, it is difficult to tell at this early writing just what the generative force of the decision will be. Much will probably depend on the future make-up of the Court, as well as on the willingness of Congress to proceed with care in determining and explaining the constitutional basis for legislative action. My own hunch at this stage is that, given the wealth of existing precedent in the last six decades, as well as the special problems raised by this particular statute and the sharp division within the Court, the impact of the decision on broader questions of federal power will be limited. But even if that hunch proves wrong, I believe my central arguments—about the overall scope of national discretion and its proper exercise, as well as about the political, social, and economic values that are furthered by the continuing dialogue engendered by American federalism—remain intact.

Selected Bibliography

Ackerman, B. *We the People* (1991).

Advisory Commission on Intergovernmental Relations. *Emerging Issues in American Federalism* (1986).

———. *Readings in Federalism: Perspectives on a Decade of Change* (1989).

———. *Reflections on Garcia and Its Implications for Federalism* (1986).

Akzin, B. Where Do We Stand, in *Constitutional Design and Power-Sharing in the Post-Modern Epoch* 239 (D. Elazar ed., 1991).

Althouse, A. When to Believe a Legal Fiction: Federal Interests and the Eleventh Amendment, 40 Hastings L.J. 1123 (1989).

Amar, A. The Bill of Rights as a Constitution, 100 Yale L.J. 1131 (1991).

———. The Consent of the Governed: Constitutional Amendment outside Article V, 94 Colum. L. Rev. 457 (1994).

———. Of Sovereignty and Federalism, 96 Yale L.J. 1425 (1987).

American Law Institute. *Complex Litigation: Statutory Recommendations and Analysis* (1994).

Anderson, A. The Meaning of Federalism: Interpreting the Securities Exchange Act of 1934, 70 Va. L. Rev. 813 (1984).

Areen, J. *Family Law* (3d ed. 1992).

Baird, Z. State Empowerment after *Garcia,* 18 Urb. Law. 491 (1986).

Bator, P. Finality in Criminal Law and Habeas Corpus for State Prisoners, 76 Harv. L. Rev. 441 (1963).

Bator, P., Meltzer, D., Mishkin P., & Shapiro, D. *Hart & Wechsler's The Federal Courts and the Federal System* (3d ed. 1988 and 1993 Supplement). (Also cited as *Hart & Wechsler.*)

Bebchuk, L. Federalism and the Corporation: The Desirable Limits on State Competition in Corporate Law, 105 Harv. L. Rev. 1435 (1992).

Beer, S. The Idea of the Nation, in *How Federal Is the Constitution?* 109 (R. Goldwin & W. Schambra eds., 1987).

———. *To Make a Nation: The Rediscovery of American Federalism* (1993).

Berger, R. *Federalism: The Founders' Design* (1987).

Berkovitz, D. Waste Wars: Did Congress "Nuke" State Sovereignty in the Low-Level Radioactive Waste Policy Amendments Act of 1985?, 11 Harv. Envtl. L. Rev. 437 (1987).

Brant, I. Mr. Crosskey and Mr. Madison, 54 Colum. L. Rev. 443 (1954).

Brennan, W. State Constitutions and the Protection of Individual Rights, 90 Harv. L. Rev. 489 (1977).

Brown, G. Has the Supreme Court Confessed Error on the Eleventh Amendment? Revisionist Scholarship and State Immunity, 68 N.C. L. Rev. 867 (1990).

Calhoun, J. *Papers* (R. Meriwether ed., 1959).

Cappalli, R. Restoring Federalism Values in the Federal Grant System, 19 Urb. Law. 493 (1987).

Choper, J. Federalism and Judicial Review, 21 Hastings Const. L.Q. 577 (1994).

———. *Judicial Review and the National Process* (1980).

Coase, R. The Problem of Social Cost, 3 J.L. & Econ. 1 (1960).

Collins, R. Economic Union as a Constitutional Value, 63 N.Y.U. L. Rev. 43 (1988).

Cottrol, R., ed. *Gun Control and the Constitution* (1993).

Cover, R., & Aleinikoff, T. A. Dialectical Federalism: Habeas Corpus and the Court, 86 Yale L.J. 1035 (1977).

Crosskey, W. *Politics and the Constitution in the History of the United States* (1953).

Davenport, J. The Federal Structure: Can Congress Commandeer Nevada to Participate in Its High Level Waste Disposal Program?, 12 Va. Envtl. L. Rev. 539 (1993).

Davis, J. *Papers: 1841–1846* (J. McIntosh ed., 1974).

Diamond, M. *The Federalist* on Federalism: "Neither a National nor a Federal Constitution but a Composition of Both," 86 Yale L.J. 1273 (1977).

Ducayet, J. Publius and Federalism: On the Uses and Abuses of the Federalist Papers in Constitutional Interpretation, 68 N.Y.U. L. Rev. 821 (1994).

Dye, T. *American Federalism: Competition among Governments* (1990).

Easterbrook, F. Antitrust and the Economics of Federalism, 26 J.L. & Econ. 23 (1983).

Elazar, D. *American Federalism: A View from the States* (3d ed. 1984).

———. Fiscal Questions and Political Answers in Intergovernmental Finance, in *Federalism and Intergovernmental Relations* 158 (D. Wright & H. White eds., 1984).

———. International and Comparative Federalism, 26 Pol. Sci. & Politics, No. 2 (1993), at 190.

———, ed. *Federal Systems of the World* (1991).

Elkins, S., & McKitrick, E. *The Age of Federalism* (1993).

Elliot, J., ed. *The Debates in the Several State Conventions on the Adoption of the Federal Constitution* (2d ed. 1901).

Elliott, W. Electoral College, in 2 *Encyclopedia of the American Constitution* 617 (1986).

Engdahl, D. The Spending Power, 44 Duke L.J. 1 (1994).

Epstein, R. Exit Rights under Federalism, 55 Law & Contemp. Probs. (Winter 1992), at 147.

———. *The Federalist Papers:* From Practical Politics to High Principle, 16 Harv. J.L. & Pub. Pol'y 13 (1993).

Eskridge, W., & Frickey, P. Quasi-Constitutional Law: Clear Statement Rules as Constitutional Lawmaking, 45 Vand. L. Rev. 593 (1992).

———. Cases and Materials on Legislation (2d ed. 1995).

Fallon, R. The Ideologies of Federal Courts Law, 74 Va. L. Rev. 1141 (1988).

Farber, D., & Frickey, P. *Law and Public Choice* (1991).

Farrand, M., ed. *The Records of the Federal Convention of 1787* (1911).

Federalist Papers: No. 2 (Jay); Nos. 8 and 9 (Hamilton); Nos. 10, 39, 45, 46, 51 (Madison); and No. 84 (Hamilton).

Feeley, M., & Rubin, E. Federal-State Relations and Prison Administration, in *Power Divided: Essays on the Theory and Practice of Federalism* 63 (H. Scheiber & M. Feeley eds., 1989).

Feldman, L. The Interstate Compact: A Cooperative Solution to Complex Litigation in the State Courts, 12 Rev. Litig. 137 (1992).

Fineman, M. *The Illusion of Equality: The Rhetoric and Reality of Divorce Reform* (1991).

Fischel, D. The "Race to the Bottom" Revisited: Reflections on Recent Developments in Delaware's Corporation Law, 76 Nw. U. L. Rev. 913 (1982).

Fletcher, W. A Historical Interpretation of the Eleventh Amendment: A Narrow Construction of an Affirmative Grant of Jurisdiction rather than a Prohibition against Jurisdiction, 35 Stan. L. Rev. 1033 (1983).

Fordham, J. *Local Government Law* (2d rev. ed. 1986).

Frankfurter, F., & Landis, J. The Compact Clause of the Constitution—A Study in Interstate Adjustments, 34 Yale L.J. 685 (1925).

Freyer, T. Hugo Black and the Principles of "Our Federalism," in *Federalism and the Judicial Mind: Essays on American Constitutional Law and Politics* 75 (H. Scheiber ed., 1992).

Friendly, H. In Praise of *Erie*—and of the New Federal Common Law, 39 N.Y.U. L. Rev. 383 (1964).

Frug, G. The City as a Legal Concept, 93 Harv. L. Rev. 1057 (1980).

———. Decentering Decentralization, 60 U. Chi. L. Rev. 253 (1993).

Gardbaum, S. The Nature of Preemption, 79 Cornell L. Rev. 767 (1994).

Gibbons, J. The Eleventh Amendment and State Sovereign Immunity: A Reinterpretation, 83 Colum. L. Rev. 1889 (1983).

Goebel, J. Ex Parte Clio, 54 Colum. L. Rev. 450 (1954).

Golembiewski, R. Organizing Public Work, Round Three: Toward a New Balance between Political Agendas and Management Perspectives, in *The Costs of Federalism* 237 (R. Golembiewski & A. Wildavsky eds., 1984).

Graglia, L. From Federal Union to National Monolith: Mileposts in the Demise of American Federalism, 16 Harv. J.L. & Pub. Pol'y 129 (1993).

Greene, F. Madison's Views of Federalism in *The Federalist*, 24 Publius 47 (1994).

Gunther, G. *Constitutional Law* (12th ed. 1991).

Halbrook, S. What the Framers Intended: A Linguistic Analysis of the Right to "Bear Arms," 49 Law & Contemp. Probs. (Winter 1986), at 151.

Harrington, J. *Political Works* (J. Pocock ed., 1975).

Hart, H. M. The Power of Congress to Limit the Jurisdiction of Federal Courts: An Exercise in Dialectic, 66 Harv. L. Rev. 1362 (1953).

Hay, B. Conflicts of Law and State Competition in the Product Liability System, 80 Geo. L.J. 617 (1992).

Head, J. *Public Goods and Public Welfare* (1976).

Heckscher, A. *Woodrow Wilson* (1991).

Howard, A. E. D. The Values of Federalism, 1 New Europe L. Rev. 142 (1993).

Inman R., & Rubinfeld, D. A Federalist Fiscal Constitution for an Imperfect World: Lessons from the United States, in *Federalism: Studies in History, Law and Policy* 79 (H. Scheiber ed., 1988).

Jeffrey, W. The Constitution: "A Firm National Government," in *How Federal Is the Constitution?* 16 (R. Goldwin & W. Schambra eds., 1987).

Jensen, M. *The Articles of Confederation* (1940).

———. *The New Nation: A History of the United States during the Confederation, 1781–1789* (1950).

Kaden, L. Politics, Money, and State Sovereignty: The Judicial Role, 79 Colum. L. Rev. 847 (1979).

Kalman, L. Abe Fortas and Strategic Federalism in Law and Politics, in *Federalism and the Judicial Mind: Essays on American Constitutional Law and Politics* 109 (H. Scheiber ed., 1992).

Kelman, M. Consumption Theory, Production Theory, and Ideology in the Coase Theorem, 52 S. Cal. L. Rev. 669 (1979).

Kennedy, D. Federalism and the Force of History, in *How Federal Is the Constitution?* 67 (R. Goldwin & W. Schambra eds., 1987).

Kenyon, C. *Men of Little Faith: The Anti-Federalists on the Nature of Representative Government,* in Wm. & Mary Q. 3d ser. vol. 12 (1955).

Kincaid, J., ed. *Political Culture, Public Policy and the American States* (1982).

Kitch, E. Regulation, the American Common Market and Public Choice, 6 Harv. J.L. & Pub. Pol'y 119 (1982).

Kramer, L. Understanding Federalism, 47 Vand. L. Rev. 1485 (1994).

Krislov, S. Oliver Wendell Holmes and the Federal Idea, in *Federalism and the Judicial Mind: Essays on American Constitutional Law and Politics* 37 (H. Scheiber ed., 1992).

Lama, L. The Wall on a Straw Foundation: The Mythical Wall vs. The Reality of Controlled Intertwinement, 5 St. Thomas L. Rev. 581 (1993).

LaPierre, B. The Political Safeguards of Federalism Redux: Intergovernmental Immunity and the States as Agents of the Nation, 60 Wash. U. L.Q. 779 (1982).

Lawson, G., & Granger, P. The "Proper" Scope of Federal Power: A Jurisdictional Interpretation of the Sweeping Clause, 43 Duke L.J. 267 (1993).

Leboeuf, J. The Economics of Federalism and the Proper Scope of the Federal Commerce Power, 31 San Diego L. Rev. 555 (1994).

Leedes, G. Rediscovering the Link between the Establishment Clause and the Fourteenth Amendment: The Citizenship Declaration, 26 Ind. L. Rev. 469 (1993).

Levy, L. Articles of Confederation, in *1 Encyclopedia of the American Constitution* 75 (1986).

Levy, R. *New York v. United States:* An Essay on the Uses and Misuses of Precedent, History, and Policy in Determining the Scope of Federal Power, 41 U. Kan. L. Rev. 493 (1993).

Lincoln, A. *Collected Works* (R. Basler ed., 1953).

Llewellyn, K. The Constitution as an Institution, 34 Colum. L. Rev. 1 (1934).

Lowry, W. *The Dimensions of Federalism: State Governments and Pollution Control Policies* (1992).

Luttwak, E. *The Endangered American Dream* (1993).

Macey, J. Federal Deference to Local Regulators and the Economic Theory of Regulation: Toward a Public-Choice Explanation of Federalism, 76 Va. L. Rev. 265 (1990).

Madison, J. *Papers* (D. Mattern et al. eds., 1991).

Malcolm, J. *To Keep and Bear Arms: The Origins of an Anglo-American Right* (1994).

Maltz, E. The Dark Side of State Court Activism, 63 Tex. L. Rev. 995 (1985).

Marcus, M. Louis D. Brandeis and the Laboratories of Democracy, in *Federalism and the Judicial Mind: Essays on American Law and Politics* 75 (H. Scheiber ed., 1992).

Maxwell, J. *The Fiscal Impact of Federalism in the United States* (1946).

McConnell, M. Federalism: Evaluating the Founders' Design, 54 U. Chi. L. Rev. 1484 (1987).

McManamon, M. Felix Frankfurter: The Architect of "Our Federalism," 27 Ga. L. Rev. 697 (1993).

McMaster, J., & Stone, F. *Pennsylvania and the Federal Constitution* 229 (1888).

Merrill, T. Chief Justice Rehnquist, Pluralist Theory, and the Interpretation of Statutes, 25 Rutgers L.J. 621 (1994).

Merritt, D. The Guaranty Clause and State Autonomy: Federalism for a Third Century, 88 Colum. L. Rev. 1 (1988).

Miller, J. *Last One over the Wall: The Massachusetts Experiment in Closing Reform Schools* (1991).

Minow, M. Putting up and Putting down: Tolerance Reconsidered, in *Comparative Constitutional Federalism* 77 (M. Tushnet ed., 1990).

Montesquieu. *The Spirit of the Laws* (1748).

Note. Clear Statement Rules, Federalism, and Congressional Regulation of States, 107 Harv. L. Rev. 1959 (1994).

Note. Federalism Myth: States as Laboratories of Health Care Reform, 82 Geo. L.J. 159 (1993).

Note. Federalism, Political Accountability, and the Spending Clause, 107 Harv. L. Rev. 1419 (1994).

Note. A Public Choice Perspective on the Debate over Federal versus State Corporate Law, 79 Va. L. Rev. 2129 (1993).

Oaks, D. Legal History in the High Court—Habeas Corpus, 64 Mich. L. Rev. 451 (1966).

Ofierski, R. Nuclear Waste Policy Act, 22 Envtl. L. Rev. 1145 (1992).

Orth, J. *The Judicial Power of the United States: The Eleventh Amendment in American History* (1987).

Ostrom, V. Can Federalism Make a Difference?, 3 Publius 197 (1973).

———. *The Meaning of American Federalism* (1991).

Ottosen, G. *Making American Government Work* (1992).

Patchel, H. K. Interest Group Politics, Federalism, and the Uniform Laws Process: Some Lessons from the Uniform Commercial Code, 78 Minn. L. Rev. 83 (1993).

Peller, G. In Defense of Federal Habeas Corpus Relitigation, 16 Harv. C.R.–C.L. L. Rev. 579 (1982).

Peterson, R., Rabe, B., & Wong, K. *When Federalism Works* (1986).

Post, R. Justice Brennan and Federalism, in *Federalism: Studies in History, Law and Policy* 37 (H. Scheiber ed., 1988).

Powell, H. J. The Compleat Jeffersonian: Justice Rehnquist and Federalism, 91 Yale L.J. 1317 (1982).

———. The Modern Misunderstanding of Original Intent, 54 U. Chi. L. Rev. 1513 (1987).

———. The Oldest Question of Constitutional Law, 79 Va. L. Rev. 633 (1993).

———. The Original Understanding of Original Intent, 98 Harv. L. Rev. 885 (1985).

Rakove, J. *The Beginnings of National Politics* (1979).

Rapaczynski, A. From Sovereignty to Process: The Jurisprudence of Federalism after *Garcia*, 1985 Sup. Ct. Rev. 341.

Redish, M. *The Constitution as Political Structure* (1995).

———. Doing It with Mirrors: *New York v. United States* and Constitutional Limitations on Federal Power to Require State Legislation, 21 Hastings Const. L.Q. 539 (1994).

———. Federal Common Law, Political Legitimacy, and the Interpretive Process: An Institutional Perspective, 83 Nw. U. L. Rev. 761 (1989).

———. *The Federal Courts in the Political Order* (1991).

Revesz, R. Rehabilitating Interstate Competition: Rethinking the "Race-to-the-Bottom" Rationale for Federal Environmental Regulation, 67 N.Y.U. L. Rev. 1210 (1992).

Riker, W. *Federalism: Origin, Operation, Significance* 145 (1964).

———. Six Books in Search of a Subject or Does Federalism Exist and Does It Matter?, 2 Comp. Pol. 145 (1969).

Ritt, L. Political Cultures and Political Reform, *Political Culture, Public Policy and the American States* 143 (J. Kincaid ed., 1982).

Rivlin, A. *Reviving the American Dream: The Economy, the States and the Federal Government* (1992).

Roche, J. Constitutional Convention of 1787, in 1 *Encyclopedia of the American Constitution* 360 (1986).

Romano, R. The State Competition Debate in Corporate Law, 8 Cardozo L. Rev. 709 (1987).

Rose, C. Planning and Dealing: Piecemeal Land Control as a Problem of Local Legitimacy, 71 Cal. L. Rev. 837 (1983).

Rose-Ackerman, S. Risk Taking and Reelection: Does Federalism Promote Innovation?, 9 J. Legal Stud. 593 (1980).

Rubin, E., & Feeley, M. Federalism: Some Notes on a National Neurosis, 41 UCLA L. Rev. 903 (1994).

Scheiber, H. Constitutional Structure and the Protection of Rights: Federalism and the Separation of Powers, in *Power Divided: Essays in the History and Practice of Federalism* 17 (H. Scheiber & M. Feeley eds., 1989).

———. Federalism and Legal Process: Historical and Contemporary Analysis of the American System, 14 Law & Soc. Rev. 663 (1980).

———. Federalism and the American Economic Order, 1789–1910, 10 Law & Soc. Rev. 57 (1975).

———. Federalism and the Constitution: The Original Understanding, in *American Law and the Constitutional Order* 85 (L. Friedman & H. Scheiber eds., 1988).

———, ed. *Federalism: Studies in History, Law, and Policy* (1988).

Shannon, J. The Return to Fend-for-Yourself Federalism: The Reagan Mark, in Advisory Commission on Intergovernmental Relations, *Readings in Federalism: Perspectives on a Decade of Change* 119 (1989).

Shapiro, D. Continuity and Change in Statutory Interpretation, 67 N.Y.U. L. Rev. (1992).

———. Jurisdiction and Discretion, 60 N.Y.U. L. Rev. 543 (1985).

———. Mr. Justice Rehnquist: A Preliminary View, 90 Harv. L. Rev. 293 (1976).

———. Reflections on the Allocation of Jurisdiction between State and Federal Courts, 78 Va. L. Rev. 1839 (1992).

Simon, J., & Skolnick, J. Federalism, the Exclusionary Rule, and the Police, in *Power Divided: Essays on the Theory and Practice of Federalism* 75 (H. Scheiber & M. Feeley eds., 1989).

Stewart, R. Federalism and Rights, 19 Ga. L. Rev. 917 (1985).

———. Pyramids of Sacrifice? Problems of Federalism in Mandating State Implementation of National Environmental Policy, 86 Yale L.J. 1196 (1977).

Stoker, R. *Reluctant Partners* (1991).

Storing, H. *The Complete Anti-Federalist* (Vol. 1, 1981).

Sutherland, A. Establishment according to Engel, 76 Harv. L. Rev. 25 (1962).

Symposium. Federal Courts, 12 Pace L. Rev. 227 (1992).

Symposium. Federalism, 6 Harv. J.L. & Pub. Pol'y 1 (1982).

Symposium. Federalism's Future, 47 Vand. L. Rev. 1205 (1994).

Tarlock, A. D., ed. *Regulation, Federalism, and Interstate Commerce* (1981).

Tarr, G. A. The Past and Future of the New Judicial Federalism, 24 Publius 63 (Spring 1994).

Tiebout, C. A Pure Theory of Local Expenditures, 64 J. Pol. Econ. 416 (1956).

Tribe, L. *American Constitutional Law* (2d ed. 1988).

Tushnet, M., ed. *Comparative Constitutional Federalism* (1990).

Van Alstyne, W. The Second Death of Federalism, 83 Mich. L. Rev. 1709 (1985).

Wechsler, H. The Political Safeguards of Federalism: The Role of the States in the Composition and Selection of the National Government, 54 Colum. L. Rev. 543 (1954).

Weinberg, L. Federal Common Law, 83 Nw. U. L. Rev. 805 (1989).

Wildavsky, A. A Bias toward Federalism: Confronting the Conventional Wisdom on the Delivery of Government Services, 6 Publius 95 (1976).

Wills, G. *Explaining America: The Federalist* (1981).

———. Introduction to the 1982 Bantam Edition of *The Federalist*.

Winter, R. Private Goals and Competition among State Legal Systems, 6 Harv. J.L. & Pub. Pol'y 127 (1982).

Wood, G. *The Creation of the American Republic 1776–1787* (1969).

———. *The Making of the Constitution* (1987).

Wright, V. *The Government and Politics of France* (1978).

Yackle, L. The Habeas Hagioscope, 66 S. Cal. L. Rev. 2331 (1993).

Zimmerman, J. *Contemporary American Federalism* (1992).

Citation Tables

United States Constitution

Provision	Page(s)
Preamble	17
Article I	3, 18, 20, 31, 59, 60, 110, 117
§ 1, cl. 1	19
§ 2	60, 116
§ 3	19, 116
§ 8	20
§ 8, cl. 1	20, 31–32, 71, 112
§ 8, cl. 3	2–3, 27–31, 36, 47, 51, 64, 72–74, 89–91, 112–14, 127, 130, 141
§ 8, cl. 11	52
§ 8, cls 15, 16	19, 115
§ 8, cl. 18	20, 24, 27, 59–60, 110
§ 9	19, 53, 60
§ 10	19, 126, 130, 136
Article II	20, 117
§ 1	20
§ 2	52
Article III	3, 21, 62, 66
Article IV	20, 74
§ 1	20
§ 2	20, 49, 51
§ 3	21–22, 60
§ 4	21–22, 60–61, 68, 76, 111, 113
Article V	22, 116, 117
Article VI	3, 22, 24, 31, 105
Article VII	17
Amendment I	62, 74, 95–96, 101–2, 120
Amendment II	23, 63, 129, 130
Amendment IV	55
Amendment VI	23, 62, 100
Amendment VII	62
Amendment IX	63

Cases